THE
GROWTH EXPERIMENT
REVISITED

Paul —
With thanks for years
of friendship. And do note
Footnote 7 of Chapter 14.

Best,
Larry

Also by Lawrence B. Lindsey

What a President Should Know

Economic Puppetmasters

The Growth Experiment

THE
GROWTH EXPERIMENT
REVISITED

[Why Lower, Simpler Taxes
Really Are America's
Best Hope for Recovery]

LAWRENCE B. LINDSEY

BASIC BOOKS
A Member of the Perseus Books Group
New York

Books published by Basic Books are available at special discounts for bulk purchases in the United States by corporations, institutions, and other organizations. For more information, please contact the Special Markets Department at the Perseus Books Group, 2300 Chestnut Street, Suite 200, Philadelphia, PA 19103, or call (800) 810-4145, ext. 5000, or e-mail special.markets@perseusbooks.com.

Designed by Linda Mark
Set in Dante MT Std by the Perseus Books Group

Library of Congress Cataloging-in-Publication Data
Lindsey, Lawrence.
[Growth experiment]
    The growth experiment revisited : why lower, simpler taxes really are America's best hope for recovery / Lawrence B. Lindsey.
        pages cm
    Includes bibliographical references and index.
    ISBN 978-0-465-05070-3 (pbk : alk. paper)—
    ISBN 978-0-465-06099-3 (e-book) 1. Taxation—United States.
2. Supply-side economics—United States. 3. Monetary policy—United States. 4. Fiscal policy—United States. I. Title.
HJ2381.L53 2013
339.5'250973—dc23
2013010325
10 9 8 7 6 5 4 3 2 1

Contents

PART II   UPDATING THE LESSONS: THE NEW CENTURY

Acknowledgments

THIS BOOK WAS WRITTEN IN TWO PARTS—SPACED TWENTY-FIVE years apart. This makes it an unusual undertaking, one that many individuals and organizations deserve credit for making possible. Technologically, special thanks needs to go to all the people at the Manhattan Institute and at Basic Books for re-creating the proverbial wheel for a book that was written before e-mail, at a time when word processing was in its infancy.

In terms of intellectual inspiration, Martin Feldstein bridges the entire quarter century between the original and this revisited version. He was President of the National Bureau of Economic Research and my thesis adviser at Harvard. The NBER provided a stimulating intellectual environment, and its TAXSIM model provided the ability to do the simulations contained in the original version. The original version was based on my doctoral dissertation, which Feldstein supervised. Moreover, for the past twenty-five years he has been a constant source of inspiration, advice, and friendship.

The Manhattan Institute, under the inspired leadership of its two Presidents over this quarter century, William Hammett and Larry Mone, provided crucial intellectual, moral, and financial support. It was Bill Hammett who persuaded me to write the original version and Larry Mone who suggested that the book be brought back into the public domain and updated. Then-Senior Fellow Richard Vigilante provided expert editorial work. Others at the Manhattan Institute, including Vanessa Mendoza and Bernadette Serton, also deserve my thanks. Martin Kessler, then-publisher at Basic Books, elevated and enlarged my own vision of what the book could be. Today, Tim Bartlett, Kaitlyn Zafonte, and Sandra Beris at Basic carry on this tradition.

In addition, a number of people who have worked for me over the years provided invaluable assistance. John Navratil and Andy Mitrusi provided invaluable research and technical help for the original version. The revisited version would not have been possible without the help of Andrew Sacher and Karolin Junnila of the Lindsey Group.

This book is dedicated to my children, Troy, Emily, and Tommy, in the hopes that as they now enter young adulthood, America may once again undertake a successful Growth Experiment.

Introduction

TAXES HAVE ALWAYS HELD A FASCINATION FOR ME, EVER SINCE my dad let me use his adding machine (the kind you find in museums today) when he did his taxes. But I really became hooked when I got to serve on the Council of Economic Advisers during the Reagan administration where I was Senior Staff Economist for Tax Policy. I got to watch the "sausage-making" process of crafting tax legislation up close. Ronald Reagan had challenged the notion that government could set rates as high as it wished without significantly affecting the working, saving, and investment behavior of taxpayers or, for that matter, their willingness to hire lawyers and accountants to arrange their affairs in a way that minimized the taxes they paid.

Back at Harvard my doctoral thesis was a study of the effects of the Reagan tax cuts. It had one of those impenetrable titles that many dissertations have: "Simulating the Behavioral Response of Taxpayers to Changes in Tax Rates." The main academic task of the paper was to figure out what the world would have looked like if the Reagan tax cuts had not taken place and the economy ran on "autopilot." By comparing what actually happened to what would have happened in this autopilot or "counterfactual" world, we could see what the effects of the tax cuts actually were. The study produced a "middle-ground" finding. Tax rates mattered a lot in determining taxpayer behavior, but contrary to the assertions of some supply-siders, they did not matter so much that the whole Reagan tax cut was a net revenue producer. Cutting the top tax rate from 70 percent to 50 percent did produce a revenue gain, but cutting lower rates did not. It was likely that the revenue-maximizing top rate of tax was somewhere in the 40 percent range.

Despite such an imposing title, the paper was an academic success. The National Tax Association gave it the Outstanding Doctoral Dissertation award in 1985. I assumed that it would be read only by my dissertation committee and a few other brave souls who read, say, the *Journal of Public Economics* and the *National Tax Journal*. But fortunately, Bill Hammett and Larry Mone at the Manhattan Institute were among those brave souls who saw in the thesis the potential to challenge the conventional wisdom about tax policy. They approached me, then a young Harvard professor, and asked me to turn the dissertation into a book accessible to a much wider audience. The result was *The Growth Experiment*, published in January 1990. Although no one in Hollywood ever approached me about the movie rights, I have been struck by the number of people who have come up to me over the past quarter century to tell me they had read it and how it had turned them on to the importance of tax policy. Among them was one Paul Ryan, the 2012 Republican Vice Presidential nominee, Chairman of the House Budget Committee, and US Representative from Wisconsin's first district, who told me he read it in college.

I ended up leaving academia and becoming a policy practitioner. The first President Bush asked me to serve as Special Assistant to the President for Domestic Economic Policy, where I got to observe the tax changes in the 1990 budget deal. That deal took the top income tax rate from 28 to 31 percent, raised some additional revenue, and was combined with some reductions in the long-term rate of growth of spending. Bush then appointed me to the Board of Governors of the Federal Reserve. Even though this shifted my focus from tax and fiscal policy to monetary policy, taxes were never far away. I was put in charge of Housing and Community Affairs and one of my assignments involved rebuilding America's inner-city neighborhoods, as Chairman of Neighborhood Reinvestment. There I learned the limits of tax policy. Although housing is a highly tax-favored activity, particularly through the deductibility of home mortgage interest and property taxes, that tax treatment did little to help boost homeownership in the neighborhoods in which I was involved. The people there weren't interested in a tax shelter, or an inflation shelter; they wanted just plain shelter. This was one of a wide variety of societal challenges that simply could not be addressed through tax policy. Taxes obviously matter, but a coherent and effective national agenda must go well beyond tax policy.

The experience helped me move from being an advocate of using tax policy as a way to target social change, which was the theme of the second half of *The Growth Experiment*, to one who thought of taxes in more limited terms. If tax policy was not the most effective tool to effect desired social change, it was probably best to go back to basics and recall that the main goal of tax policy was to raise revenue in a way that minimized the adverse consequences for economic growth. This meant having rates as low as possible, particularly on the entrepreneurial sector, as long as doing so was consistent with the basic revenue needs of the government. That doesn't mean that social goals aren't important, it's just that tax policy is not necessarily the best way to achieve those ends. By making the goal of tax policy revenue oriented and growth oriented, the optimal tax policy emphasizes simplicity, low rates, and a broad tax base.

This view will not win me many friends on either the Right or the Left. Many conservatives view tax policy as a way of achieving social goals in a relatively nonbureaucratic fashion. For example, the Earned Income Tax Credit was originally based on an idea of Milton Friedman's as an alternative to traditional welfare. Family groups push the child credit and the adoption tax credit. The Investment Tax Credit and Research and Experimentation Credit were designed as a way of encouraging businesses to allocate funds to the purchase of machinery and equipment and to product development, as opposed to wages, dividends, and the acquisition of other firms. These are worthy goals, and are generally better than the systems they replaced, but they further complicate an already unworkable tax code.

The Left has also grabbed onto the notion of taxes as a way of promoting its objectives, most notably a more equal distribution of income. The general view is that ever higher tax rates on the rich will produce a more equal society. The trouble is, it hasn't worked that way empirically. The single fastest rate of increase in measured income inequality occurred during the Clinton administration, after the top tax rate had been raised from 31 percent to 39.6 percent. In fact, income inequality rose almost as much in those eight years as it did in the eight years of Ronald Reagan and the eight years of George W. Bush combined—presidents who cut tax rates.

As a practical matter, issues ranging from income inequality to the remediation of social problems are driven by a variety of other government programs. Moreover, the greatest economic challenges the country faces, in the form of a destabilizing series of boom-bust cycles, are generally outside the realm of tax policy. Raising tax rates after a bust has already devastated large swathes of the economy is actually quite a bit like the proverbial locking of the barn door after the cows have gone. High income tax rates make it harder for those who are not yet rich to get that way while protecting the position of those who have already made it—including those who made it as a result of the excesses of the boom.

In 1997 I left the Fed and went into the private sector, specializing in analysis of global macroeconomic trends. At that point the bubble of the 1990s was starting to build, something that would end in tears. I became more vocal about this budding problem in the private sector, arguing somewhat sarcastically in a client letter that 1997 would be a good year for irrational exuberance. Later I became widely quoted as warning that we were seeing a dangerous bubble emerge. This caught the attention of George W. Bush, then Governor of Texas, who knew all about economic bubbles, having been in the oil business in Midland, Texas. Bush had not yet decided to run for president, but certainly had the talent around him to do so if he chose, including a fellow I hadn't met before named Karl Rove, who as a fan of *The Growth Experiment* asked me to autograph his copy.

Bush remembered the elation of the oil bubble and the pain it had caused when the bubble had burst. He remembered friends and neighbors in his hometown of Midland who had lost their businesses and their homes. And he wanted to know what could be done about a bubble after it burst. The answer came straight out of the economic textbook: After the bubble bursts you do the opposite of what they did in the 1930s. Instead of raising taxes—which they did in 1930—you cut them. Instead of raising interest rates, you cut them.

The Bush Tax Cuts

In 1999 Bush asked me to be chief economic adviser in his presidential campaign. At that time I began crafting what ultimately became known as the "Bush tax cuts." A lot of commentators have claimed that the purpose of the tax cuts was to enrich Bush's well-to-do friends. In fact, the purpose of the tax cuts was to do exactly what Bush and I had discussed back in 1997—provide a cushion for the economy when the bubble burst. On December 1, 1999, in Des Moines, Iowa, Bush unveiled the tax cuts in a speech that included this stated purpose. It was at the very peak of the bubble, and many economists were talking about the end of the business cycle and unprecedented prosperity. Bush said, "Yet I also believe in tax cuts for another practical reason: because they provide insurance against economic recession. Sometimes economists are wrong. I can remember recoveries that were supposed to end and didn't. And recessions that weren't supposed to happen but did. I hope for continued growth, but it is not guaranteed."[1]

In practice, the claim that the tax cuts were created simply to enrich the well-to-do has been proven false by recent events. Democrats and Republicans alike overwhelmingly voted to make them permanent in January 2013 for 99 percent of all taxpayers and for roughly 85 percent of the revenue they involved. As the data showed when the tax cut extension was made permanent, those at the top paid roughly a third of all taxes but got only 15 percent of the tax cut. Moreover, the rationale for the extension was exactly what Bush had said it would be when he said the country needed an insurance policy against recession. Getting rid of the Bush tax cuts would have put the economy into a recession in 2013, just as enacting them twelve years earlier had greatly minimized the economic impact of the stock market crash of 2000 and got the country back on the growth path far more quickly than would have happened without them.

The bubble of the 1990s did burst just a few months after his speech—as the stock market peaked in March 2000, followed by the

NASDAQ experiencing the sharpest percentage drop of any major stock index since the Great Depression. Then the downturn began—with the economy recording its first negative quarter in the third quarter of 2000 before Bush even took office, he had an insurance policy ready and waiting to go. On January 3, 2001, three weeks before taking office, Bush had a group of business leaders down to Austin, Texas, for a closed-door and very frank discussion of what was happening. Their unanimous judgment was that things were falling apart very quickly. Consumer confidence was collapsing as stock prices declined. Business demand for investment goods was plummeting as CEOs lost confidence that the boom would continue. Alan Greenspan had heard the same thing and that very day, in the middle of our meeting, announced the first of what would become a long series of interest rate cuts. The textbook response that Bush and I had discussed in 1998 for when the bubble burst had been put in place.

I still judge the effect of those tax cuts as a success. Despite what had up until then been the most precipitous loss of stock market wealth since the 1930s—an 80 percent drop in the NASDAQ—and the attacks of September 11, 2001, the economy began to recover as soon as the tax cut checks hit the economy. Was the tax cut perfect? No, of course it wasn't. And one of the lessons that the following decade taught me was the nature of tax reform as a continuous experiment in what works. The process of experimentation has its limitations and drawbacks, however, in the lack of continuity it provides the private sector for long-term planning.

Now, as a small businessman who has seen his company not only survive, but grow for the past ten years, I appreciate the importance of that need for long-term planning even more. I also understand how tax policy does impact business decision-making in a very direct way. This experience has led me to rethink a lot of what I believed about tax policy, and leads to a very different conclusion in this book about the appropriate design of tax policy than the ending of the original version of *The Growth Experiment*.

Lessons for the Future

The world's thinking about tax policy has changed a lot. At first the idea that lowering tax rates could make a difference was very much outside the prevailing wisdom. Most countries had tax regimes with very high marginal rates. At the extreme, Sweden found it necessary to cap the maximum amount of tax at 85 percent since the combination of the country's income and social insurance taxes had pushed the marginal tax rate over 100 percent. After the success of the Reagan Revolution in America and Thatcher's success with lowering marginal rates in Britain, lowering rates to more sensible levels became part of the consensus. Income tax rates came down globally, in some cases even more dramatically than in the United States. Then tax policy took another step: toward a tool of national economic development as countries such as Hong Kong and Singapore deliberately set rates low to attract the talent needed to build world-class financial centers. They discovered that we live in a world in which human capital is more important than ever in the growth process. And human capital, unlike the physical variety, can always pack its bags and move when tax regimes become too oppressive.

Quite recently we have witnessed a return to revisionist thinking about tax policy. Now we see a revival of the idea that giving private decision makers "too much" freedom is a bad idea. This argument became particularly strong after the financial bubble burst in 2007. It extended far beyond the need to regulate financial activities. The idea that government should take "only" 35 or 40 percent of someone's income became conflated with the notion of giving individuals "too much" freedom. High tax rates came to be seen as a tool both for punishing those who had been successful and for controlling the behavior of those who might push the envelope in the future.

Of course, freedom is merely the power to do things. And power is a zero-sum game. If the individual is not empowered, then that power goes to the government, and it should be no surprise that it is the political class that is at the forefront of demanding that individual decision-making power be limited. Those who advocate repressing individual freedom through regulation and taxation conveniently forget that it was government-created institutions such as Fannie Mae and Freddie Mac that provided the institutional mechanisms for the bubble and government-controlled central banks that printed the money to make it possible.

The new calls for higher tax rates as a means of "controlling" behavioral excesses is just the mirror image of the excesses of some supply-siders in exaggerating the use of tax policy to achieve social ends. The main focus of tax policy should be to produce the needed amount of revenue with the minimum amount of damage to the economy. This is particularly true in our current fiscal situation when the mismatch between government spending and revenue has risen to unprecedented levels and threatens to overwhelm our ability to finance our commitments in the future. In many respects, all of this change in the consensus view of taxes has brought us full circle.

This book is a story of how all of that change has taken place. It starts by leaving the first half of the original version of *The Growth Experiment*, published in 1990, in place. That half describes the analytics of how taxpayers actually respond to changes in tax rates. It is neither supply-side nor Keynesian—it suggests that both responses are important. Sensible tax policy therefore respects both the Keynesian objective of macroeconomic stability and the supply-side objective of preserving individual initiative and economic growth. This view that the Reagan tax cuts used both Keynesian and supply-side analyses to achieve success made *The Growth Experiment* controversial on both the political Left and the political Right. That original version ends with a remarkable chapter, "The Great Surplus of '99." Written when all were talking about "deficits as far as the eye can see," it stressed the key role that continuous growth, coupled with modest restraints on spending and reasonably low tax rates, can play in improving a nation's fiscal situation. It offers proof in black and white that the fiscal trends of the 1990s were already baked in the cake, and not the result of particular policy changes of the time.

The new version then takes over with a particular look at the role tax policy played in the 1990s and the 2000s. A central lesson is that tax policy does not operate in a vacuum. Both of those decades were characterized by large economic bubbles stimulated in part by activist and excessively easy monetary policies. In both decades the bubbles subsequently burst. My experience at the Federal Reserve has left me quite skeptical about the role of monetary policy. Monetary policy should lean against the wind and help stabilize the business cycle. But it cannot become the wind itself, particularly one that blows at gale force. A business-cycle recession might last three quarters, and using easy money to ameliorate that cycle is sensible. But five years of record-setting monetary ease goes way beyond the bounds of normal countercyclical policy. In my view, such excess actually destabilizes the American economy, all the while pretending to stimulate it as long-term equilibrating mechanisms such as "price" and "risk" get buried in an avalanche of money.

The same is true of fiscal policy. Tax cuts and spending increases may be sensible as countercyclical policies in a time frame that resembles a normal business downturn. But year after year of record-setting budget deficits goes well beyond this normal stabilization function. In fact, the deficits of the past few years will ultimately destabilize our economy as debt service becomes an ever increasing burden on the system. So, although it is necessary, getting tax policy right is only part of the equation in producing real and lasting economic growth.

Nowhere is this lesson more apparent than in our current economic circumstances. The morass into which we are marching with misbegotten economic policy will end painfully. Whether that happens in one year or five is unknown. But the end is coming. And when it does we will need a new tax policy on which to rely for a revival of growth. So this volume ends with a description of just such a tax policy. Thank you, dear reader, for your time and patience in wading through this story of three decades of tax policy. There never will be a film version of it, so the story can be told only the old-fashioned way—through the printed word.

PART I

THE GREAT EXPERIMENT: THE 1980s

[I]

The Revolution of '81

"To tax and to please, no more than to love
and be wise, is not given to men."
—EDMUND BURKE, 1774

I N 1980 THE NATION WAS IN THE GRIPS OF THE GREATEST
economic crisis it had faced since the Great Depression. The United
States had endured a decade of chronic economic disappointment
accompanied by a series of acute political shocks, from the defeat in
Vietnam to the OPEC oil crises. Not since the Depression had the
American economy seemed so fundamentally flawed, or had so many
Americans questioned our ability to control our own economic destiny.
It was not uncommon to hear economists and political leaders arguing
that we were doomed to declining standards of living, that we had en-
tered an Era of Limits, that the new economic order was controlled by
OPEC or governed by an ever tightening supply of natural resources.

In January 1980 consumer prices rose 1.4 percent.[1] That month's
increase exceeded the average *annual* rate of inflation during the 1950s
and early 1960s. Had that rate continued for the full year, consumer
prices would have risen 18.2 percent.[2] Charles Schultze, then chairman of the Council of Economic Advisers, explained to the press that

inflation for the year would really be only about 12 percent, but acknowledged that "the Nation has for some time now experienced inflation that would have been unimaginable in earlier days."[3]

Inflation for the year was held down to 12.5 percent,[4] largely because output and employment were declining as well. In the second quarter of 1980 the nation experienced one of the fastest economic declines on record, 9.9 percent at an annual rate,[5] exceeding the rate of economic collapse during the Great Depression. It took a major reversal of policy in the third quarter of the year, including another blast of inflationary money creation,[6] to take the economy out of its tailspin. The number of unemployed rose more than 1.3 million in just two months. The unemployment rate climbed from 6.3 percent in March to 7.8 percent in July.[7]

The combination of inflation and unemployment was expressed by a statistic known as the "Misery Index," which sums up the two rates. The index, a rhetorical device invented by the Carter presidential campaign in 1976, stood at 13.5 in that year. By 1980 the Misery Index reached 20.6.[8] The prime interest rate peaked at 21.5 percent just before Carter left office.[9] The real wages of American workers plunged by 9 percent in just the two-year period 1979–81, offsetting nearly two decades of growth and reducing real wages to their 1962 level.[10] With the enormous tax increases accumulated over that period, workers in 1979 were far worse off than their counterparts in 1962. American workers had not taken such giant steps backward since the 1930s.

Two years later the nation had embarked on the longest and strongest peacetime economic expansion in history, an expansion that would eventually bring more than twenty million new jobs[11] to a once-discouraged American workforce and revitalize states and regions of the country that shortly before seemed doomed to years of frustration and decline. The prime force behind this recovery was a revolution in economic policy that was scorned by many orthodox economists. This new direction in economics, though not without its own flaws, revitalized the economy while simultaneously subduing inflation and reducing the burden of government on American businesses and families. This new wave of economic thought is still controversial. But its effects have made the US once again the leader of the world economy and inspired nations throughout the industrialized and developing world to dramatically revise their own economic strategies.

This book is about our most recent cycle of economic decline and economic renewal and the strategy that accomplished the transition from one to the other.* It is also more: the story of the clash between an *economic orthodoxy* in decline and a challenger from the fringes of economic thought. Most important, it is a story about limits: the limits of a tax that first revolutionized and then dominated public finance, and to a large extent national politics, for three-quarters of a century.

It is no coincidence that these themes all derive from the same story. In 1981 the income tax, certainly the most powerful force behind the growing size and power of the federal government in this century, had reached its economic and political limits. The national economic crisis was caused in no small part by the constraints the continuous expansion of the tax placed on the economy. The orthodox Keynesian economists who, for philosophical as well as policy reasons had pushed the income tax to and even beyond its limits, were forced by the distortions of the tax they championed into positions that became untenable. The intellectual challengers, who have come to be known as the supply-side school, were, it appears in retrospect, exceptionally clever in selecting the income tax as the issue on which to do political battle. In the presidential election year of 1980, it was the political Achilles' heel of Keynesian orthodoxy.

Among those interested in the study of intellectual revolutions, 1981 will be known as a landmark. The supply-side challenge of that year was the greatest challenge to a reigning economic dogma since the overthrow of classical economics in the 1930s. Throughout the 1970s, Keynesian economics, once the New Economics, but by then the new orthodoxy, had reigned supreme. Like many an orthodoxy, it had never seemed so secure as in the last few years before its demise.

The Keynesians, whose views had been forged in the Great Depression, with its catastrophic contraction in the supply of money and credit, believed that government could most effectively manage the economy by managing the demand for goods and services. The government could do this through fiscal policy, primarily by increasing or diminishing

---

*As noted in the Introduction, terms such as "most recent" in Part I refer to the 1980s.

government debt through changes in tax and spending policies. In times of economic contraction the government would spend more, thus increasing demand directly, and take in less taxes, thereby raising the income of consumers and boosting demand indirectly. The increase in demand for goods and services would stimulate new production and employment and the economy would expand. Under the opposite economic conditions the government would reduce spending or raise taxes to keep the economy from overheating and prices from rising.[12]

These policies were followed scrupulously throughout the 1970s. The government repeatedly stimulated the economy through spending increases or tax cuts. The latter did not reduce taxes overall, but did redistribute taxes so as to pump cash into the hands of consumers most likely to spend it. As the decade progressed, however, the inflation that resulted from these initiatives was almost always worse than expected and economic growth less. When the government reined in spending, inflation did not slow as much as it should have, and the anti-inflationary recessions seemed always to be worse than expected.[13] By 1980 this set of policy prescriptions had reached both its practical and theoretical limits.

Contemporary Keynesian theory, based on the Keynesian prescriptions of the 1930s,* simply could not account for the economic facts of the late 1970s. The Keynesians had no solution for the combination of rising prices (which to thém indicated excess demand) and a falling economy with high unemployment (which indicated too little demand). The Keynesians were accustomed to using government fiscal policy to smooth out the booms and busts of the business cycle. But by the late seventies the business cycle had twisted into a diabolic double helix, in which unemployment and inflation rose together. The new economic malady was called stagflation,[14] and the Keynesians had nothing in their medicine cabinet to cure it.

The challengers, the supply-side school, contradicted contemporary Keynesianism on almost every point. The Keynesians were macroeconomists in their approach. They believed the most effective tools of economic policy were manipulations of broad aggregate phenomena, the most important being aggregate demand. The sup-

---

*Though Keynes himself would probably not have been a 1970s-style Keynesian.

ply-siders were primarily microeconomists who believed the most important precept of economic policy making was to pay attention to how government policies affected individual decisions to work, save, and invest. Whereas the Keynesians believed in short-run economic management, the supply-siders stressed basic incentives for long-term economic growth. "In the long run we're all dead,"[15] went Keynes's most famous line. To many it seemed that the economy of 1980 had reached the long run.

The Keynesians regarded tax cuts simply as a way to give cash to consumers, or the demand side of the economy, and designed their tax cuts accordingly. The Keynesians did not believe that income taxes did much to discourage either the production of new wealth or the elements of production, such as labor and capital. The supply-siders, on the contrary, focused on the supply-side, or incentive effects of tax policy. For them, tax policy represented the key to the problems of the 1970s and the solution for the 1980s. High tax rates discouraged people from working, saving, and investing and thereby caused the economy to slow and unemployment to rise. Sharp tax cuts aimed at restoring incentives would solve the stagflation dilemma. The right tax cut would work not by stimulating demand alone but supply as well. If the government restored incentives to work, save, and invest, old businesses would be made more efficient and new entrepreneurs would be more willing to take the risks that yield higher rewards. More workers would be hired, and unemployment would fall. Though the supply-siders accepted that tax cuts could stimulate demand, their prescription for economic recovery emphasized not the spending power of the buyer, but the productive power of the seller.

A tax cut, moreover, by lowering the costs of production and increasing volume, would allow the resulting products to sell at a lower price than would be possible with high tax rates. Thus the supply-siders argued that the right type of tax cut would actually restrain inflation. To the Keynesians this seemed the ultimate heresy. Yet many supply-siders went a step further. They also maintained that the right tax cut would substantially pay for itself. High tax rates, they argued, so discouraged productive activity, and so encouraged tax avoidance and even tax evasion, that reducing rates might bring in more revenue.

It is hardly an exaggeration to say the Keynesians as well as most of the media and political establishment were horrified. Carter's treasury secretary, William Miller, argued in 1980, "It would be a great hoax on the American people to promise a tax cut that sets off a new price spiral."[16] Leading Keynesian economist Walter Heller, chairman of Kennedy's Council of Economic Advisers, argued that the huge tax cuts advocated by the supply-siders "would simply overwhelm our existing productive capacity with a tidal wave of increased demand and sweep away all hopes of curbing deficits and containing inflation. Indeed, it would soon generate soaring deficits and roaring inflation."[17]

The Keynesians might not know how to stop stagflation, but they were sure a big tax cut would make inflation worse. They were not sure how safely to restore full employment, but they knew that the high employment and inflation were inexorably linked. Almost no one other than the supply-siders themselves took seriously the claim that reductions in tax rates would pay for themselves. Thus when Ronald Reagan, who throughout his political career had advocated conventional Republican economics (conservative Keynesianism and monetarism), adopted the supply-side program by resting his campaign on a platform of substantial reductions in income tax rates, two great battles were joined: one for the health of the economy and the other for the future of economics. To most Americans, the first battle probably seemed more important. The world as most people see it is not kept spinning by the musings of economists. Yet the Great Experiment in supply-side economics ushered in by Reagan's decisive victory over an incumbent president in 1980 and the substantial reductions in income taxes enacted a few months later yielded insights into economic policy that over the rest of this century and beyond may be even more valuable than the record-setting economic expansion that followed.

Though the 1984 and 1988 elections vindicated the Reagan tax cuts politically, the economic debate over what really happened in the eighties still rages. Keynesians and other representatives of the old economic orthodoxy still insist that Reaganomics was hokum and that the recovery of the 1980s was the product of standard Keynesian demand stimulus. As careful research often shows in a dispute of such magnitude, neither side is entirely correct. Nevertheless, as we shall see in following chapters, the supply-siders proved more right than the Keynesians on every practical issue in the debate of the early eighties. While most policy prescriptions are lucky to be just a little more right than wrong, perhaps earning a "C," the supply-side experiments of the 1980s deserve at least a "B plus" if not an "A."[18]

It often happens when an orthodox theory is shaken that the protests of the true believers take on an air of desperation. Keynes, himself the subject of orthodox criticisms half a century ago, noted that such protests "will fluctuate, I expect, between a belief that I am quite wrong and a belief that I am saying nothing new."[19] In this case the belief that the challengers are wrong can be subjected to quantitative analysis and the results will speak for themselves. History is the test of the claim that the supply-side challengers said nothing new. The true believers in the old economic orthodoxy need to be reminded just how vociferous their objections were to the supply-side challenge.

The 1981 tax cuts represented as clear a test of the Keynesian and supply-side paradigms as anyone could have designed. Some of the more extreme supply-side hypotheses were proven false. But the core supply-side tenet—that tax rates powerfully affect the willingness of taxpayers to work, save, and invest and thereby also affect the health of the economy—won as stunning a vindication as has been seen in at least a half century of economics. The old orthodoxy has retreated from its first line of defense—that the supply-siders were wrong—to the claim that the supply-siders said nothing new. This is the sure sign that an economic orthodoxy has reached its limits.

But the limits discovered in 1981 were more than theoretical. The income tax had reached its practical limits as well. Like any machine, the income tax broke down from overuse and abuse. The job of the income tax, like any tax, is to produce revenue. But for decades it had been used heavily for other purposes as well: income redistribution, macroeconomic management, and social engineering. The engine of income taxation was tinkered with repeatedly in the name of fine-tuning. The tax code had been changed every other year, on average, during the 1970s. In 1980 President Carter's advisers contemplated the addition of yet another gadget: tax-based "income policies"[20] that would control inflationary wage demands at the level of the individual taxpayer. Had the vote come out differently in November 1980, it is likely that the income tax—the engine driving the nation's fiscal machine—would have continued to disintegrate, causing ever more serious economic breakdowns.

Instead, the dramatic reforms of the income tax undertaken by the Reagan administration produced results the Keynesian fine-tuners could not have expected. On the most controversial supply-side claim—that reductions in high rates would bring in more revenue than they lost—the facts are as clear as they are unacknowledged. The reductions in upper-income tax rates produced a net increase in government revenue. Tax cuts for the upper-middle class just about broke even. Only the reductions in the relatively low rates on moderate- and low-income taxpayers caused the tax cut to be a net revenue loser, though not by nearly as much as the critics had predicted and still often claim. These revenue results clearly showed that high income tax rates had passed the limits of their usefulness as revenue producers (see chapter 4).

The income tax had also reached its limit as an income redistributor. The Reagan tax cut, often denounced as a huge favor to the rich, actually reaped a larger share of tax revenue from rich and upper-middle-class taxpayers than the old tax code had and substantially reduced the relative contribution of middle-income taxpayers (see chapter 5).

The Reagan tax cut also devastated the Keynesian view of the causes of inflation. In the first five years in which the tax cuts were in effect, the inflation rate averaged only 3.3 percent,[21] the lowest rate for any five-year period since the early 1960s. To paraphrase Winston Churchill, "Rarely have so many been so wrong about so much." As we will show, inflation dropped in the 1980s not only because of the Federal Reserve's tight money policy, but also in part because of the tax cuts (see chapter 7). The income tax had reached its limits as a macroeconomic stabilizer, at least in the way the Keynesians had been using it.

As to the source of the Reagan boom, the stimulus to consumer demand was, as always, instrumental to recovery, perhaps even more so than the supply-siders expected. But careful analysis of the data shows that it was the renewed incentives to supply that caused the recovery to set peacetime records for length and strength. Recently it has been popular to argue that the Reagan boom was built on debt and consumer spending that we could ill afford. In fact, consumer spending grew at a rate about normal for a recovery, and the Reagan boom was distinguished by an especially rapid growth in business investment.[22] The recovery of the eighties was not launched on a sea of red ink. Americans are not, as Reagan critics claim, in debt up to their ears. Their financial positions improved quite substantially after the tax cut. The same cannot be said of the government. High rates of government borrowing are a long-term problem. But despite persistent claims to the contrary, the Reagan tax cuts contributed only trivially to the booming deficits of the 1980s. The profligates of the 1980s were not the tax cutters or the consumers but the politicians whose vast spending produced huge deficits they now blame on the tax cuts.

These conclusions are still widely denied by those with a stake in the old orthodoxy. In part the continuing argument is a product of philosophical disagreements about human nature and the role of government and can never be fully resolved by economists no matter how sound their data. But in part the argument has persisted for lack of the data or methods of analysis to settle important disputes of fact. This book will remedy that deficit.

For instance, the job of figuring out whether a tax cut lost or gained revenue turns out to be extremely complex. It is not possible simply to compare the old pre–tax cut revenue estimates with the post–tax cut revenue report. A tax cut changes not only the government's share in the economy but the economy itself. To assess the effects of a tax cut requires a complex and dynamic model of economic decisions and the analysis of large numbers of actual tax returns, totaling tens of millions of bits of data. Practically speaking, the computer technology to do all this has not been available until this decade, and our analytic methods have only recently caught up to the technology.[23] As the data roll in, however, the results of the great Reagan experiment are likely to revolutionize economics and government policy for many decades to come. Crafting incentives for individuals will displace the gross management of economic aggregates as the key to successful economic policy. The creation of wealth will displace its redistribution as the prime concern of government. The scope of state economic power will shrink in the face of mounting evidence that aggressive state intervention, like high tax rates themselves, distorts the natural productive impulses of the people.

In its simplest form the supply-side claim has been, "Taxes matter." In large part this is because the income tax, once a levy on the elite, now profoundly affects the economic lives—and economic behavior—of the vast majority of the population. The nearly universal application of the tax means that federal policies on issues ranging from child care to capital formation to home ownership can be implemented simply by adjusting tax rules. Of course, just because tax policy is a powerful tool for changing behavior does not mean that using it for that purpose is a good idea. President Reagan's underlying policy in cutting tax rates was to reduce the power of taxes over our lives, and in so doing he struck the key blow for a less intrusive government and for more freedom for individual decision making.

Taxes matter because economics is not finally a science of aggregate numbers but a study of human nature. The founders of modern economics in the eighteenth and nineteenth centuries had a high regard for human nature. The intricate mechanisms of the free market model they first developed depend on the assumption that people will react acutely and intelligently to incentives and opportunities, risks and rewards. Those who argue that taxes do not matter are really saying that workers and savers, taxpayers and risk-takers are insensitive to the price of government and that citizens will passively allow governments to solve all its problems by writing another invoice to the people.

It is crucial that we learn the right lessons from the great experiment of the 1980s. Not every Reagan tax initiative worked, and those that did work brought costs as well as benefits. Understanding what worked in the 1980s and before will help us make successful tax policy for the 1990s and beyond. The task is an urgent one: Now that tax policy has taken center stage in the economic debate we can expect as many foolish tax initiatives as wise ones. The 1981 tax rate reductions took a meat axe to the tax code. Future operations are going to require a scalpel. But to wield the scalpel effectively we must first learn how the meat axe did its job.

The tax policy debate to come will not be over the level of tax rates. Reaganomics has been so successful in practice that only a handful of ideologues advocate a return to dramatically higher tax rates. Future tax policy debates will address the fine-tuning of specific provisions, to reduce inefficiencies in the economy; to hone the nation's competitive edge in a world in which many other nations have learned the lessons of Reaganomics; to encourage investments that help us work smarter, not harder; and, perhaps most pressing of all, to help middle-and working-class families with desperately needed tax relief.

The 1980s tested our willingness to experiment with a radical new approach to economic policy. The 1990s will test our willingness to learn from our mistakes and from our successes. The time has come to set the record straight regarding the great tax-cutting experiments of the 1980s and, in so doing, set the agenda for the tax reforms of the 1990s.

[2]

The Psychic Taxpayer

"In this world nothing can be said to be
truly certain except death and taxes."
—BENJAMIN FRANKLIN IN A LETTER
TO JEAN BAPTISTE LEROY,
13 NOVEMBER 1789

*A*PRIL 15. NO OTHER DATE ON THE CALENDAR, SAVE POSSIBLY December 25, is as indelibly etched in the national psyche. Yet the proverbial visitor from Mars might wonder what all the hoopla is about. Although income tax returns are due on April 15, most of the taxes people owe were paid during the preceding year and determined by decisions even farther in the past. And though many of us resolve on April 15 to do things differently next year, these resolutions are often forgotten in the wave of relief that comes when the tax form is finally dropped in the mailbox.

The trauma of April 15 symbolizes the cumulative effect of the tax system on our lives. Like the Judgment Day, April 15 settles all accounts. Our sins and our good works are placed in balance and our fiscal fate decided. If we have been good, we sing a chorus of hosannahs and await our reward, the refund check. If we have been bad, we usually wait until the last minute, search deep in our files for that extra deduction, that forgotten act upon which the IRS may smile, hoping that it will mitigate our guilt and our balance due.

April 15 is such a red-letter day because the income tax is designed to change our behavior as well as to collect tax revenue. As such, it is an adjunct to the judicial system. Threats of legal action, fines, or prison are meant to make us obey the explicit dictates of the law. But the tax system goes beyond the simple categories of lawful or unlawful. Within the category of lawful activities, the tax system introduces many shades of gray, ranging from lawful and untaxed to lawful but heavily taxed. The ability of the tax system to change our behavior in this nuanced way, without the cumbersome mechanics of arrest and trial, gives the government a power in some ways far more extensive than that of the criminal system.

The tax system influences us in ways that are subtle, often subliminal, and frequently difficult for individuals to measure. Taxes influence us by changing the relative costs of the goods we buy and the rewards we receive for working, saving, and taking risks. We take these tax effects into account just as we take the prices of chicken and beef into account in deciding what to buy at the grocery store, or the salary offered in deciding which job to take. Economists often say that people don't *know* their tax rates but *act* as if they do. Tax-induced changes in behavior may be too small for individuals themselves to recognize and yet result in economic changes worth billions of dollars in the aggregate. Like a psychic in his trance, taxpayers responding to tax rates deliver loud and clear a message they may never hear themselves.

For example, economic studies have established beyond any shadow of a doubt that taxes have a dramatic effect on how much people donate to charitable organizations.[1] When tax rates go up, the value of the deduction a taxpayer receives for making a charitable gift also rises. This causes taxpayers, in the aggregate, to increase the amount they contribute. Yet when people are asked in surveys if taxes influence their charitable giving, they usually deny it, maintaining they are motivated only by their means and the worthiness of the cause.[2] However, these surveys also reveal that most people believe other donors are influenced by the prospect of a tax deduction, particularly those in different economic circumstances.

When Chief Justice John Marshall said, "The power to tax involves the power to destroy,"[3] he was underscoring the potential of any tax to alter the behavior of the taxpayer. A tax will destroy the taxed activity completely if it is sufficient to eliminate all of the profit in that activity. Typically we think of this as occurring at a very high rate of tax, but this need not be the case. Marshall's famous dictum from *McCulloch v. Maryland* refers to a tax rate of only about 2 percent that the State of Maryland proposed to levy on bank notes issued by non-Maryland banks. Thus a dollar bill issued by a Maryland bank would cost $1.00, but a dollar bill issued by another bank would cost $1.02. It was obvious—indeed it was the intent—that non-Maryland bank notes would soon disappear from Maryland, for no one would use dollar bills that cost $1.02 if dollar bills costing only $1.00 were available.

As the Maryland tax shows, the damage done by a tax depends not only on the rate at which it is levied, but also on the base on which it is being imposed. Non-Maryland bank notes were a fragile and narrow base on which to impose a tax because it would be very easy to substitute Maryland bank notes and pay no tax. Even if the Maryland law had not been struck down it would soon have collected no revenue, for no one in Maryland would have used out-of-state or federal notes. Of course, that would not have bothered Maryland; the state's aim was not to collect revenue but to protect Maryland banks.

The Maryland tax illustrates the two most important consequences of making a tax rate too burdensome for the base on which it is raised. The first consequence is that the base itself—usually some form of economic activity—will shrink. In this case, the base was non-Maryland bank notes, which would have disappeared altogether. The second consequence of excessive tax rates is that revenues will be lower than expected or even, as in this case, the revenue actually would have vanished.

These two costs of excessive taxation are quite distinct, yet they go hand in hand. The shrinking of the base causes the decline in revenues, and the decline in revenues is a sign (though not a one-for-one measurement) of the shrinking of the base. For an example somewhat more realistic than the Maryland case, consider the tariffs and excise taxes on which federal revenues were based until the early twentieth century. The base on which a tariff is levied, say imported steel, is usually much broader and less sensitive than non-Maryland bank notes. Importing steel is a substantial and risky enterprise that will be undertaken only when foreign steel has sufficient advantages in price, quality, or other factors to outsell domestic steel at a profit. A 5 percent tariff on imported steel would probably not destroy the steel import business. Nevertheless, as the tariff rate was raised the amount of imported steel would gradually fall and revenue would shrink by that degree. If a 5 percent tariff raised $50,000 on $1 million worth of imported steel in a year, a 10 percent tariff would probably not raise $100,000. Since somewhat less steel would be imported under the higher tariff, it might raise only $80,000 or $90,000. Push the tariff high enough and revenues will not only be lower than expected, but will fall below the original $50,000. Push the tariff higher still and both imported steel and tariff revenues will disappear.

Shrinking revenue on rising rates is a sure indication that a tax has been pushed too far. But even if revenue does not shrink absolutely, but rises somewhat, the increase may come at too high a price. When we raise the tariff on imported steel, we not only get somewhat less additional revenue than we expected, we lose the economic value of the steel not imported. People were importing that steel for a good economic reason; its loss will have an economic cost. If it was cheaper than domestic steel, steel prices will now rise and fewer projects requiring steel will go forward. If the foreign steel had special qualities, those qualities will be lost to the economy.

It is not my purpose to argue for or against tariffs; these extra economic costs may very well be offset by other benefits. My point is that when tax rates cause the tax base to shrink, that is, diminish some economic activity, the loss of that activity has a cost over and above the revenue produced by the tax. These additional costs, beyond the tax payment itself, imposed on society by a tax are called the "excess burden" of a tax.[4] We must have taxes, and all taxes impose some excess burden. The key to sensible pro-growth tax design is to raise the needed revenue with the least excess burden on the economy.

The broader and more durable the tax base, the higher tax rates can rise before taxpayers change their behavior enough to narrow the base and reduce revenue significantly. Even a modest tax on Ford automobiles would considerably change taxpayer behavior: Ford customers would buy Chevys. Because there is not much cost to the individual in switching from a Ford to a Chevy, Fords alone (like non-Maryland bank notes) make a narrow and fragile tax base. By contrast, even a rather stiff tax on all automobiles would not bring back the horse and buggy.

For many years most economists believed that personal income, the tax base for the income tax, was so strong and broad a tax base that it was not very sensitive to tax rates.[5] They reasoned that choosing to earn income is not like choosing between a Chevy or a Ford: Income is not optional. Everyone needs it no matter how high it is taxed.

Within limits these economists were right. The income tax base is less sensitive to rate changes than many other taxes. Nevertheless our seventy-five years of experience with the income tax in the United States, the dramatic results of the Reagan tax cut after the similar results of the Kennedy tax cut twenty years before, along with mounting evidence from abroad, suggest that the income tax base is far more fragile than most economists believed even a few years ago.[6] There are numerous alternatives to earning taxable income. Wealthy investors can switch from high-yield, risky, and productive but taxable investments into municipal bonds, real estate, or tax shelters. Very high tax rates make a life of leisure look even more attractive to such people than it might otherwise. At the lower end of the economic scale, even middle-class taxpayers will discover the advantages of leisure when their overtime pay is taxed at 40 and 50 percent. Union negotiators understand full well the advantages of pay settlements that substitute untaxed fringe benefits for taxable cash.[7]

All these tax-driven decisions burden not only the treasury, which receives less revenue than expected, but the economy as a whole. Under excessive tax rates taxpayers may be driven as much by the desire to hide production as by the need to produce. A decade ago, the top US rate of 70 percent was about average for the developed countries. At that rate, a taxpayer benefited as much by avoiding 30 cents in taxes as by earning an additional dollar.

The observation that high income tax rates may discourage the activities that produce income seems so commonsensical that we may wonder why governments would ever let taxes get so high. Of course, they need the money. Moreover the counterargument—that people must have income and so will produce even when tax rates are high—seems commonsensical as well. The trick of tax policy is to find where one principle leaves off and the other takes charge. Is it at 20 percent, 50 percent, or 70 percent that taxes cause too much pain to taxpayers and damage to the economy for the additional revenue they produce? Through most of the history of the income tax it has been impossible precisely to measure taxpayers' responses to rates. Only now with computer analysis of detailed tax return data can we accurately measure the true effect of tax rate changes.

Nevertheless, our first fifty years' experience with the income tax offers circumstantial evidence of the levels to which income tax rates can safely be raised. Those lessons did not take hold with many economists or most politicians in part because for many years the income tax did not have nearly as much power over the lives and work of Americans as it has today. When the tax was first established in 1913, it applied only to rich or upper-middle-class taxpayers. Though the reach of the tax has since broadened continuously, only since World War II has it been a permanent and powerful force in the lives of nearly all Americans. Only in recent decades have most Americans faced for extended periods tax rates high enough to profoundly influence their behavior. It is hardly surprising that many economists have denied the power of high income tax rates over the economy when our experience of their broad application has been so brief.

In its infancy the income tax searched for limits, political and economic. In recent years it has found them. When high rates applied only to the rich, they brought few political consequences and their economic consequences were more easily ignored, even as the economic consequences of a tariff may be ignored when only a few people are directly involved in paying the bill. Income taxes can be raised to a much higher level than most tariffs before they do noticeable damage, but we have long since passed the point when they can be raised with impunity. Today every working American pays a significant tariff on his or her labor. The contemporary income tax places a tollgate at every workplace, savings institution, or investment house. Raise the tolls too high and the entire economy suffers directly and rapidly. Perhaps even more important, raise the toll too high and voters will rebel. In very large part the political limits of the income tax have forced us to learn its economic limits.

At the birth of the income tax in 1913, over 98 percent of American families were exempt from its levies. The standard tax rate was 1 percent on the first $20,000 of taxable income, but single taxpayers earning under $3,000 and married taxpayers earning under $4,000 (which included almost everyone) were exempt.[8] The 1913 income tax also included various "surtax" brackets that could add as much as six percentage points to the tax rate. The combined top rate of 7 percent began at a taxable income of $500,000. Today this income would be equal to $5 million in purchasing power and $15 million in relative position in the income distribution.[9]*

Taxes rose moderately in 1916, but the increase left nearly all American families still altogether exempt. World War I brought the first real tax increase and began transforming the income tax from a class tax into a mass tax. The exemption for low-income earners was slashed to $1,000 for singles and $2,000 for married couples. The number of taxpayers increased more than tenfold, and the surtaxes were applied to lower income levels. The standard rate was raised to 6 percent and the top rate reached 77 percent. It was wartime, and patriotic zeal for the boys over there greatly muted opposition to the new rates.

This wartime expansion permanently changed both the public image and the political character of the income tax. It established that income taxes would ordinarily be paid by the moderately prosperous as well as the rich and that truly confiscatory rates were politically feasible. Levying confiscatory rates on the rich probably made it easier to convince the middle class that rates of 5 to 10 or 15 percent were reasonable. Moreover, the flood of revenue produced by Wilson's wartime rates revealed resources previously undreamt of by politicians or the public and permanently changed the political agenda of this country. Never again would the number of income taxpayers shrink to a small minority of the population. Though Progressives still spoke of the income tax as a "rich man's tax," most of the additional revenue did not come from the relative handful of wealthy taxpayers exposed to high rates but from the vastly increased

---

*Expressed in 1990 dollars.

ranks of citizens paying the 6 percent tax rate. In 1916, with a top rate of 15 percent, the income tax produced $173 million in revenue, 73 percent of which came from taxpayers earning over $100,000. By 1918, with the top rate at 77 percent, the income tax was producing $1,127 million in revenue. Only 42 percent of that money came from taxpayers earning over $100,000. While the revenues collected from the very rich jumped fourfold, taxpayers earning under $10,000 upped their contribution thirty-four-fold, from $7 million to $238 million.

In 1918 4.4 million Americans filed tax returns, eleven times the number that had done so in 1916. It was this much broader tax base, not the rise in rates, that produced the extra revenue. In fact, in spite of record wartime prosperity, and an enormous inflation of incomes between 1916 and 1918, the number of taxpayers reporting incomes over $100,000 dropped by nearly one-third between 1916 and 1918. The amount of income reported by these upper-bracket taxpayers fell by nearly half. Though most of these taxpayers had seen their tax rates rise eight or nine times 1916 levels, tax *revenues* from these taxpayers were only 3.7 times higher.[10] World War I thus brought the first demonstration in the United States of high income tax rates dramatically shrinking the tax base.

When peace came in 1919, taxes were barely reduced. In the wake of a postwar recession, Republican Warren Harding promised a "Return to Normalcy," including a return to previously normal rates of tax, and won election to the White House in a landslide. Harding delivered only a modest tax cut, more by fiddling with the exemption than by cutting rates, which stayed quite high. An increase in the amount of income exempt from taxes lowers taxes on the first dollars a taxpayer earns but not the additional dollars he earns. Such a reduction provides no incentive to earn more and thus no extra incentives for economic growth. The results were predictable—a major decline in tax revenue with minimal economic improvement.*

---

*The tax rate that has the most effect on a taxpayer's behavior is the marginal rate, the rate on the next dollar he will earn. Take a fairly typical four-person family of today with an income of $35,000. On their first $13,000 of income, they pay no taxes. They pay 15 percent on the remainder for a total tax payment of $3,300. Though on average they give the government only 9 percent of their total income, their marginal rate is the 15 percent they pay on their next dollar earned. That is the tax rate a wage earner in the household considers in deciding whether to work overtime.

Harding's death brought Calvin Coolidge to office. Coolidge, with his secretary of the treasury, Andrew Mellon, engineered the first dramatic tax rate reduction in American history, and justified his decision by what we might today call supply-side arguments. In his 1924 state of the union address Coolidge argued that "the larger incomes of the country would actually yield more revenue to the Government if the basis of taxation were scientifically revised downward. . . . There is no escaping the fact that when the taxation of large incomes is excessive they tend to disappear."[11] Coolidge's proposal reduced the top rate from 73 percent to 25 percent (to start at a taxable income of $100,000), with similarly dramatic cuts for most other brackets. The lowest tax rate was cut from 4 percent to only 1.5 percent, and special exemptions for labor income reduced that rate even further, to 1.125 percent for most taxpayers. These reductions, together with an increase in the standard exemption, eliminated tax liability altogether for 2.5 million Americans.

Though the total tax package lost revenue at first, the results clearly vindicated Coolidge's supply-side intuition. Total tax receipts did decline from $861 million in 1922 to $734 million in 1925, a loss of $127 million. But this overall loss obscures more important events. The loss resulted entirely from cuts in the lower brackets, where rates had already been fairly low, and so had little effect on taxpayer behavior. A reduction in rates from 4 percent to 1 percent is a nice gift for the middle-class worker, but hardly changes his incentives. The higher exemptions and lower rates cost the government $340 million in revenue from taxpayers earning less than $10,000 a year. But families earning over $100,000 paid more in income tax than they had previously: $359 million in 1925, up from $300 million in 1922. By 1928 taxpayers earning over $100,000 per year were paying $714 million in income taxes, or 61 percent of the total. Taxpayers earning under $10,000 were paying only $36 million, or less than 4 percent of the total.

The tax rate reductions of the Coolidge era turned the income tax from a mass tax back into a class tax, and did so by sharply cutting the tax rates on the rich. Moreover, after the initial drop, total revenue growth continued strong for the next several years. In effect rich taxpayers had paid for a tax cut for the middle class, and had done so by having their own rates cut dramatically.

The Hoover administration started off with a dramatic tax increase, the Hawley-Smoot Tariff Act, which fueled a worldwide trade war. Along with inappropriate Federal Reserve policies, the tariff helped trigger the financial collapse that eventually became the Great Depression. Government revenues collapsed along with the economy. In short order the political establishment agreed that income taxes should be raised. They were, drastically. The government more than doubled all tax rates to two and a half times their previous level. (The bottom tax rate rose from 1.5 percent to 4 percent and the top tax rate went from 25 percent to 63 percent.) This increase in rates was coupled with a $1,000 reduction in the exemption for married couples and a $500 reduction for single taxpayers. Whatever the reasoning behind this draconian increase, it has been judged by history a blunder of the highest magnitude. Keynesians and supply-siders alike now argue that the tax rate increase of 1932 helped turn what was a deep recession into the Great Depression.

Though the tax increase was a disaster for the economy, it could claim modest success as a budgetary measure. Income tax revenue rose from $246 million in fiscal 1931 to $330 million in 1932 and $374 million in 1933, when the tax increases were fully effective. Though this represents a 52 percent increase in income tax revenues, a closer look at the data undercuts even this modest success. Though incomes were falling rapidly as a result of the depression, the reduction in the standard exemption was so great as to increase the number of taxpayers. This increase in the base offset the decline in incomes[12] and should have produced a revenue increase even if rates had not been increased. Even so the 150 percent tax rate increase produced only a 52 percent increase in revenue. Once again high incomes disappeared, causing revenue to be lower than expected.[13] Though some of the reduction in high incomes can be explained by the economic collapse, most cannot.

Over the ensuing decade, as the economy emerged from the Great Depression, income tax revenue never fully recovered. By 1939 the economy had substantially recovered but reported personal income remained below the 1928 level. The tax base had broadened substantially, the number of taxpayers nearly doubling from 4.1 million to 7.7 million, and tax rates had been increased yet again in 1936. Still, in 1939 tax revenue lagged 20 percent behind its 1928 level. Taxpayers earning over

$100,000 paid 58 percent less in taxes than they had in 1928, in spite of the higher rates. By contrast, the reduction of the standard exemption sharply increased taxes paid by taxpayers earning under $10,000. In 1928 these taxpayers paid $36 million; by 1939 they paid $174 million. Their share of the total income tax revenues rose from 4 percent to 19 percent while the government was supposedly trying to soak the rich and make life better for the common man.

Each major adjustment in the income tax code up through the late 1930s produced similar effects: Very high income tax rates on high incomes caused that portion of the tax base to shrink, in most cases sufficiently to reduce revenues. Tax cuts on the upper brackets actually raised revenues. Clearly income tax rates can be raised higher than the rates of other taxes without rendering the tax ineffective or dangerous to the economy, but there are definite limits.

World War II further changed the character of the income tax. The base was broadened until income taxation became a nearly universal requirement for the working population. Tax rates at the lower end of the scale were hiked roughly fivefold. For the first time top rates were pushed over 90 percent. Nor did the end of the war bring back peacetime taxes. Tax rates were slightly reduced in 1946 and 1948, but then raised again for the Korean War. After Korea, rates settled at 91 percent at the top and 20 percent at the bottom and stayed that way until 1963. Inflation gradually eroded the personal exemption. By 1963 the bottom rate of 20 percent was producing 85 percent of all revenue, and if all rates above 50 percent had been abolished only 2 percent of revenue would have been lost. The top rates served not to produce revenue but as political camouflage, kept to reassure middle-class taxpayers that they were not paying rich people's rates. Very high top rates shifted the whole structure upward, justifying middle-class levies that might otherwise have provoked political revolt. As incomes rose, partly as a result of real growth and partly because of inflation, the number of middle-class Americans encountering marginal rates in the 30, 40, and even 50 percent range increased every year.

In 1963 at age fifty, the income tax was clearly so overbearing in both scope and reach that it was damaging the economy. The class tax had decisively and permanently become a mass tax. Tax rates that ratcheted up in a series of national emergencies never came all the way back down after the emergencies passed. Rates first intended for the rich were soon applied to the less affluent, and justified by ever higher rates on the rich. By the 1960s the "psychic" responses of taxpayers to tax rates had become one of the most powerful forces in the economy as millions of taxpayers adjusted their behavior in the face of tax rates once confronted only by the rich and their accountants.

Not all taxpayer reactions were "psychic." As the burden of taxation became apparent the nation underwent a political transformation. The income tax, regarded benignly by the generality of voters when it applied primarily to the rich, threatened to become a liability to every politician as ever more taxpayers felt its burden.

[3]

Camelot Capitalism
and Keynesian Crisis

"I am convinced that the enactment this year of tax
reductions and tax reform overshadows all other domestic
problems in this Congress. For we cannot lead for long
the cause of peace and freedom if we ever cease to set
the pace at home. . . . I am not talking about giving the
economy a mere shot in the arm to ease some temporary
complaint. This [tax cut] will increase the purchasing
power of American families and business enterprises. . . .
It will, in addition, encourage the initiative and risk-taking
on which our free system depends; induce more investments, production, and capacity use; help provide the two
million jobs we need every year; and reinforce the American principle of additional reward for additional effort."
—JOHN F. KENNEDY,
STATE OF THE UNION ADDRESS, 1963

THE KENNEDY TAX CUT PROPOSED IN 1963, PASSED IN
1964, and named after the martyred president, is the real starting point of the supply-side-Keynesian debate about the effect of tax

rate reductions. For the Keynesians, then in ascendency as the purveyors of the New Economics, the 1964 tax bill represents a masterstroke in economic demand management. For the supply-side school, unborn in 1964, the Kennedy tax cuts exemplify the power of microeconomic incentives. Most important, the fight over the Kennedy tax cuts set the tone for the next fifteen years of tax policy. Though the cuts were successful in themselves, a misreading of their results prompted policies that brought the postwar income tax to endgame and precipitated a crisis for the economy, the taxpayer, the treasury, and the electorate that would only be resolved in the Reagan Revolution.

The year preceding Kennedy's 1963 state of the union address was not the best of years. The Cuban missile crisis gave our competition with the Soviet Union a new urgency and, against glowing reports of Soviet economic growth, the recent mediocre performance of our economy seemed all the worse. In the nine-year period 1947 to 1956, the American economy had grown at a 4 percent annual rate, but in the six following years, growth of the real US GNP dropped to less than 2.3 percent, less than half the alleged Soviet rate. The year 1958 brought a steep recession, with a milder one following in 1960. Unemployment rose to 6.5 percent in 1961, from an average 4.4 percent during the previous decade. Something clearly was wrong, and very worrisome for the generation that had lived through the Great Depression.

The political news was no cheerier. When in the summer of 1962 the economy appeared to be experiencing some difficulty just two years after the 1960 recession,[1] it seemed the administration would face the 1964 elections with a recession on its hands. The Republicans had turned over the White House to the Democrats by the narrowest of margins in the recession year of 1960, and the Democrats had no wish to return the favor. Toward the close of the year, the president and his advisers decided to try to revive the economy with a major tax cut. Announcing his plan in the state of the union address a few months later, the young president proclaimed, "We cannot lead for long the cause of peace and freedom if we ever cease to set the pace at home," thus putting the flag on the side of the largest tax cut in American history.

In 1963 nearly all working families paid income tax. Tax rates were quite high, starting at 20 percent and topping out at a confiscatory 91 percent. The 50 percent tax bracket started at $36,000 of taxable income for married couples and only $18,000 for single persons. Of course, a lot of inflation has passed under the bridge since then. In 1963 dollars, $18,000 would be worth about $63,000 today. Nevertheless, even in 1963 there was certainly room to "reinforce the American principle of additional reward for additional effort," as Kennedy put it.

The tax cuts President Kennedy proposed in 1963 were the most dramatic since the Coolidge-Mellon tax cuts of the 1920s. But in the 1920s, before the Mellon cuts, only 7 million people paid any income tax at all. By 1963 the number of taxpayers had grown to 64 million. Though the earlier tax cuts affected only the top quarter of American society, the Kennedy tax proposal would put more money in the pockets of virtually every American family. That fact had a profound effect on the structure of the Kennedy tax reductions.

Kennedy proposed to cut taxes most steeply at the top and bottom of the income distribution, and relatively modestly in the middle (see table 3.1). In dollar terms some 70 percent of the apparent reduction, or $5.5 billion, would go to taxpayers making $10,000 or less. In 1963 these taxpayers composed 84 percent of the total taxpaying population and paid 48 percent of the income tax. Thus the vast majority of the tax cut was focused on persons of relatively modest means.

On the other hand, the largest percentage point reductions in tax rates came at the top of the scale: Kennedy's proposal to lower the top personal income tax rate a whopping twenty-one points from 91 percent to 70 percent meant that the largest individual tax reductions would go to a relatively small number of high-income taxpayers. Assuming the tax cut did not otherwise affect their earning behavior, taxpayers earning $500,000 would get a $123,000 tax cut while those making $20,000 would get only $600. To offset the political indelicacy, the Kennedy people put great stress on the aggregate volume of the tax cut for those of modest means.

The political motive for adding deep cuts in the bottom rates to sharp reductions on top is obvious. But there was also an economic motive for this two-track approach, or rather two very different motives. What we might call the demand-side objective was to stimulate the economy by putting more money in the pockets of consumers so that

TABLE 3.1 The Kennedy Tax Cut Proposal*

Taxable Income	Old Tax	Proposed Tax	Proposed Cut
$2,000	$400	$300	25%
4,000	800	660	18
8,000	1,680	1,452	14
12,000	2,720	2,388	12
20,000	5,280	4,692	11
50,000	20,300	18,210	10
100,000	53,640	47,028	12
200,000	134,640	105,528	22
500,000	404,640	281,028	31

*Reduction as reported in *Newsweek*, 14 January 1963, 18.

they would spend more. This strategy was particularly popular with the president's economic advisers, Keynesians all, who believed the economy was underperforming because not enough goods were being purchased by consumers. The development of Keynesian theory and practice over the previous three decades had taught the Kennedy men to target the majority of the tax-cut dollars toward lower- and moderate-income taxpayers for maximum effect. They believed these people were the most likely to spend any windfall, thus increasing demand and stimulating production. Taxpayers who already had ample resources might save more of the extra money. Thus a family with taxable income of $2,000 would get a 25 percent reduction but a family earning $20,000 only 11 percent.

The second or supply-side objective of the tax cut proposal was to increase the incentives to work, save, and invest, especially for high-bracket taxpayers. Taxpayers at the 91 percent bracket who earned but 9 cents for a dollar's worth of work might easily find a better way to spend their time. For them, an investment producing a 10 percent return would yield but 1 percent after taxes, hardly enough to justify any risk at all, not to mention the sort of high-risk investments that fuel real economic advance. A substantial reduction in these rates, restoring incentives to work, save, and invest, would increase the *supply* of the economic factors of production: labor, capital, and entrepreneurship.

Kennedy clearly believed in the importance of the supply-side initiative, as his 1963 address made clear. In 1963, however, neither the supply- nor the demand-side strategies won much support. *Business Week* and other free market voices argued that the upper-bracket reduction was too little and too late. As *Business Week* editorialized, "The stultifying effects of the present tax system have been demonstrated again and again in the past five years. . . . The net reductions [the Kennedy bill] proposes are too small and too slow to give a substantial lift to production and employment."[2]

On Capitol Hill most of the critics argued that the tax cut was too large. Congressional leaders such as Wilbur Mills, the Democratic chairman of the House Ways and Means Committee, were not at all comfortable with what was still called the New Economics and feared that the Keynesian plan for stimulating demand would only worsen the existing federal deficit. As it was, the federal deficit in 1962 was 1.3 percent of GNP, the equivalent of a $65 billion deficit today.[3] Kennedy was proposing a tax cut that would apparently reduce revenues by an additional 2 percent of GNP[4] or, in today's terms, another $100 billion. Even today, we do not take $165 billion deficits lightly. Kennedy's Keynesian advisers believed that the right deficit (as determined by Keynesian theory and new mathematical models for economic forecasting) could stimulate an economy suffering from "tired blood,"[5] as Walter Heller, Kennedy's chairman of the Council of Economic Advisers put it. Heller considered unwavering opposition to deficits a vestige of our colonial heritage. "It's remarkable," he wrote in 1963, "how our basic Puritan ethic convinces people that they should deny themselves a tax cut."[6]

On Capitol Hill, the Puritans stood fast[7] and the tax cut stalled. Kennedy opposed either broadening the tax base or cutting spending to minimize the deficit effect of the tax cut, and the Congress was unwilling to give him a tax cut unless he did one or the other. On 22 November 1963, without seeing the enactment of the massive tax cut he proposed, Kennedy was assassinated.

Kennedy's martyrdom won the day for many of his programs, including the tax cuts, passed by both houses and signed by President Johnson in March 1964. Taxes would be cut in stages, in 1964 and 1965, the top marginal rate dropping from 91 to 70 percent and the bottom rate falling from 20 to 14 percent, with less dramatic cuts in between (see table 3.2).

On the supply side, the tax bill was everything that Kennedy had asked for. The sharp reductions in the upper rates were augmented with new incentives for corporate investment and capital formation. The situation on the demand side was not so clear. By itself, the tax bill provided a significant stimulus to consumer demand, providing a total apparent tax reduction of $11.5 billion, or 1.8 percent of GNP. But because of deficit worries, budget outlays for fiscal 1965 were cut below their level in fiscal 1964. Overall, federal spending declined by 1.2 percent of GNP between 1964 and 1965, offsetting two-thirds of the demand-side stimulus of the tax cut.

At the time the bill passed, Treasury Secretary Douglas Dillon proclaimed that it would "help launch a brilliant new chapter in the economic history of the United States."[8] Even treasury secretaries can succumb to hyperbole. But with the benefit of hindsight it is difficult to argue with Dillon's assessment. Real GNP grew 5.3 percent between 1963 and 1964 and a further 5.8 percent between 1964 and 1965. The civilian unemployment rate fell from 5.7 percent to 4.5 percent between 1963 and 1965 as 4.1 million new jobs were created. Productivity in the business sector jumped 4.3 percent and 3.5 percent in 1964 and 1965, respectively. The effect on personal income tax receipts was even more impressive. Though rates were cut between 17 and 30 percent between 1963 and 1965, receipts rose $1.2 billion, or 2.5 percent. The federal deficit declined from $4.8 billion in 1963 to $1.4 billion in 1965. By any economic measure, the tax cut was a solid success.

With such a success, naturally there was quite a spat over who deserved the credit: the Keynesians or the supply-siders (though no one used that term at the time). The argument intensified as the income tax was driven to its limits over the next fifteen years, and was a key part of the tax cut debates of the late 1970s and early 1980s. Walter Heller, an ardent demand-sider, wrote of the Kennedy tax cut in 1978, "The record

TABLE 3.2 The Kennedy Tax Cut as Enacted

Taxable Income	1963 Tax Rate	1964 Tax Rate	1965 Tax Rate
$0–1,000	20%	16%	14%
1,000–2,000	20	16.5	15
2,000–3,000	20	17.5	16
3,000–4,000	20	18	17
4,000–8,000	22	20	19
8,000–12,000	26	23.5	22
12,000–16,000	30	27	25
16,000–20,000	34	30.5	28
20,000–24,000	38	34	32
24,000–28,000	43	37.5	36
28,000–32,000	47	41	39
32,000–36,000	50	44.5	42
36,000–40,000	53	47.5	45
40,000–44,000	56	50.5	48
44,000–52,000	59	53.5	50
52,000–64,000	62	56	53
64,000–76,000	65	58.5	55
76,000–88,000	69	61	58
88,000–100,000	72	63.5	60
100,000–120,000	75	66	62
120,000–140,000	78	68.5	64
140,000–160,000	81	71	66
160,000–180,000	84	73.5	68
180,000–200,000	87	75	70
200,000–300,000	89	76.5	70
300,000–400,000	90	76.5	70
over 400,000	91	77	70

SOURCE: *Statistics of Income* for 1963, 1964, and 1965. Data is provided for married couples filing jointly.

is crystal clear that it was its stimulus to *demand* [emphasis his], the multiplied impact of its release of over $10 billion of consumer purchasing power and $2 billion of corporate funds, that powered the 1964–65 expansion and restored a good part of the initial revenue loss."[9] On the other hand, supply-siders used the Kennedy tax cuts as exhibit A in arguing for the Reagan tax cuts and other supply-side tax initiatives.

The truth is that both supply-side and demand-side influences contributed to the economic recovery and the very favorable revenue results. It is important, nevertheless, to assess the relative strengths of the two effects. As we shall see, the failure of the Keynesians to properly credit the supply-side effects of the Kennedy cuts was a major cause of the confused and ineffective policies of the late 1960s and the 1970s, policies that finally brought the income tax, and the economy, to crisis.

To assess the relative merits of the competing theories, let us consider two tests, one macroeconomic, using Keynesian tools, and one microeconomic, examining the effects of various incentives on taxpayers. The macroeconomic test looks at the causes of economic growth after the tax cut. To do so scientifically we must first determine how much extra economic growth the tax cut caused. Between 1947 and 1963, the American economy averaged a 3.4 percent annual rate of real economic growth. Had this "normal" rate of growth continued during 1964 and 1965 (the two years of the tax cut), real GNP would have been $667 billion in 1965. Instead, real GNP was $705 billion. So it would be reasonable to estimate that the tax cut was worth an extra $28 billion in GNP, or 4.4 percent, by 1965. This means that about 40 percent of the economic growth between 1963 and 1965 could be attributed due to the tax cut, and about 60 percent due to normal factors.[10]

The next step is to divide this $28 billion between its supply-side and demand-side causes. The demand-side stimulus is easiest to quantify: It results from the government putting extra money in the pockets of taxpayers by cutting taxes or increasing its spending. The combination of these two effects is known as the fiscal stimulus.

On the tax side, this fiscal stimulus amounted to some $11.5 billion in 1965. But, as was already noted earlier, the Congress took back some of this fiscal stimulus by cutting federal spending in 1965 instead of letting it continue to grow at its previous rate of 6 percent. The reduction in fiscal stimulus due to lower spending is $7.3 billion. Thus the net increase in fiscal stimulus in 1965 amounted to only $4.2 billion.[11]

According to demand-side analysis, each dollar of fiscal stimulus creates more than a dollar of extra GNP. This is the multiplier effect of which Heller spoke. In a 1978 report on the Kennedy tax cut, Donald Kiefer of the Congressional Research Service wrote, "The major econometric models of the US economy all have multiplier effects for various fiscal policies which range from 1.3 to 2."[12] Thus the $4.2 billion of net fiscal stimulus which occurred in 1965 could only account for a rise in GNP of about $7 billion out of the $28 billion of extra GNP, leaving $21 billion, or three-quarters of the extra economic growth, unaccounted for by the demand-side explanation.

Taking Keynesian reasoning a bit further, consider the effect of the tax cut on the composition of the economy. If the demand-side story were correct, the extra spending power in the economy should have mostly found its way into things people buy: consumer spending and housing. But these items grew only 10.5 percent between 1963 and 1965, compared to a 13.3 percent rise in total private demand. The fastest expansion of demand between 1963 and 1965 was in business spending, not consumer spending. Total business investment grew some 29 percent, and business spending on equipment, which was the target of the investment incentives in the 1964 tax bill, jumped 32 percent. Thus the composition of GNP suggests that the change in tax incentives powerfully increased the supply of financial and physical capital to the economy, a supply-side effect, and that this increase explains much of the GNP growth.

Our microeconomic test proceeds by a close examination of tax return data.[13] Though tax rates were dramatically reduced between 1963 and 1965, total tax liabilities rose from $49.2 billion to $50.6 billion. By itself, this fact is consistent with both the demand-side and the supply-side arguments. After all, GNP grew rapidly between 1963 and 1965, which would cause an expansion of the tax base, and thus in tax revenue. What tips the balance in favor of the supply-side explanation is that most of the growth in the tax base occurred among upper-income taxpayers, whom we expect to respond primarily to more powerful incentives to supply labor and capital to the economy. If the demand-side explanation were correct, most of the expansion in the tax base would have been focused on the bottom of the income distribution as unemployed workers (an existing supply of labor) entered the labor force as a result of new demand for their services.

To see more clearly how various taxpayers responded to the tax cuts, assume for a moment that the economic growth that occurred between 1963 and 1965 increased the incomes of all taxpayers proportionally, which is roughly what we would expect if demand-side effects dominated. This even distribution can then be contrasted with what actually happened to see if one effect actually was dominant. Table 3.3 presents the results. The data support the supply-side explanation. Upper-income groups, which saw a dramatic reduction in their marginal tax rates, reported substantially more income than could be accounted for if economic growth had been spread evenly across the population. On the other hand, lower-income groups reported slightly less income than we would expect if the economic growth between 1963 and 1965 had been evenly distributed. It is important to note that this does not mean that the "rich get richer while the poor get poorer." Incomes rose substantially for both upper-income taxpayers and for lower-income taxpayers. But reported taxable incomes rose substantially more for upper-income taxpayers than for lower-income taxpayers.

High-income taxpayers reported so much more taxable income that more revenue was collected under the lower rates than would have been collected under the higher tax rates prevailing before the tax cut. Taxpayers earning over $100,000, who had been subject to rates ranging from 75 to 91 percent, saw those rates reduced to a range of 62 to 70 percent yet actually paid more in taxes as a result. Taxpayers earning between $50,000 and $100,000, who saw their rates cut from 59 to 72 percent to 50 to 60 percent, paid essentially the same amount in taxes. This happened because these taxpayers reported more income, either because they actually did work harder or because they shuffled their money out of consumption or tax-sheltered investments into more productive but taxable investments, or because of some similar adjustment. Some of them may have just stopped fudging their returns as the rewards for evasion were reduced.

TABLE 3.3 Allocation of Income Reported on Tax Returns for 1965*

Income Class	Assuming Even Growth (millions of dollars)	Actual Distribution (millions of dollars)	Difference
under $10,000	$246,490	$245,864	−0.3%
10,000–20,000	123,110	121,398	−1.4
20,000–50,000	38,911	39,524	+1.6
50,000–100,000	10,676	12,400	+16.1
100,000–500,000	5,611	7,115	+26.8
over 500,000	1,569	2,308	+47.0

*The actual distribution was taken from the *Statistics of Income* for 1965. The even growth distribution was computed by taking the distribution reported in the 1963 *Statistics of Income* and increasing the total dollars in each income bracket by the growth in total income. This had the effect of shifting some taxpayers into a higher income bracket. As the data in the SOI is more detailed than that presented here, this was easily calculated. At higher income levels some interpolation was needed to calculate the new income brackets. While interpolating any function, especially a nonlinear function such as the income distribution, is necessarily imprecise, the results clearly overwhelm any imprecision.

To show this, we first calculated the amount of tax that would have been collected in 1965 if there were no tax cut and therefore no special supply-side response. To make the claim even stronger, we assume that the economic growth that occurred between 1963 and 1965 would have happened anyway and, as earlier, that the growth was spread evenly across the population. Thus, the revenue response we are measuring is in addition to the extra revenue that was collected because of the more rapid economic growth of the period.[14] Table 3.4 presents the results.

If the battle between supply-siders and demand-siders over the effectiveness of tax cuts were limited to the Kennedy experiment, the data show that the supply-siders win hands down. Not only were supply-side responses, particularly to investment incentives, the major cause of the economic expansion after the tax cuts, but the behavioral response of taxpayers at the very highest income tax brackets proved to be sufficient to cause tax revenue to rise even as tax rates declined. These findings indicate that the economic effect was three parts supply-side for every one part of demand-side stimulus. This does not mean that there were no demand-side effects or that they were unimportant, but they would have been greater had the Congress not reduced the net fiscal stimulus of the tax cut by slashing federal spending. Taking back some two-thirds

TABLE 3.4 Effect of Tax Cuts on Tax Revenue: Upper-Income Taxpayers*

	Taxpayers Earning $50,000–$100,000	Taxpayers Earning $100,000–$500,000	Taxpayers Earning over $500,000
Tax Paid Old Law	$3,622 million	$2,405 million	$701 million
Tax Paid New Law	$3,693 million	$2,780 million	$1,020 million

*These tables are compiled by taking the income distribution calculated for table 3.3 and applying the income tax bracket tables. We assumed no change in the ratio of taxable income to AGI in making the transition. The tax paid under old law was computed by taking the old high rates and applying them to the even growth income distribution. Tax paid under new law was the actual tax paid.

of the net fiscal stimulus substantially reduced the Keynesian potential of the tax change.

In retrospect this may have been sound macroeconomic policy. Had demand-driven economic growth been even faster, it is possible that inflation would have accelerated. The rapid growth of federal spending after 1965, caused by both the Vietnam War and the Great Society, was accompanied by much higher inflation. The Kennedy cuts, with the combination of demand-side and supply-side effects that characterizes most successful tax cuts, were just what was required to reinvigorate the tax system and the nation's economy. The Coolidge-Mellon cuts of the 1920s similarly both stimulated demand and unleashed an increased drive to work, invest, and take risks. The 1932 tax increase, on the other hand, collapsed demand and punished effort and risk-taking. If a close analysis of the Kennedy cut provides any specific lesson, it is that tax policy should stimulate both demand-and supply-side effects in a balanced fashion.

The tax cuts of 1964 were a major cause of the longest economic expansion then on record, which continued until 1970.[15] Unfortunately, economists seem to have benefited less than the economy. Most policy makers credited the tax cut's success exclusively to its demand-side features, and in attempts to recapture the successes of the Kennedy cuts, the government launched repeated demand-side experiments throughout the 1970s. The Congress established a new ritual: a tax cut for every even-numbered year, which by pure happenstance coincided with congressional elections. These tax cuts were aimed purely at stimulating demand. The Congress left rates essentially the same and focused relief at the bottom of the scale by raising personal exemptions and the standard deduction. In addition to cutting taxes the Congress repeatedly raised spending levels, usually to fund new social programs but also with the intention of stimulating demand. The results, almost always disappointing, culminated by the end of the 1970s in a crisis for which the Keynesians had no cure: chronic and serious stagflation, a paradoxical (for the Keynesians) combination of high inflation and high unemployment.

The orthodox Keynesians of the post–World War II period held that unemployment and inflation were contrary, not complementary economic conditions. High unemployment and slow economic growth were thought to be caused by too little demand in the economy and curable by increasing government spending or reducing taxes. High inflation was caused by too much demand in the economy and could be cured by reducing government spending and increasing taxes. There was no orthodox economic prescription for simultaneous high unemployment and high inflation, in part because the Keynesians considered them cures for each other.

The key to the stagflation paradox is that the repeated inflations of the 1970s in themselves dramatically increased taxes over the course of the decade, since in a progressive tax system inflation raises taxes automatically. In the absence of a tax cut powerful inflation raises rates brutally. Never during the 1970s did the Congress cut upper- or even upper-middle bracket rates, even though millions of taxpayers of relatively modest means were gradually being forced to pay tax rates once meant for the upper-middle class and the rich. Years of demand-side tax cuts were thus accompanied by years of unlegislated supply-side tax increases, erecting ever greater disincentives to supply capital or labor to the economy.

To see how this happens, imagine a tax system with only two rates: 10 percent on income below $10,000 per year and 20 percent on any additional income. Further suppose that ten years ago Fred earned $10,000 and thus paid 10 percent of his income in tax. If over the course of the ten years inflation had doubled his nominal income to $20,000, he would now be paying the 20 percent tax rate on the top half of his income. His average tax rate would be 15 percent, and his marginal rate 20 percent, even though he had not become one dollar richer in real terms. In fact, this "bracket creep" left him poorer in real terms after taxes, and the government richer.

That is exactly what happened in the 1970s and early 1980s. By the late seventies, ordinary taxpayers were paying "rich people's taxes." In 1980 the median-income four-person family earned about $30,000. After deductions and exemptions they found themselves at the top of the 28 percent tax bracket, fast approaching a 32 percent marginal rate. By contrast, in 1965 a family in the same relative position had been in the 19 percent tax bracket. In 1965 the 28 and 32 percent income tax brackets were reserved for people who were doing quite well. A family of four would not have hit the 32 percent tax bracket until they made 3.8 times the median family income, the equivalent of $114,000 in 1980. The rise in tax rates was even more dramatic for families who, though not rich, were doing a bit better than average. For example, a four-person family earn-

FIGURE 3.1 Tax Rates for Four-Person Family
Earning the Median Income, 1965 to 1980

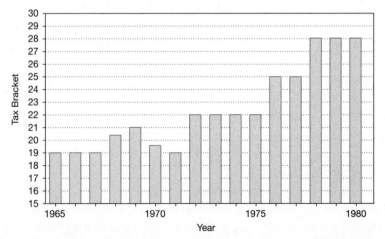

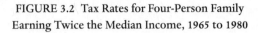

FIGURE 3.2 Tax Rates for Four-Person Family
Earning Twice the Median Income, 1965 to 1980

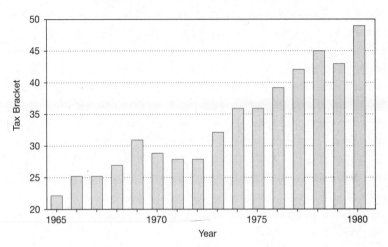

ing $60,000 in 1980, or about twice the median income, faced a top rate of 49 percent. Just fifteen years earlier, a family in the same relative economic position faced a 22 percent top rate. Figures 3.1 and 3.2 show the upward path of tax rates over this fifteen-year period.

The dramatic tax increase on the middle and upper-middle classes extended the behavioral controls of the income tax much farther down the income distribution, exposing a much larger share of the nation's earning, spending, saving, and investing decisions to destructive tax distortions. In 1963 the major problem with tax rates had been the nearly confiscatory level of taxes imposed on a few taxpayers. By 1980 very high but not quite confiscatory rates were distorting the behavior of a broad section, perhaps a majority of the taxpaying population. The income tax had been pushed beyond its limits both politically and economically. This time the excesses applied not just to a few elite taxpayers but to the vast majority. The resulting perversities and distortions gradually became a pervasive force in the behavior of both individual taxpayers and the economy as well as in national politics.

As inflation steadily increased taxes, taxpayers who had never before spent much on tax avoidance began to do so. Tax shelters, once the preserve of the very rich, were advertised in periodicals with mass circulation, such as the *New York Times* and *Money* magazine. Lawful tax avoidance became one of the great growth industries of the nation. Middle-class taxpayers facing upper-class tax rates hit upon shelters of their own, such as taking more of their pay in tax-free fringe benefits. In 1965 fringe benefits represented only 4.9 percent of wage and salary payments. By 1980 this figure had risen to 10.1 percent, and in itself, by reducing the 1980 tax base by $72 billion, cost the government between $20 billion and $25 billion in tax revenue, or between 8 and 10 percent of the revenue collected that year. Other tax revenue figures confirm the seriousness of the problem. In 1965 personal income taxes took 10.3 percent of personal income. By 1980, though typical taxpayers had seen their marginal tax rates rise by 50 to 100 percent, income taxes still took only 11.4 percent of personal income. A drastic increase in tax rates, combined with a modest increase in revenues, proves beyond doubt that the tax base was shrinking.

A shrinking tax base may seem an abstract peril. It is not. To say that the tax base is shrinking is to say people are doing less of all those things—working, saving, and investing—by which we maintain prosperity. The shrinking of the tax base in turn makes traditional Keynesian demand management obsolete. Under the traditional prescriptions, raising taxes is supposed to cure inflation by cutting purchasing power, thus reducing the *demand* for goods and services in the economy. But if tax rates are already high enough to distort taxpayer behavior and discourage work, savings, and investment, any further tax increase will also reduce the *supply* of goods and services to the economy. Supply and demand will remain out of balance and the inflation rate will stay stubbornly high. The economy, suffering from cuts in both demand and supply, will shrink. The result is stagflation.

Nor will Keynesian strategies for stimulating the economy help in these conditions. Traditional Keynesians focus their demand-side stimuli (either tax cuts or higher spending) on lower-income taxpayers, who can be relied on to spend the money and raise demand. But if excessive upper-bracket rates continue to discourage effort and risk, there will be no commensurate increase in the supply of goods and services to the economy. Higher demand coupled with stagnant supply will produce only higher inflation, not economic growth: again, stagflation. The nation scrupulously followed Keynesian advice between 1965 and 1980.[16] Fifteen years of faithfully stimulating demand and ignoring the growing penalties on supply increased the inflation rate from 1.9 percent to 12.4 percent and the unemployment rate from 4.4 percent to 7.0 percent.

By 1980 tax rates were clearly damaging the incentives to supply both labor and capital to the economy, though the disincentives for capital were particularly obvious. Consider, for example, the case of the middle-income family and its savings account, an important source of investment capital. The account earned 5.5 percent interest, but after taxes the family kept only 3.7 percent. Moreover, consumer prices rose 13.5 percent between 1979 and 1980. The real purchasing power of the money left in the savings account after taxes actually fell nearly 10 percent that year, leaving little incentive to save.

Much the same story could be told of the typical stock portfolio. A couple earning $60,000 who invested $10,000 in the stocks that composed the NYSE Composite Index in 1974, when the stock market hit its low for the decade, would have seen their investment grow to $15,500 in 1980. Assuming they sold out and took their profit, federal capital gains taxes, which are lower than ordinary income taxes, would have left them $14,400. Unfortunately, consumer prices rose 67 percent in that same time, leaving our couple $1,400 poorer in purchasing power, though they had timed their stock purchases perfectly. Most investors did worse.

The combination of high taxes and high inflation also encouraged borrowing (dis-saving) for current consumption. Since consumer interest such as the 18 percent rate on credit card purchases was deductible, the effective interest rate dropped to 9.2 percent for a family in the 49 percent tax bracket. With inflation pushing up prices by 13.5 percent per year, it was cheaper to buy now on credit than to wait a year, save the money, and pay cash.

High taxes and high inflation directly discouraged business investment in new plant and equipment. The tax code allows businesses to deduct from their taxable profits, over time, the costs of the gradual wearing out of their plant and equipment. This deduction quickly loses its value in times of persistent inflation, because it is based on the original purchase price of the tools, not the inflated cost at which they will have to be replaced. The erosion of this depreciation deduction causes business profits to be overstated and overtaxed, discouraging business investment, particularly for capital-intensive businesses.

By the late 1970s the tax penalties on the suppliers of capital were so severe that there was strong sentiment on Capitol Hill for reducing them. The 1978 Steiger amendment reduced by nearly half the top effective rate of the capital gains tax, the tax on the increase in the value of an investment, such as stock shares, paid only after the investor chooses to cash in his or her investment. After this reduction the government actually took in more capital gains tax than before; 45 percent more in 1979 than in 1978, new confirmation that high tax rates had been shrinking the tax base, penalizing supply, and punishing the economy.

The results of the Steiger amendment certainly strengthened the growing supply-side movement as well as making some converts to tax cutting on Capitol Hill. But the Carter administration, believing that high and rising taxes would slow inflation and help to cure the nation's economic ills, remained firmly opposed to any broad, significant change in tax policy. In the 1980 *Economic Report of the President*, Carter's economic advisers argued,

> Fighting inflation continues to be the top priority of economic policy, and hence the President has not recommended any legislated changes in tax rates in the 1981 budget. Since individuals will be moving into higher tax brackets as their incomes increase, the share of personal income taken by Federal income taxes will rise. Social security tax liabilities are scheduled to increase in January 1981 by $18 billion. The resulting rise in effective tax rates, combined with limited growth of Federal outlays, will cause the Federal budget to move significantly toward restraint in the next fiscal year.[17]

In the midst of an economic and political crisis, the president sought refuge in the bosom of orthodoxy. He would fight fire with more fire, deliberately using bracket creep to raise taxes yet higher so as to brake the rise in prices.

Carter's stand-pat approach did not sell. Ronald Reagan was a relative newcomer to supply-side ideas, but as he would show repeatedly in the years to come, he had a fine sense of the ripening of a crisis and the opportunities thereof. He ran for president largely on a promise of dramatic reductions in personal tax rates, which he promised would revive first the American spirit of enterprise and then the American economy. And it was largely for those promises that he was elected.

The campaign called for a reduction in rates and in rates alone. Reagan's speeches included no complicated lists of minor adjustments; exemptions; loopholes; or subsidies for the poor, the powerful, the rich, or the well connected. Yet by the time the Economic Recovery Tax Act of 1981 (ERTA) became law, it seemed to address nearly every social wrong or economic woe known to the nation. The final bill not only cut tax rates but extended the tax incentives for charitable deductions to all taxpayers, increased the subsidy for child care, provided a deduction for adoption expenses, increased the tax-free profit a retired couple could realize from the sale of their home, and made dozens of other major and minor adjustments to the tax code. These included numerous special tax favors for businesses or individuals represented by key members of Congress. The Joint Committee on Taxation estimated that by 1986 fully half of the revenue cost of the bill would come from provisions other than the personal tax rate reductions.[18]

Not all of the additional changes were unrelated to the central crisis of the tax system. The Accelerated Cost Recovery System (ACRS), the Individual Retirement Account (IRA), and the Two Earner Deduction, each of which we examine fully in the coming chapters, directly addressed the dilemmas of the late 1970s and powerfully contributed to the recovery and expansion of the 1980s. In brief, ACRS reduced the impact of inflation on the depreciation deduction for business plant and equipment, curbing the overtaxing of business profits and encouraging business investment. The IRA, aimed at increasing national savings, allowed taxpayers to deduct from their taxable income up to $2,000 in annual contributions to a retirement account and to accumulate earnings tax free until withdrawal. The Two Earner Deduction reduced the marriage penalty, under which the earnings of married working women effectively were taxed at a rate much higher than the earnings of single working women. The deduction was intended to give working women equitable tax treatment, to provide tax relief for families, and to raise the labor force participation of married women, who have been shown by economic research to be very sensitive to tax rates in deciding whether to work.[19]

All these provisions, as we shall see, were relatively successful. But the most important additional change of ERTA was the indexing of the tax code for inflation, ending the bracket creep that had drastically raised federal tax rates over the previous fifteen years even while the Congress "cut" taxes five times.

As the congressional staff noted in its *General Explanation* of ERTA,

> The Congress believed that "automatic" tax increases resulting from the effects of inflation were unfair to taxpayers, since their tax burden as a percentage of income could increase. . . . In addition, the Federal Government was provided with an automatic increase in its aggregate revenue, which in turn created pressure for further spending. . . . Indexing will prevent inflation from increasing that percentage and thus will avoid the past pattern of inequitable, unlegislated tax increases and induced spending.[20]

No words could better express why the introduction of indexing was such an important change in tax policy. Bracket creep is the twentieth-century version of "taxation without representation." Not only does it raise taxes without a vote of the Congress, it generally raises them most fiercely for people of modest means. In almost any progressive income tax schedule, rates climb most steeply at the bottom of the scale; typically a few thousand dollars of additional income will move a taxpayer from the 15 to the 20 percent bracket, while it may take tens or hundreds of thousands of dollars to move a taxpayer from the 60 to the 70 percent bracket. Of course, taxpayers in the very top bracket can go no higher. Inevitably brackets creep fastest at the bottom.

Indexing leaves tax rates unchanged, but in case of inflation adjusts the income levels to which each tax rate applies, effectively eliminating bracket creep. Indexing not only compensates for inflation, it removes a clear incentive for a government to pursue it. Without indexing a government in fiscal difficulty may be tempted to inflate its way out of the crisis. This was essentially the fiscal strategy tried by the Carter administration. The Carter administration reduced the budget deficit of the late 1970s not by cutting spending, which increased faster than inflation, but through an enormous unlegislated tax increase, courtesy of bracket creep.[21] Indexing shifted power back from the government to taxpayers and voters. Its passage, probably only possible at a time of political crisis, was perhaps the most powerful symbol of the revolt against the postwar tax system.

There is no such thing as a free lunch. The cost of the various special provisions of ERTA, good and bad, was smaller tax rate reductions than those the president had endorsed during his campaign. Nevertheless, rate reduction remained the centerpiece, however diminished, of the Reagan strategy and the Great Experiment.

The Reagan tax cut really got its start in 1977 when Senator William Roth and Representative Jack Kemp proposed the "Tax Rate Reduction Act," calling for income tax rate reductions of 33 percent over a three-year period. Candidate Ronald Reagan endorsed the Kemp-Roth legislation during his campaign in 1980, but the proposal President Reagan sent to the Congress was more modest. It called for three consecutive 10 percent tax rate reductions, the first to be retroactive to January 1981. In the political shorthand of the time, this came to be known as ten-ten-ten. To most people, three reductions of 10 percent add up to a 30 percent reduction, quite close to the Kemp-Roth scheme. In the arithmetic of tax experts, it does not work out that way. The first 10 percent cut is worth 10 percent. But the second 10 percent cut is applied to tax rates already reduced to 90 percent of their original level. So the second 10 percent cut is really only a 9 percent reduction in the original tax rates, and the third cuts rates by only 8.1 percent. Ten-ten-ten adds up not to 30 but 27 percent.

Not even the 27 percent cut survived. Despite a convincing Reagan victory in November and a stunning twelve-seat turnaround in the Senate—giving the Republicans control of that body for the first time in a generation—the Reagan proposal ran into stiff opposition. Congressional hearings dragged on until Memorial Day, and the entire package came closer to defeat than is now generally remembered. Finally in early August the House and Senate approved the bill, but only after the rate cuts had been trimmed further to five-ten-ten. And just as ten-ten-ten did not add up to 30, five-ten-ten did not add up to 25 but 23 percent. Nor were the reductions retroactive to January 1981 as the president had hoped; the first cut would not go into effect until 1 October 1981.

Reagan had wanted to move more quickly because he feared, rightly as it turned out, that the country was headed for a full-scale recession. The signs of economic decline were everywhere as he took office. Unemployment remained at 7.5 percent and real GNP declined in the second quarter of 1981. The economy was clearly headed for trouble. But

TABLE 3.5 Tax Rate Schedules Under Prior Law and the Act for 1982, 1983, and 1984 (Joint Returns)*

Taxable Income Bracket	Under Prior Law	Under the Act 1982	1983	1984
0 to $3,400	0%	0%	0%	0%
$3,400–$5,500	14	12	11	11
$5,500–$7,600	16	14	13	12
$7,600–$11,900	18	16	15	14
$11,900–$16,000	21	19	17	16
$16,000–$20,200	24	22	19	18
$20,200–$24,600	28	25	23	22
$24,600–$29,900	32	29	26	25
$29,900–$35,200	37	33	30	28
$35,200–$45,800	43	39	35	33
$45,800–$60,000	49	44	40	38
$60,000–$85,600	54	49	44	42
$85,600–$109,400	59	50	48	45
$109,400–$162,400	64	50	50	49
$162,400–$215,400	68	50	50	50
$215,400 and over	70	50	50	50

SOURCE: *General Explanation of the Economic Recovery Tax Act of 1981* (Joint Committee on Taxation. Washington, D.C.: US Government Printing Office), 405–11.

*These tables are compiled by taking the income distribution calculated for table 3.3 and applying the income tax bracket tables. We assumed no change in the ratio of taxable income to AGI in making the transition. The tax paid under old law was computed by taking the old high rates and applying them to the even growth income distribution. Tax paid under new law was the actual tax paid.

since the first 5 percent cut would be in place for only a quarter of the year, the net effect of ERTA in 1981 was to reduce income tax rates by a derisory 1.25 percent. The first 10 percent cut was scheduled to take effect 1 July 1982. On average 1982 taxes would be only about 10 percent lower than 1980 rates. The second 10 percent rate reduction was scheduled to take effect 1 July 1983, making 1983 rates, on average, still only 19 percent lower than those of 1980. Not until 1984 would tax rates drop fully 23 percent below those of 1980.

There was one encouraging break in all these delays: At the initiative of some congressional Democrats who seemed to accept supply-side arguments about the hazards of very high rates, rates were capped at 50 percent as of January 1982.[22] All rates in excess of 50 percent, including the former top rate of 70 percent, were immediately reduced to 50 percent, with additional reductions to follow on the established schedule. The top effective tax rate on capital gains was also reduced from 28 to 20 percent, a reduction of just over 28 percent. (The schedule of reductions is shown in table 3.5.)

Delaying the tax cuts almost certainly contributed to the very severe recession of 1981–82. The economy declined most precipitously in the fourth quarter of 1981 and the first two quarters of 1982. As soon as the first big tax cut hit workers' paychecks in the third quarter of 1982, consumer demand began to rebound. The economy as a whole began to expand in the next quarter.

In sum, the president got smaller tax rate reductions than he asked for, and got them too late to forestall the 1982 recession. Nevertheless, the Great Experiment was in place. Over the next five years the economic paradigms and policies, the fiscal strategies, and the public finance principles of a generation would be weighed in the balance.

[4]

The Great Experiment

"It is increasingly clear—to those in government,
business and labor who are responsible for our economy's success—that our obsolete tax system exerts too
heavy a drag on private purchasing power, profits, and
employment. Designed to check inflation in earlier
years, it now checks growth instead. It discourages
extra effort and risk. It distorts the use of resources.
It invites recurrent recessions, depresses federal
revenues, and causes chronic budget deficits."

—A PRESIDENTIAL STATE OF THE UNION MESSAGE

"It is not credible that the more Reagan cuts taxes the
sooner we reach budget balance. Here is an easy way to
call Arthur Laffer's bluff: cut tax rates and don't cut spending programs. Conservatives will not like the result."

—PAUL A. SAMUELSON, *NEWSWEEK*, MARCH 2, 1981

THIS STATE OF THE UNION ADDRESS WAS DELIVERED NOT
by Ronald Reagan but by John F. Kennedy, who numbered
among his principal economic advisers Paul Samuelson. Eighteen years

later Samuelson found himself a vigorous opponent of the Reagan tax cut proposal, though it was inspired in large part by Kennedy's great success. Samuelson was joined in his opposition to the Reagan proposal by Kennedy economic advisers Walter Heller and John Kenneth Galbraith as well as most of the Democratic political and intellectual establishment.

Why the change? Politics, like the heart, has its own reasons. Politics aside, the Kennedy and Reagan tax cuts were made in very different economic circumstances. When Jack Kennedy argued that high marginal tax rates were destroying incentives to work and invest, injuring the economy, and depressing tax revenues he could point to a top tax rate of 91 percent as exhibit A. Though the dominant view among economists was that tax rates could go quite high without serious consequences, few economists could argue that 9 cents on the dollar would incite anyone to work weekends or pry any family fortunes out of cozy tax shelters.

At the time of the Reagan proposal the top marginal rate was 70 percent. Though fairly stiff, it nevertheless gave top-bracket taxpayers more than three times the incentives they had in 1963 to work an extra hour or make an extra investment. It was harder to argue that top tax rates were a significant drag on productive activity, and it was much harder to argue that the top rates might actually be losing revenue.

Moreover, despite the recessions of 1958 and 1960 and some worrisome employment figures, the Kennedy tax cuts had come at a time of relatively favorable economic conditions. The tax cuts of 1981, by contrast, were proposed in an era of stagflation: low or negative growth paradoxically combined with a steep inflation. Under these circumstances, the Keynesians believed an expansion of demand (which they regarded as the only significant likely result of the proposed tax cut) would increase inflationary pressure while producing little or no additional real growth. The result would be a big drop in revenues, a deepening deficit, and more pressure on prices. Under this scenario the potential inflationary impact of the tax cut would make the Federal Reserve's job more difficult and dangerous. The Fed, which was already tightening money to fight inflation, would have to tighten still further, sending interest rates up yet higher and crowding out business investment. If on the other hand the Fed failed to act, inflation, already in the double-digit range, would spiral out of control. Though the Keynesian view provided no clear path out of stagflation, it did suggest that tax cuts would get us deeper into trouble. The Keynesians' assumption that tax rates in roughly the 40 to 70 percent range have only a modest effect on taxpayer behavior led them to believe that the only significant economic effect of a reduction in tax rates would be an untimely expansion of demand.

On these premises, the Reagan tax cuts were a bad idea. But the supply-siders believed that cutting tax rates would also increase the productive activities of taxpayers and thus the supply of labor and capital. If the supply-siders were right, the tax cuts might be the way out of stagflation. An increase in productive activity would put downward pressure on prices by increasing the supply of goods and services available for purchase. This might offset the upward pressure on prices caused by increased demand. The right tax cut would increase overall economic activity by increasing supply and demand simultaneously, and avoid an increase in prices. As taxpayers increased—or exposed—their productive activities, tax revenues would increase, decreasing the cost of the tax cut and perhaps paying for it outright.

As often happens in politics, the argument between the supply-siders and Keynesians soon narrowed to a single point: Would the Reagan tax cuts be big revenue losers, or would the tax cuts largely or entirely pay for themselves? Although this emphasis on revenue led to distortion and hyperbole in debate, it was not without use in concentrating discussion on a key fiscal issue: Could we afford a tax cut? However much economists may seem to bicker, they agree about quite a number of things. Most recognize that to some degree taxes are a drag on economic activity and a burden on the happiness of the people, an evil we tolerate only to obtain necessary government services. (Most also regard taxes as a necessary tool for redistributing income.) If it were true that the tax cuts would largely pay for themselves, the Keynesians, though not sharing the enthusiasm of the supply-siders, could have few objections. Without a big revenue loss, the deficit would not get significantly worse, and the pressure on the monetary policy of the Federal Reserve would be minimal. If the supply-siders were correct about revenues, the argument that we ought to have the lowest tax rates we can afford would carry the day.

To this day, economists and politicians who criticize the 1981 tax cuts claim that the Reagan policy cost the government a great deal of revenue. When, in the 1988 vice presidential campaign debate, Senator Lloyd Bentsen argued the Reagan recovery was built on "hot checks," or debt, he was depending ultimately on the claim that the tax cuts lost lots of money.

There was, however, another and deeper motivation for this focus on revenue, for more was at stake than a single tax bill. The supply-siders were challenging a paradigm that had dominated economic thought for nearly a half century. The revenue effects of the tax bill would show to what extent taxpayers change their behavior in response to tax cuts. Whoever turned out to be right about the effect of taxes on taxpayer behavior would gain a big advantage in the overall debate about the effect of tax rates on the economy and the proper course of economic policy. Most positive revenue effects would indicate that taxpayers had changed their behavior in ways that would be good for the economy (or at worst neutral) over the long term as well as the short. Positive revenue effects would indicate that taxpayers were working either harder or smarter and investing more or making their current investments more efficiently.

By a "positive revenue effect" we do not mean that the tax cut necessarily would be fully self-financing, but merely that some of the anticipated revenue loss was recovered by the treasury. The extent to which the tax cut cost less than anticipated would be the true measure of how much taxpayer behavior was affected: The larger the revenue feedback, the more the point would be proved that taxes affect taxpayer behavior and are a decisive policy tool.

Nearly a decade after the tax cuts were passed, public perceptions over the revenue results vary considerably, in part because so many people have a political stake in showing that the numbers support different positions. But the disagreement rages for another reason as well: Until quite recently we simply lacked the technological and analytical tools to assess the precise effects of tax law changes. Absent good data analysis, the debate on the tax cuts produced more heat than light.

Only very detailed computer modeling can pin down the behavioral effects of tax cuts. Such detailed analyses of tax changes were simply impractical in the 1920s, 1930s, and even the 1960s. Economic research, like politics, is an art of the possible: Without the technological tools for detailed analysis there was little point in developing analytic method. Only since the technology has been generally available have we begun to develop analytic methods to take advantage of it.

The method used here, developed for the express purpose of evaluating the effects of the Reagan tax cut, is based on the actual tax returns of more than 34,000 taxpayers in each of six tax years.[1] The actual analysis was done using the National Bureau of Economic research TAXSIM model, developed by economists including Daniel Feenberg, Martin Feldstein, Daniel Frisch, Lawrence Lindsey, and Andrew Mitrusi. This computerized model, like the tax models used by the Treasury Department and the Joint Committee on Taxation, relies on the Individual Tax Model developed by the Internal Revenue Service. With nearly one hundred items of information about each taxpayer, computers enabled us to employ some twenty million items of tax data. By contrast, the analysis of the 1964 tax cuts had to be done using only a few pages of published data from the period.

Although modern computers are great at generating answers, we humans still have to frame the questions. Much of the confusion regarding the effect of the 1981 cuts on tax revenue is the result of critics considering only *some* of the effects of the tax cut, neglecting others that failed to fit their preconceived notions. To get a useful answer, we must carefully think through what happens to the overall economy as well as to individual taxpayers when tax rates are cut.

The numerous responses to tax rate changes seem to fall into four interacting and occasionally conflicting sets, which we will term "effects." The first and simplest—though it is in some ways misleading—is what we will call the "direct effect."

The direct effect of a tax cut is the revenue change that would result if nothing else changed. The direct effect assumes that if everyone were taxed at, say, a 40 percent rate, and that rate was cut to 30 percent, revenues would decline by exactly 10 cents on the dollar. In figuring the direct effect, both taxpayer behavior and the economy are assumed not to change as a result of even a substantial tax cut. The direct effect provides a ballpark estimate of the revenue effects of tax changes. It can be useful in the case of small tax changes but is not very accurate for changes of any significant size. Whether by changing taxpayer behavior, the level of economic activity, or both, tax changes almost always do change the size of the tax base. These changes are summarized by the three indirect effects, in combination with which the direct effect does yield an estimate of the true amount of revenue lost or gained in a tax cut.

The first indirect effect is the "demand-side effect." The demand-side effect is based on the assumption that, at least in the short run, a tax cut will increase consumer demand and thus economic activity. After a tax cut, taxpayers have more money to spend and demand more goods; with more demand for goods, more people are employed and those already employed work more hours. As a result of this increased economic activity, the government collects higher tax revenue. This is hardly a new idea, and Keynesian economists, quite rightly, have argued it for many years. In fact, the demand-side effect might be called the Keynesian indirect effect.[2]

The next indirect effect is the "supply-side effect." The supply-side effect measures revenue changes that result from a change in the supply of factors of production (capital and labor) as a result of tax changes. At lower tax rates, each taxpayer keeps more of each additional dollar earned. This tends to make him more willing to work longer hours, to work harder and more efficiently in hope of a raise, to save or invest more, or—if he is an entrepreneurial type—to take greater risks in pursuit of now higher after-tax rewards. These extra efforts and investments yield more economic activity, more income, and thus more tax revenue. These are considered supply-side effects because they are due to an increase in the resources *supplied* to the economy rather than to increased demand for the economy's output.

Consider a single self-employed electrician, Fred, earning $20 per hour. Prior to the 1981 tax cut, he was taxed at the 44 percent rate on his last hour of earnings, leaving him $11.20 after taxes. After the tax cut was in place, his tax rate fell to just 34 percent, leaving him $13.20; the tax cut gave him a $2.00 per hour "raise." Common sense suggests that his raise will make Fred more willing to make a house call on Saturday or work longer hours.[3]

Married women exemplify a supply-side response backed by particularly strong economic evidence. Consider an $18,000 per year secretary,

Jane, who gets our electrician to the altar. In 1980 the new bride would have discovered that after her federal and state payroll taxes she would henceforth keep but 45 percent of her income. This was because of the "marriage penalty" rule, which combines the income of married persons for tax purposes, in effect stacking her income on top of his to determine her tax bracket. Rather than work full time for $8,100 per year after taxes, Jane might well have decided it would be more worthwhile to stay home and renovate the house or take care of the children, activities that, while valuable, produce no taxable income.

By the 1980s married couples in which both spouses worked formed the core of the nation's middle and upper-middle class. In 1984 two-thirds of the married couples earning between $30,000 and $75,000 were two-income couples. The unlegislated tax increases of the 1970s were particularly hard on these people. As brackets crept upward, the marriage penalty levied a very stiff tax on the lower earner. The evidence suggests that the most common reaction to the growing marriage penalty was for married women to work less than they otherwise would have. No other group in the population reduces its labor force participation more in the face of high taxes than married women.

The Two Earner Deduction of the Economic Recovery Tax Act substantially reduced the marriage penalty by allowing Jane and Fred to deduct 10 percent of Jane's earnings, up to $30,000. This change, combined with the general reduction in tax rates, gave married working women a substantial after-tax "raise," in Jane's case more than $2,300 a year. The results were impressive: With sharply increased incentives to work, married women not only increased their labor force participation, but also took on jobs that, on average, paid more than those they had previously held. In 1982, the year the Two Earner Deduction began, the adult female unemployment rate fell below the adult male unemployment rate for the first time since 1949. In the eight years preceding the passage of ERTA, the earnings of year-round full-time female workers were only 60 percent of those of year-round full-time male workers. In 1982, the first year during which ERTA was in effect, this figure jumped to 63 percent, and averaged 64 percent in the five years during which ERTA was the tax law of the land.

If Jane's "raise" were to convince her to keep working, the government would continue to collect taxes on her $18,000 salary, all of which it would otherwise have lost. As with Fred's willingness to work longer hours after his tax cut, the extra tax revenue produced by Jane's extra work would be a supply-side effect, since it would come from a taxpayer supplying more labor to the economy. Supply-side responses by investors work much the same way: When a tax cut raises the after-tax reward of investment, people move capital out of consumption (a bigger house, a faster car, a longer vacation) and into investment, increasing the capital available to the economy and, ultimately, the revenue available to the treasury.

Our final entry, the pecuniary effect, measures changes in taxpayer behavior that change tax revenue but do not change the amount taxpayers work or invest or the supply of any factor of production. The pecuniary effect is the result of taxpayers' tax-driven decisions about how to arrange their given financial condition, such as choosing taxable or tax-exempt bonds, or one stock over another, or more cash over fringes in salary negotiation, or how much to contribute to charity. Unlike supply-side effects, such decisions have neither clear nor direct impacts on the size of the economy. These are known as pecuniary changes because they change the allocation of money without necessarily increasing or decreasing production.

Consider the decision to buy a bond. Suppose a taxable bond yields 10 percent and a tax-exempt bond, issued by a state or municipal government, yields only 4 percent. For a taxpayer in the 70 percent tax bracket, the taxable bond yields only 3 percent after taxes. The tax-exempt bond is the better investment. On the other hand, if this taxpayer's tax rate is cut to 50 percent, the after-tax yield on the taxable bond rises to 5 percent, more than the tax-exempt bond. Thus one pecuniary effect of tax cuts is to cause investors to hold more taxable securities and fewer tax-exempt securities, producing more tax revenue.

Another example would be a shift away from nontaxable fringe benefits and toward taxable money payments in employee compensation. After a tax cut, the effective bonus from taking income as tax-free benefits drops. Workers are likely to ask for more in regular wages, which they can spend as they see fit. This shift will show up as an increase in national taxable income and will increase revenues without evoking significantly more labor supply.[4]

It is worth noting that while the pecuniary effect does not assume any increase in factors of production, certain pecuniary responses are likely to be beneficial to the economy. In the first example, lower taxes allowed the investor to move capital around more freely and efficiently (that is, in response to genuine market forces rather than tax rules). Over the long term the more efficient use of capital certainly helps the economy. On the other hand, such increases in efficiency cannot be quantified reliably and play no role in a study of the revenue effects of a tax cut over a four-year period. The economic impact of other pecuniary responses, such as shifting income from tax-free fringe benefits to taxable income, are even harder to assess.

To summarize these four responses to tax changes: the supply-side effect is produced by changes in both the behavior of the taxpayer and the size of the economy; the demand-side effect is produced by changes in the size of the economy but not taxpayer behavior; the pecuniary effect is a product of taxpayer behavior alone; and the direct effect ignores both the size of the economy and taxpayer behavior (see figure 4.1). Estimating the total impact of these various effects of the tax change is a bit like solving a puzzle. It must be done piece by piece. Only when we have all of the various pieces in place will we be able to tell what the true revenue results of ERTA were and, just as important, how those results were produced.

It sounds complicated. In some ways it is. Even though we present here only a summary of the actual calculations used in the full model, the next few pages are certainly the most difficult in this book. There is no getting around that. But I can offer two encouraging thoughts. First this section lasts for only a few pages and the rest of the book can be read independently of those pages. Second, these next few pages will be less difficult if the reader remembers that we are doing something that, in concept at least, is fairly simple and quite straightforward. We are separating the effects of ERTA on taxpayer behavior and economic growth from all other economic events of 1981–85. Only after we do that can we tell how much revenue the government really would have reaped in the absence of the tax cuts, and thus how much the tax cuts cost.

FIGURE 4.1 Taxpayer Responses to Tax Rate Changes

	Static Economy	Dynamic Economy
No Taxpayer Behavior	Direct Effect	Demand-side Effect
Taxpayer Behavior	Pecuniary Effect	Supply-side Effect

We start with the assumption that the tax cut had no effect on the economy (whether by boosting demand or by changing taxpayer behavior): We assume that everything that happened between 1981 and 1985 would have happened even without the tax cuts. This assumption allows us to estimate the direct effect of the tax cut.

To obtain a base for comparison, we apply the old tax rates and rules to the actual events of 1981–85 by means of the 34,000 sample tax returns employed in the computer model.[5] The computer takes actual tax returns from 1979, before the tax cut was in place, and extrapolates the income and deduction items on each tax return to reflect the size of the economy in the years 1981–85, in effect completing tax returns for each of these taxpayers in each year, but using the old tax law. This yields a figure for the income tax revenue the government would have received in each year if it could have had both the old tax code and the new economy (as produced by both expansion of demand and changes in taxpayers' willingness to supply factors of production). These figures are shown on the "Old Law, New Economy" line of figure 4.2.

The second step in estimating the direct effect of the tax cut is to run the same sample tax returns (still adjusted for the economy of 1981–85) through the computer, this time applying the new tax rates and the rest of the changes included in the new tax law. This procedure

FIGURE 4.2 Direct Effect of Tax Law

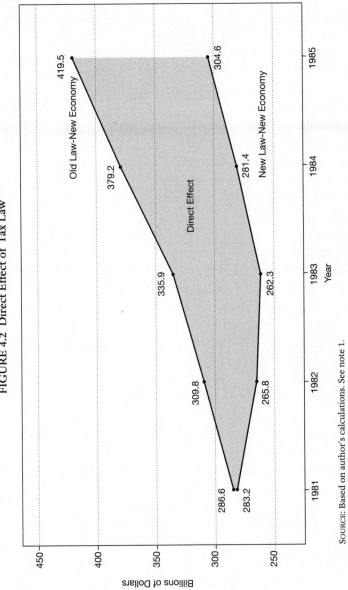

SOURCE: Based on author's calculations. See note 1.

yields projected revenues from the new tax law under the actual economy of 1981–85. (See the "New Law, New Economy" line on figure 4.2.) The difference between the "Old Law, New Economy" figures and the "New Law, New Economy" figures is the direct effect of the tax cut: It is the result you get by pretending that a change in tax rates and rules will not affect the economy. In figure 4.2, the direct effect of the tax cut from 1981 through 1985 is the region between the upper ("Old Law, New Economy") and lower ("New Law, New Economy") lines. Note that the direct effect of ERTA is quite large, rising from $44 billion in 1982 to $115 billion in 1985.

You may feel that estimating revenues from the old law under the new law's economy has a certain never-never-land quality, and so it does. This estimate is something called a counterfactual, an economic scenario that runs counter to the events that actually took place. Counterfactuals are used to isolate specific economic effects. But this direct effect estimate, or a set of similar numbers, is what many ERTA opponents use when they criticize the alleged high cost of the tax bill. They are using assumptions from never-never land.

We use those assumptions also, but only as a starting point in the process of isolating the real effects of the tax changes on tax revenues. Our job is to calculate the extent to which this direct effect is an exaggeration of the true cost of the tax bill. Step by step, we will correct our estimate downward from how much revenue the government would have collected under the counterfactual "Old Law, New Economy" assumption. We will do this by separating out the revenue effects of the tax-induced changes to the New Economy. Our goal is a reliable estimate of the revenue the government would have reaped under the old law and the old economy, the revenue the government would have collected had the tax cuts never happened. Then we will be but a few short steps away from estimating the true revenue cost of the tax cut.

The old economy that we will use for our "Old Law, Old Economy" revenue estimate is also a counterfactual construct. Building it is a matter of some educated guesswork. We can estimate what the old economy (the economy absent the tax changes) would have looked like by examining the effects of other, smaller tax changes made in other years and studied by other economists, extrapolating those effects to the tax changes enacted in 1981 and then subtracting those extrapolations from the new economy.

The demand-side, or Keynesian, effect is the least controversial aspect, because both Keynesians and supply-siders agree that it occurs. To estimate the demand-side effect we first estimated the additional funds ERTA made available to taxpayers (assuming no change in their behavior). We then apply to that figure the estimates of the multiplier effect used by the DRI model of the US economy, among the oldest and most respected of all economic forecasting models.[6] As noted in the previous chapter, the multiplier accounts for the fact that each dollar of a tax cut produces more than a dollar of demand-induced GNP growth. Since there is a consensus that the multiplier tends to be large when there are many unemployed workers available to the economy, and since the ERTA tax cuts came at a time of very high unemployment, the figures were adjusted accordingly. Economists agree that over time, as there remain fewer additional workers to be hired, the multiplier effect tends to diminish toward zero. We employed that assumption. Thus, although the tax cuts may have contributed significantly to the demand-induced growth in the early 1980s, the DRI model assumes that the effect of the tax cuts on demand have been largely dissipated by now.

The results indicate that had these demand-side effects not occurred, the economy would have been 2.1 percent smaller in 1982, 3.2 percent smaller in 1983 and 1984, and 2.7 percent smaller in 1985. The recession of the early 1980s would have continued past the last quarter of 1982 into the middle of 1983. This smaller economy was then incorporated into the computer model of the taxpayer population. Had the economy been smaller, taxpayers would have received smaller incomes. Some would have been unemployed, others would have worked shorter hours. Small businesses would have seen lower profits, and taxpayers who receive corporate dividends would have gotten smaller dividend checks. It is impossible to allocate precisely these various effects among each of the 34,000 representative taxpayers in our sample, but because these taxpayers are representative of the whole population, we can safely assume that the 2 to 3 percent reduction in the nation's GNP would have translated into a 2 to 3 percent reduction in their incomes as well. After adjusting for these demand-side changes, we find that

FIGURE 4.3 The Demand-Side Effect

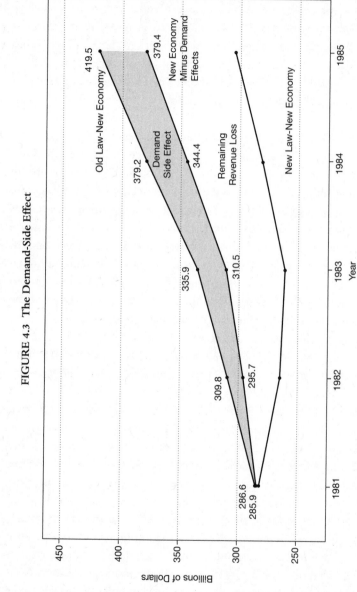

SOURCE: Based on author's calculations. See note 1.

income tax collections under the old law would have been $14.1 billion lower in 1982 and $40.1 billion lower in 1985. Those figures represent the extent to which the "Old Law, New Economy" line overestimated tax revenues by incorporating demand-side changes in the economy that would not have occurred without the tax cut.

Subtracting this demand-side effect from the "Old Law, New Economy" line, we get an "Old Law, New Economy, Minus Demand Effects" line. This line shows that after taking demand-side revenue increases into account, the revenue cost of ERTA falls sharply (see figure 4.3). Instead of costing $44 billion in 1982, the tax cut cost only $29.9 billion. Instead of costing $115 billion in 1985, the actual revenue forgone was only $74.8 billion. Over the early 1980s roughly one-third of the direct effect revenue loss was recaptured by the demand-side response to the tax cuts.

The second effect of the tax cut on GNP was the supply-side effect. As in the case of the hypothetical electrician and secretary, the reduction in marginal tax rates had the effect of giving a raise to most workers in the economy. Previous economic studies have estimated the effects of such tax cut–induced raises on labor supply.[7] These studies suggest that males in their prime earning years tend to be quite unresponsive to wage changes, while the response of married females is quite high. This different response of men and women is important because ERTA provided an extra marginal rate reduction for the lower-earning spouse in a two-earner family, the worker in the family likely to be most responsive to a tax rate change.

To estimate the effect on labor supply, we assumed that a 10 percent rise in after-tax wages would cause the primary earner in the family to work 1 percent more while a 10 percent rise in the secondary earner's wages would cause that earner to work 10 percent more. We then tested whether these responses seemed plausible in light of the actual results of the tax change; they appeared to be on the cautious side of the estimates.[8]

Of course, how much any particular taxpayer responded to the tax rate changes depends on how much of a raise he or she received. We estimated the after-tax income of each of the taxpayers and their spouses covered by our 34,000 tax returns and used the above response estimates to estimate how much less they would have worked had they not received a tax cut. The value of the extra work effort from the tax cut amounted to $38 billion, or about 2.5 percent additional labor supply, from 1981–85. Of this figure, about three-fifths, or $23 billion, was due to the response of secondary earners in two-earner families. We performed the same type of calculation for entrepreneurial income to see how much more self-employed people chose to earn as a result of the tax rate reduction and found it to be around $6 billion.

In addition we calculated the effect the tax cuts would have on how much of their compensation workers take in the form of tax-free fringe benefits. A leading estimate of the responsiveness of workers' choice of fringe benefits to tax rates was performed by Professor Robert Turner at Colgate University, who found that each percentage point rise in the tax rate causes workers to increase the fringe share of their total compensation by 0.18 percent.[9] Applying this estimate to the actual tax rates faced by our representative 34,000 taxpayers yielded an increase of about $30 billion in taxable wage income. Technically this fringe benefit response is part of the pecuniary effect rather than the supply-side effect, because the taxpayers did not work any more as a result of the compensation change. However, it does have an effect on the amount of taxable income reported by taxpayers after tax rates were cut. We include it among the supply-side effects because it appears so directly in the labor-supply response, though, as we shall see, most pecuniary effects show up much more indirectly.

All this extra taxable income produced extra tax revenue. Falsely assuming that this extra income and extra revenue would have appeared even in the absence of the tax cut caused the direct effect estimate of the cost of the tax cut to be too high by about $20 billion in 1985. Subtracting that $20 billion from the "Old Law, New Economy Minus Demand Effects Line," produces the "Old Law, Old Economy Line" in figure 4.4.

With the construction of this line we have achieved most of what we set out to do. We have created an "Old Law, Old Economy" revenue estimate. This new revenue estimate gives us an internally consistent picture of how much income tax revenue the government would have collected had it not passed ERTA. A comparison of the "Old Law, Old Economy" line with the "New Law, New Economy" line shows just how powerful the economic effects of a tax cut can be. The difference

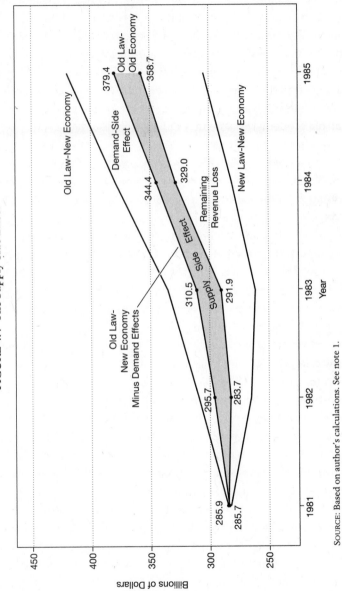

FIGURE 4.4 The Supply-Side Effect

SOURCE: Based on author's calculations. See note 1.

between these two lines is only $17.9 billion in 1982, less than half the direct effect revenue estimate of $44 billion. In 1985, the difference is $54.1 billion, again less than half of the direct effect of $115 billion.

One final step remains. We have not yet estimated the pecuniary effect of the tax cut, that which results not from any change in the size of the economy but merely from taxpayers reshuffling their assets. The pecuniary effect played no part in producing our "Old Law, Old Economy" line: We could not back pecuniary effects out of the new economy to get the old economy, because they did not significantly affect the size of the new economy in the first place. Since we have already computed all the ERTA-induced revenue effects that we can account for by examining observable changes in the economy, everything else is a pecuniary effect by default.[10] We can calculate the pecuniary effect with a reality check by comparing our estimates for how much money "should" be collected under the new law and the new economy with actual revenue results (see figure 4.5). Our "New Law, New Economy" line shows taxpayers paying $265.8 billion of income taxes in 1982. In fact, as the "Actual Revenue" line in figure 4.5 shows, they paid $277.6 billion. In 1985 this difference is greater, with actual payments of $325.7 billion and predicted payments of only $304.6 billion. The pecuniary responses to the new tax law provided $12 billion of additional tax revenue in 1982, rising to $21 billion in 1985.

Why the difference? The "New Law, New Economy" line reflects, for the most part, ERTA-induced changes in taxpayer behavior that show up in the size of the economy. It does not, for the most part, reflect the revenue results of changes in behavior that do not affect the size of the economy. As we have seen, there are many such changes, from the decision to switch from tax-exempt to taxable bonds to the decision to give less to tax-exempt charities (as people do when tax rates drop) and therefore pay more in taxes. Though such rearrangements change the relative size of various sectors of the economy, they do not materially alter the size of the economy as a whole.

There are some important exceptions to the statement that the pecuniary effect section of the graph indicates revenue changes that are not explained by an improved economy. Recall, for example, that in our discussion of supply-side effects we noted that tax cuts increase the return

FIGURE 4.5 The Pecuniary Effect

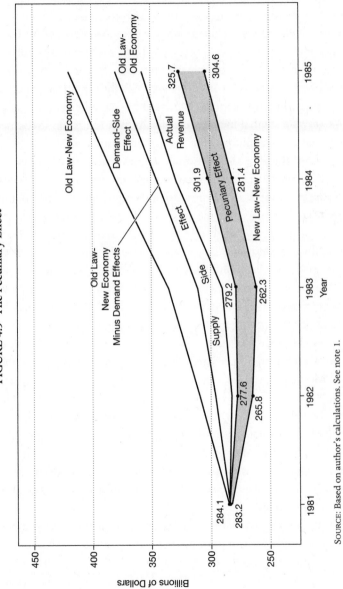

SOURCE: Based on author's calculations. See note 1.

on savings, investment, and risk-taking, as well as on labor, and therefore can be assumed to increase the supply of capital to the economy even as they increase the supply of labor. But in our estimate of supply-side revenue effects we included only the revenue effects of additional labor supply. That is because the short-term revenue effects of even quite large increases in the supply of capital are often very small.

Suppose, for instance, that in 1985, with all the tax cuts in place, productive investment of all sorts increased by $20 billion as a result of ERTA's very substantial increase of the after-tax return on investment. Such an increase would provide very great long-term benefits to the economy. Yet the short-term revenue effects would be negligible. Assuming a 10 percent real return on business investment,[11] a $20 billion increase in investment would increase national income by $2 billion in one year. The average marginal tax rate on investment income in 1985 was about 30 percent. Thus, our hypothetical $20 billion increase in capital would yield additional 1985 revenue of only $600 million. That is just too small a needle to find among our haystack of revenue figures, so instead of trying to break it out, we include it and any similarly small revenue responses increases in the pecuniary effect. This is worth noting because it is the one important case in which revenue figures do not help us establish the tax cut's positive effects on the economy. Recall that we are interested in revenue figures not only because they show how much the tax cut cost, but also because certain positive revenue effects indicate that the tax cut changed taxpayer behavior in ways that benefit the economy. That tax cuts increase risk-taking and investment was one of the strongest supply-side arguments for ERTA, yet the claim cannot be either proved or disproved by revenue evidence. Intellectually, this is disappointing. As we shall see in later chapters, however, there is other very substantial evidence that ERTA was a boon to savings, investment, and risk taking.

This process of eliminating the demand-side, supply-side, and pecuniary effects leaves us with the true cost of the tax cut. Figure 4.6 shows this as the difference between the "Old Law, Old Economy" line and the "Actual Revenue" line. The "Old Law, Old Economy" line shows how much the government would have collected had we not cut taxes, and the "Actual Revenue" line shows how much it actually collected. ERTA

FIGURE 4.6 The Actual Revenue Effect

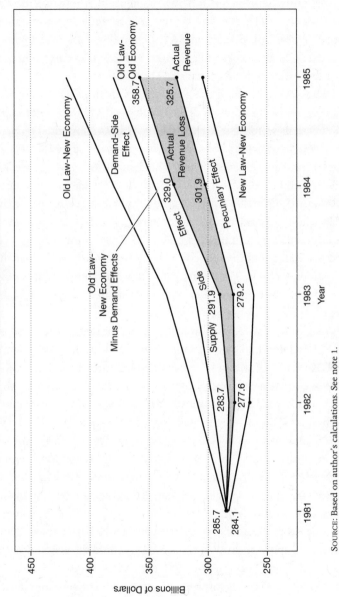

SOURCE: Based on author's calculations. See note 1.

cost less than one-third as much as implied by the naively calculated direct effect estimate, which is roughly the figure that most political and media critics of ERTA cite. In 1982 this true revenue cost amounted to only $6.1 billion, compared to the $44 billion direct effect estimate. By 1985 the true revenue cost had grown to $33 billion as compared to the direct effect estimate for that year of $114.9 billion.

So who was right about the effect of tax changes on the economy, the Keynesians or the supply-siders? The answer is both, at least in part. The Keynesians were right in claiming that such a substantial reduction in rates would powerfully boost demand, a point the supply-siders never denied but perhaps underestimated. The demand-side revenue feedback and the combined behavioral feedbacks (supply-side and pecuniary) turned out to be roughly equal. On the other hand, the revenue results vindicate the supply-siders' most important claim: The tax cut produced quite large changes in taxpayer behavior. That claim, strongly confirmed by results, ran directly contrary to Keynesian theory and most Keynesian predictions. The combined supply-side and pecuniary effects recouped well over one-third of ERTA's estimated direct cost, a very powerful response.

ERTA did not pay for itself as some of the most enthusiastic supply-siders claimed it would. Personal income tax collections were lower under ERTA than they would have been had tax rates never been cut. As we shall see in the next chapter, however, the reductions in very high tax brackets easily paid for themselves and produced a rather sizable increase besides. This increase helped finance a large part of the reduction in taxes from lower-and middle-class taxpayers. Though this is not what some enthusiastic supply-siders predicted during the political fight for the tax cuts, it is what basic supply-side theory would predict.

The Reagan tax cuts put supply-side economics on the map intellectually and politically. The evidence certainly favors the fundamental supply-side proposition that taxes matter: They distort taxpayer behavior, limit the supply of productive factors, and hold the economy below its potential. The effects of the 1981 tax changes shift the burden of proof to those who claim government can raise taxes with impunity.

Putting theory to one side for a moment, were the Reagan tax cuts a good idea? More specifically, could the country afford them? By 1985, at a revenue cost in that year of $33 billion, economic output was between 2 and 3 percent higher than it would have been without the tax cut. That extra growth stands for millions of new jobs and a higher standard of living. Moreover, as we shall see in the next few chapters, the tax cuts had salutary effects on inflation, investment, and savings and contributed only marginally to the deficit. By the standards of government programs this one would have to be judged a bargain.

Critics persist in arguing that the 1981 tax cut lost huge amounts of revenue and brought few benefits. This is not surprising. The analysis we have used here can be difficult to accept for the simple reason that nearly all the numbers involved are hypothetical and relative. The only real number on any of our figures is the actual revenue amount. The supply- and demand-side effects, which "reduce" the revenue shortfall, do not make the actual revenue any larger; they simply correct downward the direct effect estimate of how much more revenue could have been reaped without the tax cut. However, the direct effect numbers on which the critics rely actually involve the most drastically counterfactual assumptions.

All these counterfactual calculations do give the enterprise an unreal quality. One yearns for down-to-earth numbers. There are none to be had. By any method for determining the effect of the tax cuts, there will be only one real number: actual revenue. All others will be estimates derived from events that did not happen.

To see more clearly the problems with apparently more straightforward ways of figuring the loss in tax revenue, let us imagine that the direct effect estimate really does represent the revenue the government ought to have received, as critics of the tax cuts maintain. This would mean that the 1985 actual income tax revenue figure of $325 billion really should have been $94 billion higher, or $419 billion. Remember you can get this figure only by assuming that the tax cut had absolutely no effect on anything, either the size of the economy or the behavior of taxpayers.

A $419 billion income tax take for 1985 would mean that income taxes that year would have taken more than 26 percent of the tax base (that is, of the income on which taxes are paid after deductions and exemptions), instead of just the 21 percent actually absorbed by taxes. It would also mean that the average marginal tax rate on the base would have been roughly 44 percent instead of just 34 percent. To be consistent, the critics of ERTA or of the analysis presented in this chapter must believe that we could have imposed a 44 percent marginal tax rate on the tax base, instead of a 34 percent rate, without affecting the size of the base.

For the government to have actually collected $419 billion in tax revenue, consider what would have had to happen, for example, in consumer spending. In 1985 disposable personal income, or income after taxes, was $2,841 billion. Of this, consumers spent $2,629 billion on purchases and paid $85 billion in installment interest and transfers to foreigners, which left them $127 billion in personal savings, or 4.5 percent of their income. If we really believe that the tax cuts had no demand-side effect, then we would have to assume that the extra $84 billion the government would have collected in taxes would have left consumer spending unaffected. Stated differently, consumers would have been able to save only $43 billion, or 1.3 percent of their incomes. To believe that the government actually would have collected $419 billion in tax revenue if the tax cuts had not taken place, we have to believe that households would have cut their savings rate by 70 percent.

That is implausible, to say the least. And nearly all economic analysts accept that there would be a demand-side feedback from the tax cuts. Some critics accept the demand-side argument but reject all alleged supply-side or pecuniary effects. Consider some of the assumptions these "pure" demand-siders must make. In 1981, just before the tax rates were cut, roughly four million taxpayers were in the 49 percent or higher brackets of the income tax. By 1985, absent the tax rate cuts, that figure would have grown to more than seven million taxpayers. In order to assume that we really would have collected $94 billion more tax revenue had we not cut taxes, the demand-siders must assume that the three million taxpayers who would have become eligible to share half their income with the government would have done so cheerfully, without increasing their tax avoidance behavior at all. They must also assume that a 10 point rise in the nation's average marginal tax rate, from 34 percent to 44 percent, would have had no effect on taxpayer behavior. They must assume, contrary to all existing empirical evidence, that taxpayers would have contributed no more to charitable organizations, realized the same amount of capital gains, and refrained from switching from taxable investments into tax-exempt bonds. They must assume that labor-force participation rates would have moved strongly upward, as happened throughout the 1980s, even if workers had been taking home steadily less after-tax income rather than steadily more. They would have to believe, contrary to common sense and the empirical evidence, that lower wages cause people to work more while higher wages cause them to work less. They would have to believe that the sudden jump in the labor-force participation and taxable income of married women, which occurred in the 1980s, would have happened without ERTA's quite dramatic reduction in tax rates for working spouses. They would have to believe that the sudden halt in the decade-long trend toward more fringe benefits and less taxable cash in pay settlements would have occurred even if the taxes on that cash had continued to rise instead of being dramatically decreased. In short, they would have to assume away most of the microeconomic research on the effects of taxes over the past ten years.

The real never-never land is the one of revenue projections that do not take behavioral and macroeconomic repercussions into account. The direct effect estimates used by those who maintain that ERTA cost "hundreds of billions of dollars" presume that the world would have been the same regardless of the level of taxes. Their world is also a counterfactual one. To decide who to believe, one must decide which counterfactual assumption is more plausible. Does it make sense to believe that taxes have no effect on behavior or that they have the kind of effect demonstrated by various economic studies? Clearly the latter. The challenge to policy makers for the coming years is to remain true to the principles that common sense suggests and the evidence has now established: taxes matter. When they are too high, they impair not only the happiness of the people, but the wealth of the nation and the resources of the treasury.

[5]

Did the Rich Get Richer?

> "Mr. Reagan's individual tax cuts were skewed
> to the rich and Congress added more
> goodies for corporations."
> —*THE NEW REPUBLIC*, JULY 4, 1983

W E OFTEN HEAR THAT "UNDER RONALD REAGAN THE RICH
got richer and the poor got poorer," and that the 1981 tax
cuts were a big windfall for the rich and only for the rich. It would seem
to be common knowledge. But what everyone knows isn't always true,
and in this bit of common knowledge there is no more than a tiny ker-
nel of truth.

During the early part of Reagan's first term, the rich did get richer
while most of the rest of the country stayed even.[1] Some lost ground.
The causes were not the tax cuts but record high interest rates and the
back-to-back recessions of 1980–82. When interest rates go up, lenders
get richer and borrowers get poorer. Since the lenders tend to have
more money than the borrowers in the first place, high interest rates do
make the rich richer. Recessions reinforce this process because recessions are costliest to middle- and working-class people who lose their
jobs, while the rich rarely become unemployed.

Common knowledge stumbles at this point because rising interest rates and higher unemployment began well before Reagan became president. For example, a common bit of evidence used by Reagan critics is that the poverty rate rose after the tax cuts. Actually, the poverty rate bottomed out at 11.4 percent in 1978.[2] It hit 13 percent in 1980 and 14 percent in 1981, the year Reagan took office but before his economic program was in place. The poverty rate peaked at 15.2 percent in 1983, by which time the tax cut was still only three-quarters in place. In short, two-thirds of the rise in the poverty rate occurred before Reagan's tax and budget policies could take hold, and all the rise occurred before ERTA was fully in place. By 1985 the poverty rate was back down to the level it was at when Reagan took office. It dropped even further during his last three years in office. Thus, though the poverty rate rose in three of Carter's four years as president, it fell six of Reagan's eight years.

Consider the "rich got richer" critique.

When interest income rises as a share of national income, the rich get richer compared to everyone else. This is because the rich derive more of their income from investments than most people. Interest income did increase its share of national income during Reagan's first term. Again, however, the trend had started under Carter. In 1976, the year before Jimmy Carter took office, interest income was 9.2 percent of personal income. By 1981, when Ronald Reagan entered the White House, it was up to 13.3 percent. The interest share of personal income peaked in 1985 at 14.4 percent of income. Thus three-quarters of this windfall to the rich occurred before Reagan took office. Like the poverty rate, interest income as a share of personal income fell in the latter half of the Reagan presidency.

Who got richer under Reagan? Taking into consideration data from both Reagan terms, the answer is that, on average, everyone did. The real income of the median family rose over $3,000 under Reagan, after falling that same amount between 1973 and 1981 (the largest such retreat since the Great Depression). Continuing the trend of the late 1970s, families above the median did best early in the administration, with everyone else catching up later as the economic recovery continued apace. This situation had more to do with macroeconomic trends than with the direct effect of the tax cuts, however.

The phrase "tax cuts for the rich" has become a staple of the rhetoric of anti-Reagan politicians. Even the most cursory look at the evidence, however, shows ERTA raised the share of the tax burden borne by the rich. As figure 5.1 shows, the top 0.1 percent of all taxpayers (roughly speaking, those making over $200,000 a year) saw their share of income tax payments rise from 7 percent in 1981 to 14 percent in 1986. The share of taxes borne by the top 2 percent of taxpayers (roughly those making over $60,000) rose from 26 percent in 1981 to 34 percent in 1986. By contrast, taxpayers on the bottom half of the income scale saw their share of tax payments fall from 7 percent at the start of the decade to only 6 percent by 1986. The great American middle class, people earning between $20,000 and $60,000 in the early 1980s, saw their tax share fall from 67 percent to 60 percent between 1981 and 1986. It was they who received the vast bulk of the Reagan tax cuts. The rules of arithmetic dictate that if the rich ended up paying a bigger share of taxes, everyone else must have taken a bigger tax cut than the rich. So much for common knowledge.

This simple demonstration does not settle the argument. Presented with these facts, the Reagan critics switch gears. They point out that the

FIGURE 5.1 Share of Taxes Paid by the Rich 1979–86

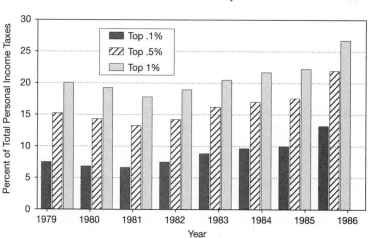

rich, having had a tax rate cut, could be paying more in taxes only if they had gotten a lot richer compared to everyone else. This is true by definition. The rich will pay more taxes at lower rates only if their *reported taxable* income goes up, which it did. This conclusion, however, is not very interesting in itself. The more important question is: Why did the rich report more taxable income? If it happened because Reagan shifted the nation's economic playing field in favor of the rich (say, by permanently increasing interest income as a share of national income, that is, favoring capital over labor), then the critics have a point: The Reagan policies would have unfairly favored the rich over the poor. But if the change occurred because the tax cuts simply encouraged the rich to expose more income to taxation or, even better, to work harder at producing more income, then the Reagan administration can hardly be accused of unfairly boosting the rich. In fact, the supply-siders had defended the tax cuts on the grounds that a reduction in rates would cause the rich to shift from tax-free to taxable activity and to work harder. Before the tax cuts the critics had agreed this would be a good thing; they simply denied it would happen.

If the rich got richer mostly because of underlying economic currents, and not because they worked harder or rearranged their finances, that would imply that the Reagan tax cuts failed to change taxpayer behavior. But if underlying economic currents cannot explain the rising share of taxable income reported by the rich, then the changes in the taxable income must be the result of the kind of behavioral responses to tax rate cuts that supply-siders predicted.

The question can be resolved by the analysis described in the last chapter because it takes account of underlying economic currents, assuming changes in the share of interest and other capital income in national income to have occurred under all scenarios. What is left are the changes in tax revenue from the various effects of the Reagan tax cuts. To the extent that the higher tax payments (and, implicitly, higher reported taxable income) result from behavioral responses to the tax cut, the supply-side case is vindicated: The rich paid more because their behavior changed, not because the economy was shifted in their favor.

Rerunning the model used in the last chapter, this time only for taxpayers earning more than $200,000, gives the results shown in figure 5.2.

As before, the "Old Law, New Economy" line represents estimated revenues, assuming that the pre-ERTA tax rates had stayed in place but the economy still boomed as if rates had been cut. The "Old Law, Old Economy" line shows this revenue if that growth never happened. The difference between these two lines is the demand- and supply-side effect of the tax change. The "New Law, New Revenue" line estimates tax revenues with the ERTA tax rates but with no behavioral response by taxpayers. The "Actual Revenue" line shows how much was actually collected.

As figure 5.2 indicates, the supply- and demand-side effects combine to recoup about one-fourth of the supposed direct revenue loss from high-income taxpayers. This is much less than for the general taxpayer population. The benefits of the demand-side stimulus to employment went almost entirely to the non-rich. And the increase in the labor supply to the economy, mostly from ERTA's after-tax "raise" for married women, also was disproportionately large among the non-rich. But what is most striking about figure 5.2 is the huge "pecuniary" effect (the region between the "New Law, New Economy" line and the "Actual Revenue" Line). The pecuniary effect is so large for the rich that it drives the "Actual Revenue" line above the "Old Law" line. From the rich, ERTA reaped not only a relative increase in the share of the tax burden but an absolute increase in tax revenues, derived almost entirely from the pecuniary effect.

Recall that the pecuniary effect is the result of taxpayers rearranging their finances in response to tax changes, but not always in ways that clearly increase the supply of labor or capital to the economy. Here these pecuniary changes were so large that the government collected more tax revenue from upper-income taxpayers at a 50 percent top rate than it would have at 70 percent. The model also indicates that upper-middle-class taxpayers, with incomes ranging from $75,000 to $200,000, whose rates were cut from a range of 54 to 69 percent to a range of 38 to 50 percent, paid about 92 percent of what they would have paid under the old law. For these taxpayers also, the pecuniary effect plays a larger than average role. Only middle-class and working-class taxpayers paid substantially less taxes (about 18 percent less for taxpayers earning $20,000 or less and 14 percent less for taxpayers earning between

FIGURE 5.2 Effect of Tax Cuts on Taxes Paid by the Rich

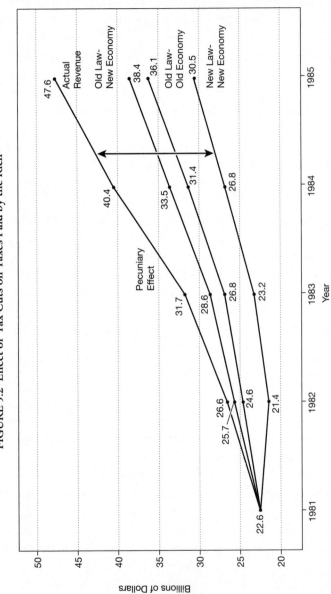

SOURCE: Based on author's calculations. See note 1, chapter 4, for details.

$20,000 and $50,000) under the new law. These latter groups were almost entirely responsible for ERTA's revenue losses.

These results show that high tax rates do affect taxpayer behavior dramatically. This increased taxable income represents a behavioral response by taxpayers above and beyond any underlying macroeconomic trends that might have caused the rich to get richer. The data are quite clear: The principal reason the rich paid a bigger share of taxes was not underlying economic trends, but a behavioral response by the rich to lower marginal tax rates. The Congressional Budget Office, which has not generally supported supply-side theories, reached essentially the same conclusion:

> The data show considerable evidence of a very significant revenue response among taxpayers at the very highest income levels. This finding of a strong revenue response in the top income groups holds true for both projection methods and all target years.[3]

The implications of these findings are enormous. Tax rates over 50 percent are counterproductive from the view of collecting tax revenue. The old high rates were purely punitive; they discouraged taxpayers from earning or reporting high incomes while simultaneously lowering government tax revenues.

The very large pecuniary effect for upper-income taxpayers thus drives home an essential lesson: Upper-income taxpayers have enormous discretion over how and when they receive income, and over whether it will be exposed to taxation. Tax cuts that prompt them to take more income in taxable form will improve government revenues. But such changes may also make the rich appear much richer statistically without considerably increasing their share of the nation's wealth.

Consider the owner of a very successful business consulting firm in the 70 percent tax bracket. How should he take his compensation? His twelve-hour-a-day job requires extensive travel around town. His company could buy a red Maserati for his use for $60,000, a fully justified deductible business expense: It is important to impress those clients. The consultant also gets some nontaxable satisfaction from his business-owned toy, but at a 70 percent tax rate, his company would have had to pay him $200,000 in salary in order for him to buy the same car for him-self. Cut this fellow's tax rate to 50 percent and things change a bit. The after-tax cost of the Maserati will be lower in terms of forgone salary, but so will the after-tax costs of a lot of items that he could not have jus-tified as business expenses: mink coats, backyard swimming pools, etc. He might very well decide that the company should spend only $30,000 on a car, a Cadillac, say, and pay him $30,000 more in cash. The govern-ment takes $15,000, which is brand-new revenue because he would not have exposed that $30,000 to taxes at the 70 percent rate. With the $15,000 he has left after taxes, he buys a mink coat for his wife or a swimming pool for the whole family. He might make other adjustments as well, such as redecorating the office less frequently and less lavishly—paying himself still more cash.

After these adjustments, the government is richer, and the business-man and his family are happier. But are they richer? In an absolute sense the answer is yes: He has more choice over how to use the resources un-der his control over his money. His well-being has increased because he has more control, but the rise in his income greatly exaggerates the rise in his well-being. The rise in his well-being is measured by the increased happiness gained from having the mink and Cadillac instead of the Maserati. That is clearly less than the rise in his income—the equivalent of the mink by itself.

Most important, he has made no one poorer in the process. In fact, he has made his less prosperous fellow citizens somewhat better off by helping to finance a reduction in their taxes or an increase in their gov-ernment services. Yes, we might call him "richer," but this is not the sort of picture people usually have in mind when they angrily complain that "the rich get richer and the poor get poorer."

This example shows a classic pecuniary response because there is no clear benefit to the economy when our businessman switches from Maseratis to minks and Cadillacs. However, as noted in chapter 4, in many other versions of this story the economy does benefit. If, for in-stance, the tax cuts also prompted our businessman to rearrange his per-sonal investments in ways that increased both their exposure to taxation and their productivity for the economy, not only the government and the businessman would be happier, but so would future generations.

The businessman's reported taxable income would rise quite a bit, but it would seem even more unreasonable to say he was substantially richer, especially in the short term.

The greater after-tax reward of entrepreneurship would probably cause more people to emulate the businessman of our example and to put in the enormous personal investment required to strike out on their own, or to really excel at a high-paying job. In other words, some of the not-so-rich will get rich, though national income statistics won't distinguish them from the rich who get richer.

High tax rates not only harm the economy, they fail to soak the rich. They neither net appreciably more tax revenue from the rich nor redistribute wealth. Indeed, the evidence suggests that high tax rates help ossify the class structure rather than break it down. In 1960, when the top rate was 91 percent, the income of the rich was drawn disproportionately from interest and dividends. The top 2 percent of taxpayers received 48 percent of interest and dividends but only 8.7 percent of wage, salary, and entrepreneurial income. By 1985, with a 50 percent top rate, the share of interest and dividends received by this group was cut in half while the share of wage and entrepreneurial income had risen 28 percent. The real losers from soak-the-rich taxation aren't the presently rich, but the would-be rich. High income tax rates bar access to the upper class. At a 91 percent rate it is hard to accumulate enough after taxes to make the upper-class club. As the rates come down, so do the barriers to entry.

The data from the early 1980s show conclusively that governments that play soak-the-rich to win votes do so at the treasury's expense. Politicians of both political parties now favor tax rates much lower than those of the late 1970s. One still sees the politics of envy, but it seems much more common in campaign speeches than in legislation. Instead of trying to soak the rich, politicians now more commonly seek something they call the "revenue-maximizing tax rate." Just their use of that phrase is a triumph for supply-side reasoning. Conceptually, the revenue-maximizing rate is the peak of the once-derided "Laffer Curve."

Nevertheless, the revenue-maximizing rate, like the Laffer Curve itself, is a poor guide to tax policy. Consider taxpayers with incomes slightly below $200,000. Taxpayers earning between $75,000 and

$200,000 did not produce more revenue under ERTA than they would have under the old law. The government cut their tax rates by 25 percent and their tax payments fell by about 8 percent. Their new tax rates, ranging from 38 percent to 50 percent, seem to be generally below the revenue-maximizing rate.

Does that mean we cut their taxes too much? To answer that question, let's rephrase it. Would it be wise to increase tax rates 25 percent to gain 8 percent more tax revenue? An 8 percent revenue increase after a 25 percent rate increase suggests the tax base shrank by 14 percent. Is it worthwhile reducing overall economic activity by 14 percent in order to transfer 8 percent more money from taxpayers to the treasury? Remember, the 8 percent is no increase in national wealth but only a transfer from citizens to the government, while the 14 percent shrinkage is a real reduction in the tax base.

We can show this trade-off more graphically by considering an economy worth $10. The government currently collects a 40 percent tax on the economy, or $4. Wanting more revenue, it increases the tax rate to 50 percent, the equivalent of a 25 percent income tax rate increase. The economy shrinks by nearly 14 percent to $8.64. The government now has 8 percent more revenue, a total of $4.32. The people are left with $4.32. The government is 32 cents better off, but the private sector is $1.68 poorer, having paid both the cost of the tax—32 cents—and the cost of the shrunken economy, $1.36.

If it were true that the revenue-maximizing rate is always the correct rate, then it would always be correct to make the trade-off described here, charging the private sector $1.36 to make 32 cents for the public sector. In fact, it would always be right to charge the private sector $10 to make the public sector a penny. Tax rates could be considered too high only when the government actually started losing money. Unfortunately, the revenue-maximizing rate is now often referred to as the "optimal" tax rate. This is a misuse of a basic economic concept. Optimal means the best possible trade-off. The truly optimal tax rate depends on how high a surcharge or excess burden society is willing to pay in transferring resources from the private sector to the public sector. Except in times of dire emergency, few people aside from revenue-hungry politicians would consider it a good bargain to charge the private sector $1.68

to get 32 cents more in government revenue. Yet the present revenue maximizers want to do even worse.

Today, tax rates on very high income taxpayers stand at 28 percent, well below the revenue-maximizing rate. The revenue maximizers want a raise, often suggesting a new higher rate of 33 percent, the special bracket rate that now applies to some upper-middle-income taxpayers.[4] The data suggest this would shrink the tax base by at least 10 percent. The government would then collect 33 percent of a 95 cent tax base or 31.5 cents, instead of the 28 cents it now collects. The cost to the affected taxpayers totals 8.5 cents, a 5-cent loss of income and 3.5 cents more in taxes. In other words, the government would shrink the after-tax income of upper-income taxpayers by almost $2.50 in order to produce $1.00 more in tax revenue. Does a 2.5-for-1 trade-off, with all its implications for blunted incentives and shrunken demand, really make sense?

It is encouraging to see that politicians realize high tax rates can cost the government money. But the willingness of some to propose that $1 in government revenue is worth making the private sector $2.50 poorer indicates how far the debate still has to go.

[6]

Who Made the Deficit?

"I think it would not be a favor to the people to
send them a tax refund written in red ink that's going
to add to their interest rates and add to inflation."
—SENATOR LAWTON CHILES,
IN THE DEMOCRATIC RESPONSE TO
A REAGAN TELEVISION ADDRESS[1]

"All in all, I believe it is feasible to attain President
Reagan's original goal of (budget) balance in fiscal 1983,
and relatively easy to do so by fiscal 1984."
—PROFESSOR MILTON FRIEDMAN[2]

FROM THE TIME THE REAGAN TAX CUTS WERE PROPOSED, they have been linked to the problem of the federal deficit. Critics like Senator Chiles argued the tax cuts would substantially increase the deficit and add to inflation. Proponents such as Nobel Laureate Milton Friedman, no fan of deficits, maintained that the deficit could be reduced and inflation avoided by the rest of President Reagan's programs: spending cuts and monetary restraint. Now the facts are in. The deficit did increase dramatically in the wake of the tax cut. Yet, as with the revenue effects of the tax cut, what seem to be the bare facts don't tell the story very well. By reasonable standards of measurement the tax cut contributed only minimally to the deficit.

Before addressing the various did-the-tax-cuts-cause-the-deficit questions, we have to answer a semantic question. There is a big difference between contributing to a problem and causing it, and a big difference between being a minor and a major contributor. To the question "Was the deficit larger with the tax changes than it would have been without them?" there is only one answer: yes. Even with the offsetting indirect effects of the tax rate reduction on taxpayer behavior and the size of the economy, the rate reductions still caused government revenue to decline. Yet even the most cursory examination of the revenue cost of the tax cuts that ignores these indirect effects shows a revenue loss of between $30 billion and $60 billion per year. This compares with the size of the federal deficit during the 1980s between $150 and $200 billion per year. Thus, even ignoring all we have learned about tax rates and tax revenue, the rate cuts alone cannot account for the deficit.

That rather simple observation does not end the argument but shows we were asking the wrong question. The really interesting question is not whether the tax cuts caused the deficit—after all, the deficit was substantial already in 1980—but how much of the *increase* in the deficit can be blamed on the tax cuts rather than the many other major changes in fiscal and monetary policy in the eighties. To untangle the causes of the deficit growth we must measure the effects of these various changes, starting in the era before the tax cuts and the other policy changes took effect.

In 1980 the federal government ran a deficit of $61.3 billion, or 2.2 percent of GNP. By 1983 the deficit had grown to $176 billion, or 5.2 percent of GNP.[3] It is the increase, 3.0 percent of GNP, that we are concerned with here: We must measure the *change* in tax policy against the *change* in the deficit.

This analysis requires some basis for comparison, or "baseline." The fiscal policy mix in the last full year of the Carter administration offers such a baseline. The impact of Reagan policies, including the tax cut, can be measured by comparing what actually happened during the 1980s with this 1980 baseline. For example, the change caused by Reagan tax policies in 1983 is the difference between the actual taxes collected that year and the amount of taxes that would have been collected if taxes took the same share of GNP in 1983 as they did in 1980. By applying the same analysis to spending, the contribution of tax changes to the change in the deficit can be determined.[4]

First it is important to put our 1980 baseline into perspective. All the tax and spending numbers were very high to begin with. In 1980 federal receipts took 20.3 percent of GNP, the second highest level of any year up to that time, peacetime or wartime.[5] From the end of World War II to the start of the Carter administration, federal receipts averaged 18.6 percent of GNP, 1.7 percent of GNP below their 1980 level. The Reagan tax cuts reduced taxes from a historic high to a level still slightly above the postwar average, 19.3 percent at their lowest.

Non-defense spending, at 17.3 percent of GNP, was also at a record level in 1980. During the Great Society years of the Johnson administration (1965–68), non-defense spending was 11.1 percent of GNP. From 1965 to 1979, the year before our baseline, non-defense spending averaged 13.9 percent of GNP. On the other hand, defense spending in 1980 was at a record low level of 5.2 percent of GNP, compared to the post–World War II average of 7.5 percent.[6] Despite the parsimonious defense spending of 1980, total government expenditures reached 22.5 percent of GNP, the second highest level since the end of World War II.

Relative to 1980, most years in the last decade saw the tax share of GNP decline slightly, but increases in both defense and non-defense spending raised the government-spending share of GNP to new records. Figure 6.1 shows the effect of these changes with a tax bar and a spending bar for each year, giving the tax and spending contributions to the deficit as percentages of GNP. The tax bar is positive for years in which tax changes added to the deficit by taking a lower share of GNP than in 1980, negative for years in which taxes took a higher share of GNP than in 1980. Similarly, the spending bar is positive for years in which spending took a greater share of GNP than in 1980 and negative otherwise.

The delay in passing the tax bill and postponing the tax cuts until October 1981 increased the tax share of GNP for that year, reducing the deficit by $20.7 billion, or two-thirds of 1 percent of GNP. With the start of the recession that year, spending rose (to meet both added

FIGURE 6.1 Contributions to the Deficit 1981–1987
Relative to 1980 Shares of GNP

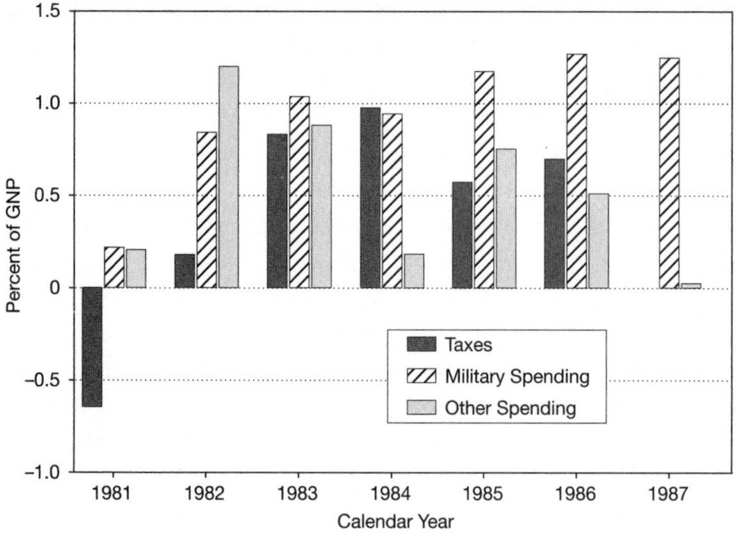

SOURCE: Historical Tables of the Budget of the United States Government.

unemployment and welfare costs and higher defense spending) by $16 billion, or about one-half of 1 percent of GNP. Overall, the 1981 deficit was therefore slightly smaller than it would have been had 1980 fiscal policies continued in place.

The first major tax cut occurred in July 1982, dropping the tax share of GNP below the 1980 level, and increasing the deficit by $6.3 billion relative to 1980. Spending continued to skyrocket, adding $68.4 billion to the deficit, again largely due to anti-recession spending. The 1982 deficit took twice the share of GNP as the 1980 deficit. Taxes were cut again in July 1983, lowering the tax share of GNP to 19.4 percent and adding $30.3 billion to the deficit. The spending share of GNP was 24.5 percent, the 2 percent of GNP excess over 1980 levels contributing $68 billion to the deficit. In total, the 1983 deficit hit a peacetime record 5.2 percent of GNP, nearly $100 billion above the level it would have been if 1980 fiscal policies had stayed in place. Yet only 30 percent of this increase was due to lower taxes. Seventy percent was due to higher spending.

The final phase of the tax cut took effect in July 1984, shrinking the tax share of GNP to 19.2 percent of GNP, the lowest level in the 1980s. This further tax cut contributed $38.5 billion to the increase in the deficit that year. Yet the tax share of GNP was still higher than in any peacetime year of American history except those of the Carter administration. Spending was trimmed to 23.7 percent of GNP that year, but the extra spending above 1980 levels still amounted to $46.4 billion. By 1985 the tax share of GNP started to rise again, reducing the contribution of the tax cuts to the deficit. Spending also rose and contributed $81.9 billion to the deficit. There was little change in 1986, but in 1987 the Tax Reform Act of 1986 increased taxes, pushing the tax share of GNP up to the 1980 level. Taxes thus made no net contribution to the deficit that year. By 1987 the *entire* cause of the increase in the budget deficit since 1980 was added spending, not lower taxes.

Between 1980 and 1987 the national debt rose $529 billion more than would have been the case had 1980 fiscal policies stayed in place. Of this $529 billion, only $112 billion, or 21 percent, was due to the tax reduction. The remaining $417 billion, or 79 percent, was caused by the spending increases. And though the tax cuts no longer contribute to the national debt, the spending problem remains unsolved. This may seem surprising given all the talk about budget cuts in the Reagan years. Some specific programs were cut. But overall spending not only increased, it increased even faster than the economy expanded.

By far the major reason for this increase was defense spending.[7] In the late 1970s, a bipartisan consensus held that defense spending had been cut too far. President Carter agreed in 1978 with the leaders of the other NATO nations that each would increase defense spending by 3 percent in real terms each year. During the 1980 campaign, President Carter committed himself to a 5 percent annual real increase in defense spending. Between 1980 and 1987 real defense spending increased by an average of 6.3 percent per year, or 55 percent total. This added defense spending increased government spending by 1.3 percent of GNP. By 1987 the cumulative increase amounted to $275 billion of the $417 billion added to the national debt by higher spending, or 52 percent of the total increase in the debt. These proportions result from the choice of 1980 as a baseline—by historic standards, the 6.5 percent of GNP spent in 1987 on defense is relatively low. Had other years besides 1980 been used as a baseline, the change in defense spending would have appeared as a *decrease* in the deficit.

The second biggest increase in expenditure during the 1980s was for interest payments on the national debt, an increase caused in part by the increase in the national debt due to the tax cuts or added defense spending. From 1981 to 1987 the tax cuts cost about $17.5 billion in extra interest and increased defense spending cost an extra $53.6 billion in interest.[8]

After accounting for defense increases, tax cuts, and the extra interest payments due to each, $71 billion of extra spending remains on non-defense programs. Although the 17.3 percent of GNP spent in 1980 on non-defense programs set a record, non-defense spending continued to grow during much of the 1980s.

In sum, all types of spending increased during the 1980s, not only in real terms, but as a percent of GNP. About 13 percent of the increase in the deficit was due to an increase in non-defense spending, although the 1980 baseline represents a record high for non-defense spending and a historically low level of defense spending. Even including the extra interest payments ascribable to the tax changes, only 24 percent of the rise in the deficit during the 1980s was tax induced. The remaining 76 percent was caused by increases in spending. The overall reduction

TABLE 6.1 Change in Taxes Relative to Constant 1980 Share (Figures in Billions of Dollars)

Year	Personal Taxes	Other Taxes	Total Taxes
1981	+10.7	+10.1	+20.8
1982	+5.4	−12.1	−6.3
1983	−26.9	−3.4	−30.3
1984	−45.7	+7.2	−38.5
1985	−32.5	+7.2	−25.3
1986	−38.6	+5.2	−31.4
1987	−21.7	+21.8	+0.1

in the tax burden was thus neither the *cause* of the deficit increase nor the major *contributor* to it.

Though personal income taxes were generally lower during the decade, other taxes increased. As table 6.1 shows, this increase in other taxes significantly reduced the tax contribution to the deficit. Personal tax cuts added $149 billion to the cumulative deficit increase during the period 1981–87, while other taxes reduced the cumulative deficit by $37 billion. In 1980 all taxes were at or near historic highs. The tax changes of the 1980s successfully lowered personal taxes toward normal levels, but other taxes continued to rise dramatically.

In its early days the Reagan administration confidently predicted a balanced budget by 1983 or 1984. The administration missed the mark so badly not because of the tax cuts, which contributed only one dollar out of every five to the deficit increase, but largely because administration officials were wildly optimistic about their ability to cut overall spending, even while increasing defense spending.

Shortly after taking office the Reagan administration, in *A Program for Economic Recovery,*[9] outlined its economic and fiscal strategy, including numerous specific proposals for reducing the federal deficit. But the administration quickly learned it could exert little influence over the fiscal 1982 budget, initially submitted by President Carter on 1 January 1981. Though the final vote on the 1982 budget did not come until summer of 1981, six months isn't enough time for a new administration to get control of the budget process, begun in the bureaucracy a year earlier.

The first true Reagan budget was the fiscal 1983 budget, submitted in January 1982 and scheduled to run from October 1982 through September 1983. The 1983 budget proposal detailed domestic spending cuts that would have pared spending $43 billion in 1983, $80.5 billion in 1985, and $105 billion by 1987.[10] The administration lost the ensuing political struggle. Few of its reductions were enacted by the Congress. Had the administration prevailed, the picture might have been quite different. In fiscal 1983 non-defense spending came to 3.9 percent of GNP more than proposed by the administration when it first came to office, exactly the amount by which the deficit increased.[11] Of course, the recession contributed to the deficit in that year, somewhat muddying the water.

By fiscal 1985, a year of healthy economic growth, the picture was quite clear. The 1983 administration proposal requested defense spending of 7.0 percent of GNP and non-defense spending of 13.8 percent of GNP, for a total level of spending of 20.8 percent of GNP. After the Congress finished with the budget, non-defense spending that year hit 17.5 percent of GNP, raising total spending to 23.9 percent of GNP. The result was a dramatically higher deficit than would have occurred under Reagan's 1983 budget.

The administration also seriously underestimated both the effectiveness and the cost of its anti-inflation policy. It underestimated the rate at which inflation would drop and, probably because of that first error, failed to allow for the 1982 recession, which also partly resulted from anti-inflationary monetary policies. Table 6.2 shows how far off the administration was in forecasting inflation and real GNP growth. Administration officials made the "First Forecast" immediately upon coming to office; the "Second Forecast," incorporated in the fiscal 1983 budget, was made late in 1982. A joke around Washington at the time had it that these forecasts were made by an administration employee named Rosie Scenario. But though the predictions for growth were definitely rosy, those about inflation were pessimistic. The 1982 rate of inflation was

TABLE 6.2 Reagan Administration Forecasts of Inflation and Growth*

	Inflation			Real Economic Growth		
Year	First Forecast	Second Forecast	Actual Level	First Forecast	Second Forecast	Actual Level
1981	9.9%	9.1%	9.7%	1.1%	2.0%	1.9%
1982	8.3	7.9	6.4	4.2	0.2	−2.5
1983	7.0	6.0	3.9	5.0	5.2	3.6
1984	6.0	5.0	3.7	4.5	5.0	6.8
1985	5.4	4.7	3.0	4.2	4.7	3.4
1986	4.9	4.6	2.7	4.2	4.4	2.8

*These data are calculated assuming an inflation elasticity of revenues of 1.6 with respect to inflation and an elasticity of 1.36 with respect to real economic growth.

SOURCES: *A Program for Economic Recovery* and 1983 *Budget of the United States Government.*

only about half what was expected, and cumulative inflation from 1983 to 1986 was just over half the predicted level.

Inflation raises taxes through bracket creep. Typically, 10 percent inflation causes personal income tax collections to rise 16 percent, for a 6 percent real increase. The dramatic reduction in the inflation rate and the corresponding slowdown in real economic growth during the early 1980s therefore caused tax collections to be lower than they would have been had inflation stayed high. Lower inflation not only causes lower revenue, it also reduces both real (that is, adjusted for inflation) tax revenue and the tax share of GNP. Thus, until tax indexing began in 1985, lower-than-expected inflation caused tax revenues also to be lower than expected.

A much larger share of GNP would have been taken in taxes for each year from 1982 through 1987 had the administration forecasts been correct. Under the administration's original economic assumptions, the income tax share of GNP would have been 0.55 percent higher in 1983, 0.58 percent higher in 1984, 0.75 percent higher in 1985, 0.78 percent higher in 1986. In a typical year, about 30 percent of the overestimation of revenue was due to overoptimism in the real-GNP forecast (Rosie Scenario), while about 70 percent was attributable to administration pessimism about the decline in the rate of inflation. Total income tax collections over the period 1983–87 would have been $73 billion higher had the administration's 1982 forecasts come true. The total value of the personal income tax cuts between 1983 and 1987 was $145 billion relative to their 1980 share of GNP. Thus it can be argued that the administration expected to reduce the personal tax share of GNP by only half the actual figure.

On average, the difference between what the administration expected to collect and what it actually collected was about $14 billion, about 10 percent of our current deficit and about 14 percent of the total deficit increase during the 1980s. The bottom line is clear. The great deficit increase of the 1980s was overwhelmingly the result of higher spending, not lower taxes. Even with the personal tax cuts, taxes remained high by historic standards. Though in 1980 overall spending hit a then record high as a share of GNP, spending continued to climb throughout the Reagan years and was responsible for at least three quarters of the increase in the deficit.

There is, however, one way in which the tax cuts contributed more to the deficit than anyone expected. For contrary to nearly all predictions, the evidence shows the tax cuts were one of the reasons inflation dropped so much more quickly than expected. But that is our next story.

[7]

Why No Inflation?

"Reagan's task of winning credibility is made more
difficult by widespread skepticism among economists
and other opinion makers who fear that his unconven-
tional program—by traditional economic standards—
could worsen inflation rather than cure it."
—*BUSINESSWEEK*, DECEMBER 1, 1980

JIMMY CARTER PRESIDED OVER THE FIRST SUSTAINED DOUBLE-
digit inflation since official US records have been kept.[1] In the
fierce debate over Reagan's Great Experiment no issue caused more
concern than the possibility the tax cuts might send inflation even
higher, with devastating effects to the economy and the nation.
Carter's treasury secretary, William Miller, argued in 1980, "Hasty tax
cutting now could be counterproductive. It would be a great hoax on
the American people to promise a tax cut that sets off a new price spiral."[2] Walter Heller warned that "a $114 billion tax cut in three years
would simply overwhelm our existing productive capacity with a tidal
wave of increased demand and sweep away all hopes of curbing
deficits and containing inflation. Indeed, it would soon generate soaring deficits and roaring inflation."[3] Charles Schultze, chairman of

Carter's Council of Economic Advisers, argued, "We want to take a careful, deliberate approach and develop tax cuts that will address both short- and long-run problems, rather than come in with some quickie program that seeks immediate stimulus, without long-term benefits."[4] These men reflected what had become the Keynesian orthodoxy: Because the prime cause of inflation is too much demand, or spending power, in the economy, tax cuts, which give consumers more money to spend, would exacerbate inflation.

Yet the record is clear as to the contrary. Consumer prices, which had risen at a double-digit pace in 1979 and 1980, increased only 8.9 percent in 1981, the year the tax cut was passed. In 1982, the year that the tax cuts first hit the spending stream, prices rose only 3.8 percent. After additional tax rate reductions in 1983 and 1984, the rate of inflation stayed below 4 percent. From 1982 through 1987 the inflation rate averaged only 3.3 percent,[5] the lowest rate for any five-year period since the early 1960s. The Reagan experiment devastated the contemporary Keynesian's view of inflation. Not since the Great Depression itself has the prevailing economic orthodoxy been proven so decisively wrong.

The fault was not that of Keynes, but of his latter-day disciples. *The General Theory* was written in the 1930s, when inadequate demand was clearly a problem and prices were actually falling, not rising. Keynes focused on solving the problem of inadequate demand, not excess demand, or inflation, neither of which were pressing problems in the midst of the Great Depression. The early postwar Keynesian model of the economy thus did not consider inflation, assuming for the sake of analysis that prices were stable. It was only much later that the disciples of Keynes tried to extend his theory to the problem of inflation. Their reasoning went like this: Keynes showed that when demand is too low, unemployment rises and prices fall. Therefore, they concluded, when prices rise it must be because unemployment is falling and demand is too high. But this inverse reasoning, which seems commonsensical, does not work as symmetrically as one might expect. Reducing inflation by raising unemployment through demand management is a slow, painful process.

To fully understand why the modern Keynesian paradigm failed, we need a new paradigm that can account for the unexpected events of 1982–86. In short, we must answer the question: Why no inflation?

We start with a clear and widely accepted model of the mechanisms of inflation, developed not by the supply-siders but by the monetarist school of economic thought and rooted in a simple observation. The amount of money in the economy, multiplied by the rate at which money is spent, must equal the total amount of spending that takes place:

$$\text{Money} \times \text{Rate Spent} = \text{Spending}$$

If this doesn't seem controversial to you, it's because it isn't. The observation is true by definition. It is complemented by another observation: The amount of spending that takes place equals the price of each good sold times the number of units of the good that are sold.

$$\text{Spending} = \text{Price} \times \text{Quantity Sold}$$

Taken together, these statements produce the conclusion that the amount of money times the rate at which it is spent equals the level of prices times the amount of goods sold.

Of course, economists have their own jargon. The amount of money is called the money supply, "M." The rate at which money is spent is called velocity, "V." The quantity of goods sold is called real output or real GNP, "Y." And the price at which these goods are sold is called the price level, "P." The money supply times velocity equals the price level times real GNP. In economists' shorthand this is:

$$M \times V = P \times Y^6$$

The nice thing about an equation like this is that it can easily express changes in the economy. Any change in one side of the equation must be matched by a change in the other side. If one side goes up by 10 percent, then the other side must also rise by 10 percent. In other words:

$$\% \text{ change M} + \% \text{ change V} = \% \text{ change P} + \% \text{ change Y}$$

To translate, "% change M" is the growth rate of the money supply, "% change V" is the change in the velocity or rate of spending, and "%

change Y" is the real growth in the economy. That leaves "% change P," the change in the price level, or what we call inflation.

Now we have a formula for figuring out the rate of inflation. Inflation equals how fast money is created, plus how much faster each dollar is spent, minus how fast the real output of the economy is expanding. Our formula is just a mathematical version of the old saw that inflation is caused by too much money chasing too few goods.

Start with money. If either the money supply or the velocity increases by 1 percent (and the other remains the same), total demand (the left side of the equation) will increase by 1 percent. But that increase must be matched by a change on the right side. If the rate at which goods are produced by the economy (Y, or real growth) goes up 1 percent, then P can stay unchanged and there will be no additional inflation. But if production does not rise, the price level must rise, adding 1 percent to the inflation rate. By the same token, if real growth goes up, and (M + V) growth stays the same, inflation must go down.

Thus, other things being equal, an increase in the rate of real growth will lead to a decline in inflation, because the same amount of money will be chasing more goods. And a decrease in the rate of real economic growth will lead to an increase in inflation—again, other things being equal—because the same amount of money will be chasing fewer goods.

With this model of inflation, we can analyze the acceleration of inflation in the late 1970s and its decline in the early 1980s. Table 7.1 presents the data for the four variables of our equation for the periods just before and just after the passage of ERTA. Again, the sum of the changes in money and velocity minus the rate of real growth will give us the rate of inflation in the economy.

The most striking fact in these numbers is that the rate of money growth, in this case measured by M2 (a measurement of money supply that includes money in cash, checking and NOW accounts, money market funds for individuals, savings accounts, and small-value certificates of deposit, all of which individuals could spend fairly readily) hardly changed over the period in question, though the inflation rate (as measured by the GNP deflator) increased in the years up to 1980 and fell sharply thereafter. This strongly suggests that the Federal Reserve's effort to control the money supply during this period cannot by itself

TABLE 7.1 Money, Inflation, and Real Growth 1978–1986

Year	Percent Money Growth	Percent Velocity Change	Percent Inflation	Percent Real Growth
1978	8.0	6.3	8.0	6.3
1979	8.0	1.5	8.9	0.6
1980	8.9	0.9	9.9	−0.1
1981	10.0	−0.7	8.7	0.6
1982	8.8	−5.5	5.2	−1.9
1983	11.8	−1.7	3.6	6.5
1984	8.3	0.2	3.4	5.1
1985	8.5	−2.0	2.9	3.6
1986	9.5	−4.7	2.8	2.0

NOTE: Money growth rates are calculated on a December-to-December basis. As GNP and the price level (the GNP deflator) are not calculated monthly, fourth quarter–to–fourth quarter growth rates are used. Velocity is calculated as an arithmetic residual for exposition, although it should more properly be calculated as a logarithmic residual; the difference, however, is small.

SOURCES: 1989 *Economic Report of the President*, and author's calculations.

explain the drop in inflation. In 1985, for instance, money growth was slightly faster than it had been in 1979, yet inflation was less than half as severe. The big changes were not in money supply but in velocity, which moved from a positive to a negative number, and in real growth. Both the slowdown in velocity and the rise in real economic activity were helped along by the tax cuts.

Velocity is the speed at which the money supply is spent on final goods and services. Over long periods of time, the velocity of the M2 money supply is relatively stable. Between 1960 and 1980, for example, M2 velocity grew at an average annual rate of only 0.1 percent. The dramatic velocity swings of the late 1970s and early 1980s are a bit of a puzzle. Why did people spend their money so much faster in the late 1970s and then slow their spending so rapidly in the early 1980s?

To solve this riddle, we must realize that money serves not only as a means of carrying on transactions, but also as a store of value. Most of our personal wealth is stored in long-term investments, whether stocks or office buildings or the family home. But for security and convenience we all store a certain amount of our worth in ready money, cash or its near equivalents. We may prefer to keep a chunk of cash sitting in our wallets so as not to use the credit card. We tend to put enough cash in the checking account to cover a few months' bills without having to draw upon savings.

The portion of the national money supply we allow to "sit" as a store of wealth in our checking accounts and in our wallets is the key to the velocity of money. If a large share is sitting, the *average* velocity of money in the economy will be low. Those dollars that stay put have a velocity of zero and pull down the average velocity for all the dollars in the economy. On the other hand, if the share of dollars that is sitting in cash or in checking accounts falls, then the average velocity of dollars in the economy rises. Over the long term there is little reason for the share of the money in the economy that is kept sitting to change much. That is why, over a long period of time, velocity is fairly stable. But velocity can change dramatically, as in the late 1970s and early 1980s, when changes in the economy changed people's attitudes toward holding money as a store of wealth.

Keeping money idle has costs. When these costs go up, the amount of idle money goes down and velocity increases. The most obvious cost is the profit we lose by failing to invest our cash. Keeping money in cash or in a checking account means sacrificing the interest one might earn by holding a bond or other interest-bearing security.[7] When interest rates rise, the cost of keeping money idle rises. People then keep less money in checking accounts and more in securities. The issuer of the securities, who gets the money, keeps some of it idle but puts most of the money to use to earn more money to pay interest to his investors and bondholders. Thus, during periods of rising interest rates, velocity tends to increase.

Individual consumers may say they do not fine-tune their finances in this way. In fact, there is evidence that the proportion of money put into money market funds instead of checking accounts does vary with interest rates.[8] The bulk of this fine-tuning, however, is done by firms, not individuals. The financial officers of major corporations manage millions of dollars in cash assets. They must balance the desire for a good return on those assets against the risk the company will be caught short of cash if too much of its money is tied up in interest-bearing investments. The higher the return from lending, the more willing they are to squeeze their cash balances to the minimum.[9] This nationwide balancing act has a significant effect on velocity.

From 1978 to 1985 interest rates closely followed velocity. Interest rates rose until 1981 and then fell, as did velocity. But why did interest rates fall? According to the opponents of the tax cuts, interest rates should have risen as the government was forced to borrow more and as consumers got more spending power. In part interest rates may have fallen because the Federal Reserve convinced people it was serious about controlling inflation. But as the data indicate, money supply creation increased in 1982. Changes in money alone simply cannot explain the changes in inflation. There is an alternative explanation: the effect of tax cuts on the velocity of money.

Before the tax cuts a taxpayer in the top 70 percent tax bracket who invested in a 10 percent bond would earn only a 3 percent return after tax. The tax cut, by reducing the top rate to 50 percent, nearly doubled this net return to 5 percent. Logic suggests that this increase in return would make more money available for investment and lower its price, that is, the interest rate. And that is just what happened. In the high inflation pre–tax cut years of 1978–81, net purchases of financial assets by households grew at an annual rate of only 3.7 percent even though personal income was rising at an annual rate of 11.5 percent and interest rates were very high. People put less and less of their earnings into financial assets despite record high interest rates. Instead, the money went to spending. After the tax cuts were passed, this trend reversed. Between 1981 and 1984, net purchases of financial assets by households grew at an astounding 19 percent annual rate while personal income grew at only 7.2 percent. The share of personal income being committed to financial assets rose from 12.7 percent in 1981 to 17.4 percent in 1984 after falling in the years leading up to 1981.[10] Because most of this increase came from increased income and decreased spending rather than a reduction in idle cash, it did not increase velocity significantly.

The increase in the funds flowing into financial assets did put downward pressure on the before-tax interest rate. Since corporate tax rates were left essentially unchanged, this decline in interest rates reduced the incentives for corporations to stretch their idle cash to the limit, and they began to keep more on hand to meet day-to-day needs. The consequent increase in idle cash reduced velocity.[11]

Tax rate reduction reduced velocity in another way as well. As we explained in chapter 3, high tax rates can encourage consumer borrowing and spending, especially in an inflationary environment. Because of the tax deduction for interest payments, an 18 percent credit card loan effectively cost a taxpayer in the 49 percent bracket only 9.2 percent. With inflation at double-digit rates, that taxpayer had a big incentive to borrow and buy now rather than wait till next year when the price might be 12 percent higher. In that environment, it was very much to people's advantage not only to spend all the money they had, but to borrow money as well. By cutting tax rates, the government cut the incentive to spend and to borrow to finance spending. Our 49 percent bracket family, for instance, saw its marginal tax rate reduced to 37 percent. That tax cut raised the after-tax cost of the same 18 percent credit card loan to 11.5 percent, a bit more than the prevailing inflation rate. The bonus for borrowing and spending had disappeared. This reduction in spending helped slow velocity somewhat. And the reduction in consumer borrowing contributed to the drop in pre-tax interest rates, further reducing the velocity of corporate funds.[12] This helps explain why interest rates and velocity fell after the tax cut was passed. It also explains why the inflation rate started to fall so rapidly: Changes in velocity, caused by a significant change in individual behavior, helped reduce inflation independent of, but in addition to, the effects of monetary policy.

In sum, cutting tax rates on the return to savings allowed before-tax interest rates to fall. The falling interest rate led to a fall in velocity that acted as a brake on inflation (and on the economy). The tax cut also reduced the incentives to borrow to finance consumption purchases. This led to a further reduction in the demand for goods and services, thus putting even more downward pressure on the inflation rate. Instead of inflation accelerating, which opponents of the tax cuts had expected, the exact opposite occurred.

The tax cuts slowed velocity and reduced inflation in another way as well. The tax cut clearly helped raise the value of the dollar as compared to other currencies. This increase meant each dollar could buy more overseas. Moreover, a rising dollar makes foreigners more willing to hold idle dollar balances: With the dollar going up, idle dollars grow in value every day. The tax bill raised the foreign exchange value of the dollar by making the United States the most profitable place in the world to invest. The next chapter details how ERTA's increased depreciation allowances and reduced tax rate on interest, dividends, and capital gains drew capital from all over the world to America in search of a profitable rate of return.

In order for foreigners to invest in the United States, they first had to purchase US dollars. After all, American investments, from factories to treasury bonds, are priced in dollars, not yen, marks, or pounds. The rush to invest in the United States thus increased the demand for dollars, which increased their price. The US dollar rose from 1.8 German marks in 1980 to 2.9 marks in 1985. Between 1980 and 1985 the value of the dollar rose 64 percent compared to the currencies of our major trading partners. As a result, each US dollar bought more foreign goods in 1985 than it did in 1980.[13] In 1985 imports from abroad composed about 11 percent of our total purchases. Since 11 percent of our purchases were 64 percent cheaper than they would have been had the dollar not risen, by 1985 the rise in the value of the dollar probably had reduced US prices by about 7 percent, or 1.4 percent per year.[14] The reduced cost of imported goods also restrained price increases on those American goods that competed with imports.

The tax cuts also reduced inflation by increasing real growth. Recall that the inflation rate equals the rate of money creation plus the change in velocity minus real growth. If inflation is more money chasing fewer goods, it can be reduced by increasing the amount of goods as well as by reducing the amount of money. In the eight years leading up to the passage of the tax cut, real economic growth averaged only 2.1 percent.[15] In the eight years following the passage of the tax cut in 1981, real economic growth averaged 3.0 percent per year, even including the deep recession year of 1982. The rate of real economic growth seems to have accelerated. It is too early to tell if this is a permanent phenomenon. But as the discussion of the supply-side effects of tax policy in chapter 4 indicates, the tax cut does explain an increase in the rate of real growth of at least 0.5 percent per year from 1982 to 1985.

One of the key ways the tax cuts add real growth is by increasing the labor force the economy has to work with. Real after-tax wages rise, making work more attractive or making it cheaper to hire workers at the same after-tax wage. Since the first reduction in withholding in July 1982, over 20 million new jobs have been created in America, twice the new jobs created in Europe and Japan combined. This record expansion in employment is a major reason real output increased and inflation declined.

The modern Keynesians failed to see that the tax cuts might restrain inflation for the same reason they failed to see that the tax cuts would earn back much of the revenue they apparently lost. They focused almost exclusively on the tax cuts' impact on aggregate demand, the increase in the amount of money in consumers' pockets, and they largely ignored the profound effect high tax rates have on taxpayer behavior. High taxes had been encouraging people to buy more, borrow more, and produce less. As inflation redoubled these bad incentives and steadily raised tax rates through bracket creep, inflation continued to get worse even as the economy declined.

The key to breaking this vicious cycle was not gross manipulation of aggregate demand, but subtle changes in individual incentives. The key to breaking the vicious double helix of stagflation was, to a very large extent, cutting taxes.

[8]

A Deluge of Debt?

"Something quite bad is going to happen
to the US economy fairly soon. Politically, the big
question is whether it will happen before or
after the 1984 election."
—THE EDITORS, *THE NEW REPUBLIC*, JULY 9, 1984

THE CONVENTIONAL WISDOM HOLDS THAT THE 1981 TAX cuts ushered in a period of profligate borrowing and consumption in America, a binge that diminished savings and investment, impoverishing future American generations and hampering the economy. The specter of looming catastrophe was raised by the critics in the 1984 election and again in 1988. It will no doubt be raised again in 1992. Yet now that the catastrophe has been postponed for nearly a decade, perhaps we should examine the great sea of red ink on which the Reagan economic recovery supposedly floats.

It is not surprising that the Keynesians believe the recovery of the 1980s was built on debt and consumer spending. Keynesian theory maintains that stimulating consumer spending is one of the most effective ways of stimulating the economy and that too much savings can actually hurt economic performance. Moreover, as we saw in chapter 4, the 1981 tax cut did stimulate spending by putting more money into the hands of taxpayers. But this is a far cry from the claim that the Reagan *recovery* was good old-fashioned Keynesianism.

The data indicate that the record-setting expansion of the 1980s was exceptional not for a binge of consumption, but for a rapid rise in investment spending.[1] It is important to note that this economic expansion, which began in the final quarter of 1982, is one of the strongest as well as one of the longest on record. During the first two years of the expansion, real GNP expanded at a 5.8 percent annual rate, compared to a 4.8 percent annual rate in the other five continuous expansions of the preceding quarter century. Typically an economic expansion lasts about three years. The present expansion is entering its eighth year as this book goes to press.

Consumption spending played a role in the current recovery, but consumption spending is an important part of any economic recovery. In the expansion of the 1980s, real consumption grew at a 5.4 percent annual rate in the first year and a 4.8 percent annual rate during the first two years. This is the evidence cited by the Keynesians. But this consumption pattern is almost identical to that of previous expansions. The five preceding expansions averaged an identical 5.4 percent increase in consumption during the first year and a slightly higher 4.9 percent increase during the first two years. In this regard, the ERTA expansion was quite average.

The real impetus to the expansion of the 1980s was investment spending. In recent history, investment spending increased an average of 23 percent during the first year of an expansion, and at a 13 percent annual rate during the first two years. But during the expansion of the 1980s investment skyrocketed 41 percent during the first year and expanded at a 27 percent annual rate during the first two years. The present expansion began with an explosion of investment spending twice as powerful as usual.

The investment incentives of ERTA were quite strong and produced marked results. ERTA's most important pro-investment provision was the Accelerated Cost Recovery System (ACRS). Governing the rate at which new investments could be depreciated for tax purposes, ACRS bolstered the depreciation deduction for business plant and equipment.

During the 1970s the erosion of that deduction by inflation and high taxation had substantially penalized business investment.

A key principle of business taxation is that a company should pay taxes only on its profits, and not on its costs of doing business. For that reason businesses have been allowed to deduct, over time, the cost of the plant and equipment used to produce their products or services. The deduction is taken over time rather than at purchase (as with materials or wages) because the expense of using a machine or a factory is considered to occur over the course of its useful life. Depreciation deductions are not based on the actual useful life of a particular piece of equipment, however, but are taken from standardized schedules for depreciating broad categories of plant and equipment.

By the late 1970s inflation and the tax rules had undermined these depreciation schedules and subverted the principle that businesses should pay taxes only on their profits. Imagine a machine that cost $100 the year it was purchased and wears out at the rate of 10 percent a year, so that it must be replaced at the end of ten years. The tax system allows the company to subtract $10 per year from its taxable profits to account for the wear on the machine: a cost of doing business. This $10 subtraction in effect allows the company to sell $10 worth of goods tax free. At the end of ten years, if the $10 in goods the machine produces has been set aside each year, the company will have accumulated $100 tax free to buy a new machine. In the absence of inflation, this system works well.

But suppose inflation enters the system and all prices rise 10 percent per year. After one year, the $100 machine will cost $110 to replace. After ten years it will cost $259 to replace. But IRS accounting rules, which ignore inflation, allow the company to accumulate only $100 tax free. The additional $159 the new machine costs comes out of after-tax profits, violating the basic principles of fair taxation and harming the economy by discouraging investment.[2]

ACRS was ERTA's solution to this problem.[3] Under the old tax law, it often took as long as eight to ten years to fully deduct the cost of new machinery. ACRS reduced the time period to five years, substantially cutting the after-tax cost of buying new equipment. ACRS did not provide precise compensation for inflation. The way to do that would have been to index the system, adjusting the original purchase prices of plant and equipment for actual inflation and increasing the depreciation allowances accordingly. Nevertheless, ACRS did substantially encourage investment in plant and equipment.

A way to quantify this investment effect is by the "hurdle rate of return"—the rate of return an investment must produce to justify the decision to make it. Hurdle rates vary for different businesses, depending on their particular circumstances and opportunities. As hurdle rates rise, fewer and fewer investments make business sense. In 1979, because of the combination of high tax rates and 10 percent inflation, an investor needed a 16.4 percent nominal rate of return in order to make a 4 percent hurdle. By 1981, with inflation down to 8 percent and the new tax law in effect, an 11.5 percent nominal return would make the same 4 percent hurdle. Of this five-point drop in the hurdle rate of return, which made a tremendous number of previously unprofitable projects quite attractive to investors, three points were directly attributable to the tax law change and the remaining two-point drop came from the reduction in inflation.[4]

(In some cases the changes may have gone too far. For certain types of investment ACRS actually produced a net tax subsidy, encouraging overinvestment in certain types of equipment. These net subsidies were subsequently eliminated in tax bills passed in 1982 and 1984.)

ACRS helped make the Reagan recovery one of the most investment-oriented on record. It is particularly significant that the investment incentives of the bill worked even though other factors in the economic environment, such as high real interest rates, were not conducive to business investment. The ACRS provisions were particularly generous in their treatment of producer durable equipment. Such investment usually expands about 8 percent in the first year and 9 percent over the first two years of an economic expansion. In the ERTA recovery it expanded 21 percent the first year and averaged 18 percent over the first two years. On the other hand, investment in structures such as factories, which was not particularly favored by the bill, behaved normally for an expansion.[5]

In sum, the recovery benefited from both consumption and investment, but it was investment that turned it from an average recovery into a record-setting expansion. The investment boom continued well into the recovery. In 1985, the last year of the ERTA investment incentives, fully 8.4 percent of the nation's real GNP went into real, inflation-adjusted investment in producer durable equipment.[6] During the 1970s this investment figure never exceeded 8.1 percent.

Investment spending is crucial to the long-term health of the American economy. If the nation devoted a greater proportion of its resources to investment spending, our living standard would rise more quickly. But ERTA was clearly part of the solution, not part of the problem. Later in the decade, when most of the incentive provisions of ERTA had been repealed, investment spending slowed somewhat; taken as a whole, however, the investment data from the 1980s hardly indicate a nation headed for economic catastrophe.

Critics of the tax cut also claim it has made us a nation of borrowers instead of savers, and that our profligacy could lead to economic ruin. Once again, it is indisputable that increasing the national savings rate would be a good idea. But most of those who criticize the effect of Reaganomics on saving use a standard of measurement that tends to substantially understate national saving during periods of strong economic growth. Better measurements show that we do not face catastrophe now, nor did ERTA make the existing situation significantly worse.

Before we get into the measurement issue, however, let us consider one way in which ERTA clearly fostered saving. As mentioned in chapter 3, ERTA established the Individual Retirement Account program (IRA) to increase national saving and to make it easier for individuals to save for their own retirement. Under this program taxpayers could deduct from their taxable income up to $2,000 in annual contributions to a retirement account. The contributed funds accumulate interest, dividends, and capital gains tax free; the participant in an IRA plan pays taxes only when the funds are withdrawn, generally after retirement.

The advantages of an IRA to an individual are twofold. First, the taxpayer's tax rate while working and contributing to the IRA will probably be greater than when the funds are withdrawn. The taxpayer thereby receives an immediate saving equal to the difference between the two tax rates. For most taxpayers, however, the biggest advantage is that the funds contributed grow tax free over time. One dollar invested in an IRA program at 8 percent interest grows to $4.66 in twenty years. If the total is then taxed at a 28 percent rate, the taxpayer is left with $3.36. On the other hand, if the dollar is deposited in an ordinary savings account paying 8 percent interest, taxes must be paid both on the initial contribution and on each year's interest as it is earned. At the end of twenty years, the retiree is left with only $2.24, or 34 percent less.

This made IRAs very attractive. Data from the first three years of the program indicate that 12 million taxpayers contributed $28.3 billion in 1982, 13.6 million taxpayers contributed $32.1 billion in 1983, and by 1984, 15.4 million taxpayers contributed $35.8 billion. Most participants contributed in all three years, and much of this money was "new" savings, not just transfers from other accounts. (Because IRA contributions must be "locked up" for many years, they cannot be readily substituted for other forms of saving that the taxpayer can use at his or her discretion.) Data from the Survey of Consumer Finances indicate that individuals who contributed to an IRA were 50 percent more likely than noncontributors to have increased their overall saving in the year their contribution was made. Careful statistical analysis of the IRA data indicate that about 45 percent of the money contributed to IRAs came from a reduction in household consumption, 35 percent from the tax savings, while 20 percent came from other forms of existing saving.[7] The first category represents new saving to the economy, while the latter two represent a reallocation of saving, either from the government to the IRA or from other savings vehicles to the IRA. Overall, in its first three years, the IRA program increased net national saving in America by some $40 billion, a very respectable figure.

Even aside from the IRA program, however, the effects of ERTA on saving were far more beneficial than is popularly believed.[8] Critics usually cite a statistical series called the personal savings rate, the percentage of after-tax income that is not spent by consumers, to prove the national savings rate has tumbled. This statistic has fallen from roughly 7 percent in the late 1970s to a low of 3.2 percent in 1987. If it accurately reflected the true behavior of households toward savings, we would be in bad shape. Fortunately, it does not.

A look at history makes obvious the shortcomings of the personal savings rate as a measure of national capital formation. The sum of all statistically reported personal savings back to the beginning of recorded

US data plus a generous allowance for personal savings from that point back to the time of the Pilgrims would indicate that Americans have saved somewhat less than $4 trillion during our nation's history. Yet the total accumulated wealth of American households was over $14 trillion at the end of 1987. The personal savings rate missed nearly three-fourths of the real savings because it does not count the rising value of personal assets ranging from houses to stock portfolios. A family that took out a $25,000 mortgage in 1950 to buy a house and has since paid off the mortgage now holds an asset that may be worth $200,000 or more. But only the $25,000 spent paying off the mortgage counts as saving. The $175,000 rise in the value of the house is considered a capital gain, which is not counted as income by the National Income and Product Accounts and therefore not included in figures for personal savings.[9]

The personal savings calculation produces another even more bizarre result. According to official calculations, the house fully depreciated during the four decades the family lived in it, and it is now carried on the nation's balance sheet as being worth zero. Even if the owner sells the house and puts the money in the bank, neither the owner nor the buyer is considered to be saving the $200,000. According to the statistics, they are simply swapping one asset (officially valued at zero) for another and not producing either income or savings. The same peculiar accounting applies to many other assets. The stocks in the family portfolio are valued at the purchase price, not their current market value. Even at the time of purchase there would have been no net saving in the economy if the seller spent the proceeds. Most Americans accumulate far more wealth than the personal savings rate suggests.

In its balance sheets for the US economy, the Federal Reserve compiles a much more accurate measure of household savings: the rise in the net worth of households, or the difference between the increase in their assets and the increase in their liabilities.[10] If after the tax cuts households had gone on a borrowing and spending binge, piling up debt without offsetting increases in assets, household net worth would have declined, and household savings would be negative.

Quite the reverse happened. Between the end of 1981 and the end of 1987, household liabilities rose more than $1.3 trillion, but household assets rose more than $6 trillion. All together, households increased their net worth by $4.7 trillion, or 49 percent, while prices rose only 23 percent. These data indicate a *rise* in the real savings rate of households: In the five years before the rate reduction took effect, using the rise in real net worth as the measure, household savings averaged 7.8 percent of personal income, but in the five years following the passage of ERTA, household savings grew to 13.5 percent of personal income.[11]

The oft-quoted but misleading personal savings rate often falls in a strong economy and rises when times get hard. During a falling stock market and high inflation people see the real value of their existing assets decline. They compensate by saving a greater proportion of their current income. But during good times, with a rising stock market and low inflation preserving or even increasing their store of wealth, people feel less compelled to save out of current income. The rising value of household wealth in the 1980s probably blunted the urge to save.

Some people worry that a stock market crash could wipe out all the gains of the 1980s or that many families have leveraged debt against paper wealth that could disappear tomorrow. But all the figures we have been using come from the end of 1987, when the market had barely begun to recover from its record fall in October of that year. More important, since the end of 1980 the share of household assets in the stock market has risen only from 11.2 percent to 12.2 percent, hardly a significant increase considering that the stock market doubled. Safer holdings such as bank deposits, money market funds, and government bonds have risen from 20.4 percent of household assets to 23.2 percent.

Nor have households run up exceptionally large credit card balances. At the end of 1980 consumer credit amounted to $355 billion or 24 percent of such readily accessible household assets as currency, checking and savings accounts, and money market funds. By the end of 1987 consumer credit had grown to $697 billion, but ready cash had also grown to $2,788 billion. Consumer credit still equaled only 25 percent of ready cash.

On the average, American households in the late 1980s could pay off all their debts, including credit card debt, auto loans, and mortgages on their homes with their ready cash. They would not have had to touch their houses, cars, stock portfolios, pension funds, life insurance, small business holdings, or other assets. Obviously not every household was in this situation, nor has there ever been a time when all were. But taken as a whole, the households of the nation were no more burdened by debt at the end of the decade than they were in 1980. The situation is hardly a recipe for catastrophe or crisis.

The nation's businesses are in a similar position, though they are not quite as comfortable as households. According to the Federal Reserve, from 1 January 1981 to 31 December 1987, American businesses increased their liabilities by nearly $1.2 trillion. But they increased their assets by nearly $2.1 trillion and their net worth rose some $900 billion, or about one-third. At the end of 1980, nonfinancial business corporations had $196 billion in liquid assets covering nearly 24 percent of their $828 billion in credit market debt. The prime interest rate was over 20 percent. At the end of 1987, these businesses owed $1,697 billion in the credit markets but had $494 billion of liquid assets. Their liquid assets covered 29 percent of their debts while the prime rate was only 8.75 percent, less than half the 1980 rate.

As to the banks, it is obvious that the savings and loan industry is in serious trouble and that commercial banks are overextended in their third-world loans. But the overall picture is not one of profligacy. Private financial institutions saw their net worth rise from $247 billion at the end of 1980 to $490 billion at the end of 1987, an increase of 98 percent. The share of their assets held in very safe US government debt rose from 9.2 percent at the end of 1980 to 15.6 percent at the end of 1987, while corporate and foreign bonds took a roughly constant share of their portfolio. On the whole, banks have increased savings and reserves and reduced the risk in their loans.

All in all, the private sector's net worth rose from $10.5 trillion at the end of 1980 to $15.8 trillion at the end of 1987, an increase of 51 percent. During the same time, the price level rose 34 percent. The real growth of the net worth of the private sector has been 13 percent, or 1.7 percent per year during this seven-year period as shown in figure 8.1. The fight against inflation clearly took its toll. Real net worth increased only 0.5 percent per year from the end of 1979 to the end of 1982. By contrast, growth from the end of 1982 to the end of 1987 averaged nearly $300 billion per year, a 2.2 percent annual rate.

The most comparable period is the 1960s, which combined moderate inflation and fairly robust economic growth. During that decade, the real net worth of the private sector increased at a 2.6 percent annual rate.

For the private sector, the savings versus borrowing record has been good but far from outstanding in the 1980s. That is not true of the public sector, where the financial position deteriorated significantly. Net financial liabilities, after adjusting for inflation, doubled from $825 billion to $1,652 billion between the end of 1980 and the end of 1987. Fully half of the $1.6 trillion of real growth in the private sector's net worth was offset by this deterioration in the financial net worth of the public sector.

Considering the private and public sector together, the overall savings performance of the country has been quite mediocre during the 1980s. Real national net worth grew only about 1 percent per year from the end of 1980 to the end of 1987. America clearly must do better. At the same time, the nation's assets are growing faster than its liabilities, and we are far from sinking in a sea of red ink.

The 1980s combined rapid growth in investment with a mediocre performance in savings. This is a bit unusual. Savings and investment usually run in tandem, since the first is a primary source of the second. ERTA changed that normally close relationship by providing very gen-

FIGURE 8.1 Real Value of Private Sector Net Worth 1979–1987

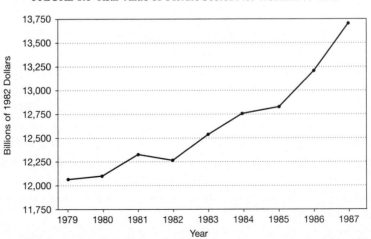

erous incentives for new investment. Despite the popularity of the IRA program and the taming of inflation, incentives to save were less successful, and any extra private savings were consumed by greatly increased public sector borrowing.

ERTA did not flood the country in red ink. But by encouraging investment much more powerfully than it encouraged savings, it created an imbalance in the credit markets. As investors demanded more funds than savers supplied, real interest rates moved sharply higher. This rise did eventually evoke new sources of capital but only partially from American households. The balance was made up in part by American businesses themselves. Gross business savings by American firms jumped 58 percent between 1980 and 1985.[12] In addition, foreign capital flowed into America at an unprecedented rate as the United States became the world's premier investment opportunity.

In the years leading up to 1980, American direct investment abroad in new plant and equipment far exceeded foreign investment here. After the tax cuts the situation reversed dramatically, with foreigners investing in new plants in the United States at three times the rate Americans made similar investments overseas. Direct foreign investment in plant and equipment in the United States rose from $109 billion in 1981 to $220 billion in 1986. Private foreign investment in financial assets rose from $93 billion in 1981 to more than $400 billion in 1986. In short, the United States was internationally recognized as the smart place to invest in the early 1980s. This trend was so powerful that by 1988 critics who had complained about US companies shipping jobs overseas by investing abroad were instead complaining that foreigners were "buying up America."

The lesson of ERTA is twofold: The investment provisions worked quite well. But any tax bill that encourages business investment should also include equivalent encouragement for private savings—one more example of the fundamental need to balance the supply and demand features of any tax cut.

[9]

The World's Tax Cut

"The reason for the world-wide trend toward
lower top rates is clear. Excessive rates of income tax
destroy enterprise, encourage avoidance, and drive
talent to more hospitable shores overseas."[1]
—NIGEL LAWSON,
CHANCELLOR OF THE EXCHEQUER, HMG

I N THE UNITED STATES THE DEBATE OVER REAGAN'S GREAT
Experiment rages on. But abroad the verdict is clear. In a shining
example of that sincerest form of flattery, nearly all the industrialized
nations as well as most of the newly developing nations have either reduced their tax rates during the 1980s or scheduled rate reductions for
the early 1990s.

The worldwide reduction in taxes is part of a larger worldwide
movement toward free markets, again led by the United States. But
though the United States, under Reagan, started this trend, Reagan's de-
parture from the scene will not reverse it. Cutting taxes and freeing markets have become essential weapons of worldwide economic
competition. The United States would find it difficult if not impossible
to return to the high tax rates of the past and still maintain its position

in the world. Indeed, international competition coupled with the technological revolutions of the recent past will likely prompt further worldwide progress to even greater economic freedom and even lower tax rates.

The 1980s were an important turning point, not an end but a beginning. And the beginning began not just in the United States, but in the United Kingdom as well. History will likely credit the worldwide resurgence of free markets and lower taxes to Margaret Thatcher as well as Ronald Reagan.

At the start of the decade one could not imagine two nations less likely to lead an economic revival. Through the 1960s and 1970s they had competed for last place in the world growth leagues. While Americans spoke of a national malaise, Europe spoke of the "British disease" afflicting a country that seemed more interested in prolonging economic decline than in reviving past glories.

In the late 1970s Britain levied a top marginal rate of 83 percent on earned income and an utterly confiscatory top rate of 98 percent on capital income. Margaret Thatcher's first budget called for a reduction in the regular top rate from 83 to 60 percent, with smaller percentage reductions in lower rates. The opposition benches cried "rich man's budget" as the chancellor read the proposal, but the Iron Maiden triumphed. In the first year of the tax rate reductions the rich did pay a smaller share of Britain's taxes, but the reduction was quite small compared to the rate cut. Though the top rate was cut by more than 25 percent, the share of taxes paid by the top 2 percent of the British taxpayers fell only from 15.4 percent to 14.7 percent. By the second year of the lower rates, the share of taxes paid by the top 2 percent of taxpayers had regained its pre–tax cut level. And by the fourth year after the tax cut, the top 2 percent were paying a greater share than before the cut: 16.4 percent. In real terms, the taxes paid by the top 5 percent rose 35 percent in the decade, compared to 5 percent for other taxpayers. Rising revenues and the beginning of a revitalization in the British economy soon emboldened the government to eliminate the 15 percent Investment Income Surcharge on all nonsalary income. By the second year of this latter cut, the share of taxes paid by the top 2 percent was at an all-time high, and headed higher.[2]

As we have learned, such profound behavioral changes generally indicate that tax rates had been a significant burden on the economy. True to form, after the rate cuts, Britain's long-comatose economy began an astounding recovery. The United Kingdom has had the fastest rate of growth of the major countries in Europe in every year but one of the last seven. Since 1981 British industrial production has grown more than 20 percent, easily the fastest growth in Europe. The British pound, long shunned, is regaining its status as a world reserve currency, and most of Europe envies the capitalist fever that Thatcher brought to Britain.

In the government's 1988 budget, Thatcher's Chancellor of the Exchequer Nigel Lawson proposed cutting the top rate of income tax to 40 percent and the basic rate of tax to 25 percent. Lawson reasoned that a 40 percent rate in the United Kingdom, which does not have state and local income taxes, would be roughly equivalent to the United States' 33 percent top rate plus the typical state rates of 5 to 10 percent. These dramatic tax rate cuts, passed in 1988 and in effect since the beginning of 1989, were derided as excessive by the opposition. At this writing, Lawson does face a budgetary problem: The British budget, long in deficit, is headed for a record surplus of some 13 billion British pounds,[3] or nearly 3 percent of British GNP. He has begun retiring the British national debt, which, coupled with a booming economy and the tax cuts, has brought a flood of foreign investment capital to Britain, driving up the pound. Prime Minister Thatcher has won two landslide reelections and is now the longest serving prime minister in modern times. Her critics still heckle, but strictly from the sidelines; the public is much too busy enjoying the record-breaking prosperity to pay any attention.

The United Kingdom represents an obvious success story for tax rate reduction. But some critics of tax cuts point to Sweden as a model of a nation where prosperity and high tax rates have long gone hand in hand.[4] Sweden is not technically a socialist country. Government ownership of industry is rare. Rather Sweden has high-tax capitalism, and taxes are high enough to make the head spin. The top marginal income tax rate takes effect at the equivalent of $35,000 income. Tax cuts during the 1980s reduced that top rate from 87 percent to 75 percent, but it is still high by almost any standard. Counting social insurance taxes and value-added taxes, a Swedish worker earning average wages faces a 73 percent combined marginal tax rate. Yet Stockholm is filled with Mercedes and Volvos; boat ownership in Sweden is among the highest in the world; and many families own summer homes. Why haven't such staggering tax rates impoverished Sweden?

First, much of the money paid in taxes comes right back in the form of subsidies. The expansive Swedish state consumes about 55 percent of GNP in taxes, overwhelmingly paid by the middle class, and then gives about 45 percent of GNP back in the form of subsidies, largely paid to the middle class. To receive a subsidy you don't have to do anything unusual: Just consume food (which is heavily subsidized), or have children (who entitle you to generous child allowances), or live long enough to collect your pension. The staggering level of taxes really doesn't reflect the government's burden on the typical Swede. After paying subsidies, the Swedish government consumes about the same share of GNP as the American government.

Still, rerouting all that money through the government via the tax system does profoundly change economic incentives. For example, the Swedish family's way to the good life is not to save. The interest paid on consumer loans is tax deductible. Given the tax rates, sensible Swedes not only do not save, they pile up debt. Borrowing is the Swedish way to enjoy a great lifestyle while sheltering income from the tax collector. So great are these incentives and so smart are the Swedes that the government's net tax take from capital income, interest, and dividends is actually negative. Only lower-income, low–tax rate individuals save. Though these spend-and-borrow tactics do help individuals in the short term, the long-term consequences are severe. The government loses tax revenue and the economy loses capital. Sweden's personal savings rate is actually negative.

Another secret to making it in Sweden is to take compensation not in salary but through the company expense account, which can buy your car, your travel, and your meals for you directly and tax free. One economist explained that Sweden has two types of money, pre-tax and post-tax. In a corollary of Gresham's law, pre-tax money drives out post-tax money.

Beating the tax system is a favorite topic at Swedish dinner parties. The dinner itself is often part of the deal. The restaurant is filled, but not with families. No children are present at all, there are three men for every woman, and everyone in the restaurant is in a business suit. As one Swedish economist told me, when you negotiate with your employer, wages don't come up. You talk about lifestyle. Once that is settled, you get together to figure out the best way of paying for that lifestyle. The objective is to have the government pick up as much of the cost as possible.

The result of all this is tremendous wage compression. Virtually no one in Sweden earns more than $50,000. Jobs that pay six figures in the United States pay one-third to one-half as much in Sweden. But the result isn't really equality. Assembly-line workers don't get a business lunch, a company car, or foreign travel. Their compensation comes in very taxable cash. Company executives pay taxes too, but on a smaller portion of their total compensation.

Even better than living off one's employer is to set up a company. The company can be a consultancy, or you can own rental housing or engage in any activity that can be done after regular business hours. The company need not make money: Its purpose is to preserve the income of one's regular job. Tax-deductible company purchases—cars, housing, etc.—can keep that lifestyle in shape, because most of the company's losses are deductible against other income. A hot conversation topic on my last visit to Sweden was the rumor that some clever accountant had found a way to deduct such business losses twice. Two deductions, each worth 80 percent, means that the more you lose, the more you make.

There are other escape routes. Tennis stars, rockers, and other high rollers become expatriates during their high earning years. Others opt for less dramatic departures. One night in Stockholm I was surprised to learn that my waiter was an electrical engineer on leave from Ericsson, the huge Swedish telecommunications firm. He was taking his three-month leave to be a waiter in order to "make some money." He made more money after taxes as a waiter than he did as an electrical engineer. The tax man has trouble getting at tips.

Talk of taxes in Sweden makes a guest feel a bit like Alice visiting Wonderland. The Red Queen would understand: The faster you run, the more you fall behind. The secret is not to run so fast. Swedes do not get ahead by working overtime and sharing 80 percent of the proceeds with the state. Instead the Swedish middle class makes it by living off state subsidies, borrowing, taking as much compensation as they can tax free, and working in the untaxed informal economy.

Even in Sweden, however, there is no such thing as a free lunch. Many of Sweden's leading economists and business leaders feel that Sweden peaked in 1970, when it held undisputed title to the world's highest standard of living. With a highly educated work force and world-class expertise in engineering, metallurgy, and telecommunications, Sweden had built for a quarter century on all industrial infrastructure left untouched by World War II. Postwar taxes were high by international standards but far lower than today; Swedish taxes in the 1950s and 1960s were roughly comparable to American taxes after Reagan. In the seventies things turned sour. Taxes rose steadily throughout the decade, hitting record levels by the early 1980s. Sweden is now fourth among Scandinavian countries in per capita income. Its economic growth since 1970 has been well below its historic trend and below average for the OECD. To remain internationally competitive Sweden has reduced the value of the krona by half compared to the German mark. But this drastic devaluation is itself an onerous tax on Swedish citizens, who must pay far more for imported products or raw materials. In recent years the krona has declined faster than any currency save those of Greece, Spain, and Portugal. Even the Italian lira has done better.

This relative decline does not mean poverty. Most Swedes remain oblivious to their nation's eroding economy. As the head of Sweden's largest private economic think tank told me, "It took the English one hundred years to wake up to their decline. Where will Sweden find itself at the start of the twenty-first century?"

It is a good question. The industries that made Sweden strong, particularly steel, are no longer growth industries. Future growth depends on new investment in new industries, particularly the high-risk high-technology start-up companies of today. Whereas the US venture capital market will take a risk on a new venture with prospects for a 25 percent pre-tax rate of return, the Swedish tax system forces this threshold up to the 50 to 60 percent range. Swedish capitalists must often turn their backs on start-up companies with payback periods of as little as three years.

The Swedish tax system, allowing people to consume today, is systematically consuming Sweden's future. Next year, Swedish companies will invest more in other countries than they will at home. High taxes are no longer merely a long-run problem. The day of reckoning comes ever closer. The Swedes themselves seem to realize this. The Swedish opposition parties have called for sharp reductions in tax rates. Now the social democratic government seems willing to go further. The government has proposed lowering the top rate to 60 percent, with further reductions to 50 percent in the 1990s. In the wake of the worldwide tax revolt, Sweden will still have one of the highest personal income tax rates in the world but should see economic incentives substantially improved. Even this bastion of the welfare state demonstrates the basic tenet of supply-side economics: Taxes matter, especially since democratic governments will almost always compensate for high taxes with loopholes and benefits that distort economic incentives even more perversely than high taxes alone.

Sweden's social planners have long been committed to equality of income, the elimination of private wealth, and the provision of economic security. The tax system established to achieve these goals has in a sense succeeded: High taxes advanced equality by prompting the very wealthy to leave the country and electrical engineers to become waiters. High taxes plus tax deductions for borrowing certainly discouraged private wealth. The personal savings rate is negative. Basic economic security, plus high taxes on profit, guarantees that few Swedes will undertake high-risk ventures, so the Swedish people and Swedish industry can grow old together. Sweden is not the exception that proves the rule. It is not an exception at all. Sweden proves that the tax system can either encourage work, saving, and risk-taking or discourage them. Sweden does not prove that incentives do not matter. Sweden proves that they work both ways.

The social democratic formula is breaking down throughout Scandinavia. Norway slashed its top tax rate from 75 percent to 54 percent over the course of the 1980s. Finland cut its top rate from 71 percent to 51 percent during the 1980s and has scheduled a further reduction in the top rate to 44 percent in the 1990s. The social democrats have not abandoned their goals of greater equality and a higher standard of living for working people, but they seem to recognize that lower tax rates help accomplish these goals. Individuals striving for personal success are the prime engine of social mobility. High taxes discourage that mobility by discouraging new money. Taxes do not break down class distinctions but perpetuate them.

Social democratic governments in Australia and New Zealand have also lowered tax rates. Australia reduced its top rate from 62 percent to 49 percent. New Zealand cut its top rate from 60 percent to 48 percent and plans a further reduction to 33 percent, the top US rate. Israel has cut its top rate from 66 percent to 48 percent, Canada (under a Tory government) from 58 percent to 45 percent, Austria from 62 percent to 50 percent, and Belgium has scheduled a cut to 55 percent, down from a high of 76 percent in 1979.

After Sweden, Japan is probably the country most often cited in evidence by those who believe tax rates have but little effect on economic performance. Japan, the greatest economic success story of the postwar era, has long maintained very high apparent tax rates, though after a few years of poor economic performance it recently cut its top rate from 75 to 50 percent.

The secret of Japanese tax rates is that few Japanese pay them. Huge tax deductions reduce real Japanese tax rates to levels comparable to or lower than current US rates. Moreover, most Japanese tax deductions, unlike those in Sweden and other high-tax countries, favor long-term economic growth. By far the greatest of these deductions has been for savings. Until 1989 Japanese could deposit money in savings accounts of up to $25,000 in value without paying any tax on the interest. Each member of a family was allowed to have such an account, greatly increasing the maximum amount of tax-free savings available to a household. In addition, few checks were placed on taxpayers who held multiple accounts. By some estimates, as much as 80 percent of total Japanese household savings were completely exempt from tax. The combination of very high tax rates and very large deductions for savings virtually forced the Japanese to maintain one of the world's highest personal savings rates. This was useful during the rapid phase of Japanese economic growth, channeling funds away from consumption into investment in new plants and equipment.

Even in Japan, however, the government's attempt to direct the course of economic life through tax rates has had its downside. As in Sweden, high Japanese tax rates encourage business consumption in place of personal or family consumption. As in Sweden, high tax rates encourage Japanese workers to negotiate lifestyle rather than paycheck, with families the losers. Any visitor to the Ginza in the evening finds its restaurants crowded with groups of males in business suits. No families in sight. A quick look at the price list tells why. The men are having a night on the firm, a tax-free benefit for the worker and tax deductible for the firm, but a luxury few workers could afford to provide for their own families. Such camaraderie has come to be considered an important part of the Japanese corporate ethic, but Japanese families are poorly housed and have what we would consider a low standard of living.

Like the Swedes also, the Japanese seem to be changing their minds. The government has cut tax rates in part because it believes the tax biases that served Japan's postwar needs are no longer as helpful. Japanese leaders now believe that in the 1990s and beyond established industries led by large corporate hierarchies will decline in importance compared to entrepreneurial knowledge-based start-ups. MITI, the Japanese ministry of trade and industry, has been encouraging Japanese businessmen to study the US entrepreneurial style, and the government is studying US entrepreneurial tax rates.

The emerging industrial nations of East Asia have been ahead of Japan in this regard. Hong Kong has always had extremely low income taxes. Singapore recently slashed its top rate from 55 percent to 33 percent. South Korea reduced its top rate from a 1979 high of 89 percent to 70 percent in 1989 and has scheduled a further reduction to 48 percent during the 1990s. Indonesia, Malaysia, and Thailand, who seek to be the Koreas and the Hong Kongs of the early twenty-first century, all slashed their top tax rates during the 1980s.

The growth of a true global market encourages the worldwide tax revolt.[5] As the resources that drive economic growth become more mobile, they gravitate toward places where they can earn the highest after-tax rates of return. The key resource behind economic growth isn't a fixed resource like gold or oil, or even capital equipment, but something far more mobile: the human mind. Nations that wish to compete for that resource must keep the price of government low and the quality of government high.

In the past, governments that controlled centers of financial, cultural, or industrial activities were able to exact high "rents," including high taxes, from those who wanted to live there. As the advantages of geography diminish with the advent of cheap communications and transportation, governments will lose some of this leverage and will be forced to cut taxes. On a recent Sunday night flight from Dublin to London, my wife and I were surrounded by young nurses. They were not traveling as part of a group, but as individuals, each returning to a job in the United Kingdom after visiting family back in Ireland. Irish income taxes, which hit 60 percent at the equivalent of an $18,000 income, have driven the economy downhill and the educated work force across the Irish Sea. The Penal Laws could never make Irishmen into Englishmen. It took Maggie Thatcher's tax cut to do that.

In the world of the future, the advantage will be to those nations that allow their populations to live and work as cheaply as possible. No country is exempt. Robert Walter, an economist at the University of Kiel in West Germany, argues, "We will see a brain drain to the US if nothing happens on taxes here."[6] The smart and prosperous regions of the world will be those that attract the talented and the entrepreneurial with low taxes and few fetters. The economic move to free markets and low taxes has just begun.

$\begin{bmatrix} 10 \end{bmatrix}$

One Step Sideways

"The prospects are pretty high that, in the end,
we'll get something called tax reform,
but it won't be real tax reform."
—RICHARD RAHN, CHIEF ECONOMIST,
US CHAMBER OF COMMERCE[1]

B Y 1984 THE COUNTRY WAS LEARNING THE LESSONS OF THE Great Experiment. The economy was recovering, inflation had dropped precipitously and stabilized, unemployment was declining, and, thanks to ERTA, Americans were enjoying bigger paychecks, in real terms, for the first time in more than half a decade. In addition, as the first detailed data on the tax cut came in, the most important supply-side contention was proving true: The rich were paying more in taxes at lower rates.

In four years, voodoo economics had traveled a good part of the distance from taboo to totem. In his first run for the Senate in 1978, Bill Bradley had vigorously and repeatedly denounced the proposed Kemp-Roth tax cut authored in part by his opponent Jeff Bell. Just five years later in 1983, Senator Bill Bradley and Representative Richard Gephardt, both Democrats, introduced a tax reform bill that would have cut the top rate of income tax to 27 percent. Ronald Reagan called, in his 1984 state of the union address, for a further reduction in tax rates and a doubling of the personal exemption.

ERTA's success also changed the economic agenda. The economic recovery made demand-side stimuli, such as demand-oriented tax cuts and spending increases, less important. And as the budgetary cost of the transition to low inflation became apparent, and the federal budget deficit made headlines, tax revenues grew more precious.

The nation had also learned an additional, rather subtle, lesson: Just as high tax rates discourage productive activities, overly generous tax incentives can produce too much of the subsidized activity. For example, ERTA's dramatic increase in the depreciation allowances for business equipment reduced the after-tax cost of some such purchases to less than their pre-tax cost. The tax system actually became a subsidy, lowering the net cost of some purchases to below what they would have been if we didn't have any taxes at all, giving a whole new meaning to the adage "you have to spend it to make it."

Because ACRS favored certain industries over others, politicians and economists put a new demand on the tax agenda: the "level playing field," a tax code that would not play favorites.[2] In a way, the concern for a "level playing field" vindicated the central supply-side argument: taxes matter. Members of Congress who never before thought a moment about taxes and incentives were turned into latter-day supply-siders by lobbyists' charts showing that the industries in their home districts were unfairly taxed. Human nature being what it is, it soon turned out that everyone was unfairly taxed and had the charts to prove it.

The success of the tax cut strategy, the new economic and budget environment, and the fair play pressures produced a groundswell of support for a different kind of tax rate reduction: rate reduction coupled with reform, which while it broadened the tax base by eliminating the "unfair" provisions would also pay for the reduction. In principle, everyone liked the idea. President Reagan and the supply-siders would get even lower tax rates. Critics of the 1981 bill would get to "close loopholes" and make everyone pay their "fair share" of taxes. And everyone could crusade to end everyone else's tax breaks, so that people back home could compete on a level playing field.

The ground rules were laid down by President Reagan in his mandate to the staff of the Treasury Department: Tax reform should promote fairness, simplicity, and growth. (A report to the president by the department in November 1984 was titled just that: *Tax Reform for Fairness, Simplicity, and Economic Growth.*) President Reagan would never concede that the budget deficit should be closed by raising taxes, but he did believe that reform should not make the deficit any larger and required that any tax legislation be revenue neutral. Revenue neutrality was also supposed to limit the tax goodies for favored constituents that had become part of just about every tax bill. With revenue neutrality, one man's goodie would be another man's tax increase.

This great movement for tax reform started as a civics class dream. It had bipartisan support, clear-cut rules of the game, including the bottom-line discipline of revenue neutrality, and was to be written by experts—the permanent treasury staff—not politicians. By the end of the two-year drafting process, a combination of politics as usual, a preoccupation with that moving target called revenue neutrality, and a greater concern for the appearance than the reality of fairness produced a bill that ignored some of the most important lessons of Reagan's first great experiment.

The treasury document that opened the process devoted many pages to lofty principles of efficient tax design and scientific reform. By the time the measure cleared the House of Representatives, most of the text was devoted to the lofty principle of constituent interest. The bill provided, for example, that "the treatment of annuity contracts as investment property under section 147(b)(2) of such Code shall not apply to any obligation issued by the South Dakota Building Authority . . . "[3] and that a parking facility met section 142(a) requirements if "such facility is for a university medical school and the last parcel of land necessary for such facility was purchased on February 4, 1985."[4] Sorry, neither 3 February nor 5 February qualify, though somewhere in the voluminous text there are undoubtedly some juicy benefits for the owners of playing fields leveled on 15 April.

Neither the principle of revenue neutrality nor the spirit of fairness was enough to entirely eliminate the customary goodie-grabbing and constituent-coddling. In fairness to those who shepherded the process, I have to say the Congress did better than usual. But the special favors that were doled out were costly, because the principle of revenue neutrality required full funding for every favor by some corresponding tax increase.

Revenue neutrality in fact is economic nonsense when applied in such detail as it was in 1986. The principle hardened into a rule that any proposal that apparently cost revenue must be coupled with a specific revenue increase. The short-term revenue numbers quickly dominated the process. As we have seen, it is not easy to estimate precisely the revenue effects of any tax change. In this case, the net effect of the procrustean matching of revenue losers and gainers was an enormous error (on the order of $15 billion per year) in the overall estimates of the tax revenue the bill would produce. At first, in 1986, the government collected far more revenue than expected. The data for 1987 suggest, however, that revenue was overestimated, and early evidence for 1988 suggests that people moved some income from 1987 into 1988 to take advantage of the lower 1988 rates. (The data consistently point to underestimation of the responsiveness of taxpayers to tax rates.) Moreover, though the joint committee predicted the tax reform would raise the share of taxes paid by upper-income taxpayers, the early evidence tends to the contrary.

The explanation is simple. Given the enormous complexity of precisely balancing all the revenue-losing and revenue-gaining provisions, the Congress took the easy way out. It ignored the overwhelming evidence for the behavioral effects of tax changes and, for the most part, made its calculations on the basis of direct-effect estimates alone. Frankly, it is hard to see how any committee of 535 governed by the revenue neutrality rule could have agreed on any more sophisticated system.

Consider the process of trading off higher rates for special tax favors to pick up key votes. The direct revenue effect of such special tax exemptions is based on the current level of activity in the favored area. But when a particular economic activity gets a new tax favor, it tends to expand at the cost of other activities. Hence the actual revenue loss will be *bigger* than anticipated by the direct-effect estimates, which ignore such changes.

To pay for the various special exemptions the top rate of the income tax had to be increased from the planned 26 percent to 28 percent, with a special 33 percent bracket for many upper-middle-class taxpayers.[5] These rates are low enough to be on the revenue-increasing side of the revenue-maximizing rate but, as we have learned, an increase in the rate from 26 percent to 28 percent will not produce two twenty-sixths more revenue. Even at relatively low rates, the tax base shrinks as the tax rate is increased. The official direct-effect revenue estimates did not take this into account and predicted higher revenues than the government actually received.

Such errors also derailed the goal of shifting a greater share of the tax burden onto the rich. Both the special exemptions and the increase in the top rate mostly affected upper-income taxpayers. Since in both cases the government overestimated revenues, tax return data for the next few years will probably show the rich paying a smaller share than the reformers intended, and perhaps a smaller share than under the ERTA regime.

Changes in the capital gains tax rate produced the same errors on a larger scale. Despite overwhelming evidence that the 1978 and 1981 reductions in capital gains taxes produced extra revenue the final 1986 bill eliminated the special treatment of capital gains income for the first time in more than a half century. The top capital gains tax rate was increased from 20 percent to the same 33 percent top rate applied to ordinary income. The effective increase was even larger than that because the new law made it much more difficult to write off investment losses against ordinary income. A risk-taking investor whose plans went bad might no longer have even the cold comfort of being able to reduce the taxes on his ordinary salary though he might just have gone through one of the worst years of his life financially.

The prime motive for this increase in capital gains rates had been to increase the share of income tax paid by upper-income taxpayers. Yet the Congressional Budget Office's own research indicated that a 33 percent capital gains rate would take in essentially the same amount of revenue that a 25 percent rate would collect, because of behavioral effects.[6] Congressional direct-effect estimates ignored this evidence and substantially overestimated capital gain tax revenues under the new law. The mistake was most pronounced in the estimates of the new tax burden on the rich.

This undue focus on the estimated direct revenue effects of the tax changes systematically biased the bill against sensible supply-side incentives. Had the reformers included behavioral changes in their estimates, they could have produced a bill with lower overall tax rates. Still, not every provision of the 1986 tax bill was adverse to the supply-side. The very large reduction in the top marginal tax rate was certainly a supply-side move. One might easily argue, as many supply-siders do, that any defects in the bill are insignificant compared to the dramatic accomplishment of cutting the top marginal rate from 50 percent to 28 percent. That dramatic reduction probably increased incentives to work, save, and invest significantly and is likely to produce both unanticipated revenue and additional economic growth for many years to come. On the other hand, the very substantial increase in capital gains taxes almost certainly did significant injury to the economy.

As the 1988 data in table 10.1 show, the 1986 law may produce a loss of much more revenue than anticipated, most of it to upper-income taxpayers. Lower-income taxpayers also ended up paying slightly less, while middle-income taxpayers paid more. Seeking the illusory goal of strict revenue neutrality throughout such a complex reform was the real culprit in these setbacks.

The second great lesson of the 1986 tax reform is that a little fairness can be a dangerous thing. In politics, the assignment "level the playing field" turns out to be not a rule of simplicity but a source of endless contention. It is only natural that members of Congress regard a level playing field to be one tilted in favor of their constituents. In the end Congress leveled the investment capital playing field not by smoothing out the rough spots in the 1981 law but by raising the cost of capital for everyone.

The 1986 reform eliminated the Investment Tax Credit, in part to pay for personal tax reductions. The Congress had anyway regarded the tax credit as a villain for promoting investment in short-lived equipment above longer-lived assets, particularly structures. A detailed study by Roger Gordon of the University of Michigan, James Hines of Princeton, and Lawrence Summers of Harvard questions this thesis and argues that the tax code had offered substantial support for investments in structures.[7] Structures are far easier to resell than most movable equip-

TABLE 10.1 Potential Revenue Impact of Behavioral Responses

Income Class	Revenue Effect (Billions of Dollars) Due to Response of			
	Wages and Salaries	Business Income	Capital Gains	All Responses
under $10,000	−0.1	−0.0	−0.1	−0.2
10,000–20,000	−1.4	−0.0	−0.2	−1.6
20,000–30,000	+0.1	+0.0	−0.5	−0.4
30,000–40,000	+2.0	+0.1	−0.6	+1.5
40,000–50,000	+0.8	+0.1	−0.8	+0.1
50,000–75,000	+2.7	+0.2	−2.7	+0.2
75,000–100,000	+2.6	+0.2	−2.3	+0.5
100,000–200,000	+3.0	+0.5	−5.3	−1.8
over 200,000	+4.4	+0.5	−18.4	−13.5
Total	+13.8	+1.6	−30.8	−15.5

NOTE: A detailed description of the methodology behind this analysis appears in Lawrence Lindsey, "Did ERTA Raise the Share of Taxes Paid by Upper-Income Taxpayers? Will TRA 86 Be a Repeat?" in *Tax Policy and the Economy*, ed. Lawrence H. Summers (Cambridge: MIT Press, 1988).

ment and they can be depreciated repeatedly. It is easier to finance structure by debt, and the interest is tax deductible. Gordon, Hines, and Summers concluded that the supposed unevenness of the investment playing field was exaggerated. Thus the 1986 increase in the corporate tax burden brought no added efficiencies to the investment market, just higher taxes, and thus worsened the single most important bias in the American tax treatment of capital. American tax law (primarily through mortgage interest deduction) greatly favors residential housing over business plant and investment, a favoritism that provides little help to homeowners of modest means, because it raises the price of houses and because in their relatively low tax brackets the mortgage interest deduction does not save them much. But the mortgage interest deduction does shift capital away from job-producing industrial plants and toward upscale housing, and the 1986 increase in corporate taxes will make it that much harder for business to compete for capital.

The level playing field argument originated not with the Congress but with the economists, and the 1980s made an interesting and useful contribution to the understanding of capital taxation. But the level playing field theme, still in its academic infancy, was seized upon by the political process, and turned into a bulldozer when economists meant it to be a hand hoe. This is another reminder that too-finely tuned theories can come to grief in a political debate. Whether the goal is a full-scale tax revolt or a series of small but essential adjustments in the code, it may be best to keep the agenda simple, or as Reagan critics liked to say of his policies, "simplistic."

The question remains open whether the 1986 tax bill will be good or bad for the economy. We will learn the answer as more tax data become available. As to politics of reform, adherents to the Reagan revolution could claim a partial victory: The claim that high tax rates matter to the economy is now widely accepted in Washington, at least in practice. Furthermore, the top tax rate is less than half of what it was when Ronald Reagan took office. But the subtle point that some parts of the tax base are more sensitive than others was lost, with higher capital gains taxes as one unfortunate result.

Because the Congress and even some in the administration ignored the dynamic effects of tax cuts on tax revenues, the government will end up with less revenue, a bigger deficit, and a distribution of the tax payments borne less by the rich, than it otherwise would have. Unfortunately, the lesson may still not have been learned. If those who resist the supply-side message run true to form, they will call for yet higher tax rates, to try to soak the rich as much as they originally had intended. If they get their way, the behavioral effects will be even more adverse, the rich will pay even less, and the deficit will grow.

One thing is certain: the need for further reform to address the problems the 1986 bill created. We will consider the direction those reforms should take after a look at first principles: the appropriate goals of any tax system.

[11]

Of Revenue
and Righteousness

"The art of taxation consists in so plucking the goose
as to obtain the largest possible amount of feathers
with the smallest possible amount of hissing."
—JEAN BAPTISTE COLBERT (1619–1683)

DESPITE THE PROGRESS OF THE 1980S THE US TAX CODE
still needs reform. The Reagan tax cuts, including the Tax Reform Act of 1986, revitalized the economy but left room for improvements in our competitive posture. The tax cuts raised the tax
contributions of the rich while lowering their rates, yet retained a number of provisions that favor upper-income taxpayers over lower. The tax
cuts increased business investment, a benefit partly lost in 1986, but did
less to encourage savings. The tax cuts made the nation wealthier but
missed opportunities to encourage the socially responsible use of
wealth.

Most important, the tax cuts, having helped rescue the US (and
world) economy from what seemed like protracted decline, provide
an opportunity to ameliorate what may be the nation's most pressing

economic and social problem: the growing economic burdens on middle- and working-class families with children. Their situation steadily worsened during the seventies but could not be addressed before the Revolution of '81. From 1973 to 1981 the real after-tax income of a typical American household declined by 9 percent. And though real wages of American workers also declined by 8 percent over the same period, the tax share of those wages rose dramatically. Many costs of establishing membership in the middle class, such as buying a house or sending the children to college, rose painfully throughout the seventies and eighties. After ERTA began to take hold in 1982, real after-tax household income rebounded, in large measure because of the success of the Reagan policies. But the fact remains that during the 1970s and early 1980s the American dream became a mirage for too many Americans.

The situation has improved. The country has exchanged economic peril for economic prosperity. Precisely because of the recent improvements, we are now in a position to do a better job of restoring the hopes of American families and extending the promise of prosperity to far more Americans. We can do much of this through tax reform. The Reagan tax cuts and the Reagan recovery got us out from behind the economic eight ball. Every era has its crises, but the late 1970s sometimes seemed like nothing but crises. It was hard to think about fine-tuning success with the news always of failure. It was hard to think about lowering the tax burden on lower-and middle-income families when the nation seemed desperately strapped for cash and the role of tax rates in causing stagflation was the subject of fierce and urgent debate.

Those days of constant crisis are gone, largely because the large tax rate cuts for upper-income and upper-middle-income taxpayers restored the incentives that drive the American economy. As shown in chapter 4, the rate cuts did not significantly reduce short-term revenues. The rich pay more, and the upper-middle class only slightly less than under the old rates. For these fortunate taxpayers, the rate cuts reduced the excess burden—the additional cost, over and above the tax payments themselves, of a high tax rate. The excess burden as explained in chapter 2 is the cost to the individual and the economy of taxpayers being forced into second or third best economic choices by excessive tax rates. By dramatically reducing the excess burden on upper-middle-class and rich taxpayers, the tax cuts increased incentives for them to work, save, and invest, benefiting the economy in both the short and long term. The reforms of the 1980s, by reducing inefficient burdens on the well-to-do, have given us the breathing space to focus on the problems of the less well-off.

In addition to providing an economic base for family tax relief, the Reagan tax cuts offer a base of economic knowledge for directing further reform. We have gained a more precise working knowledge of the relationship between tax rates and tax revenues. We have learned that tax rates above 40 or 50 percent produce no additional revenue, and we also have learned a lot about the trade-offs between rates, revenues, and excess burden at lower brackets. We can predict more confidently the revenue effects of tax increases and reductions at almost any level and how such changes might interact with various tax shelters, subsidies, penalties, and other biases of the code. The several adjustments during the 1980s to taxes on business investment have given us a better understanding of similar issues for those taxes.

This accumulated knowledge can help us design a tax code that will help the United States finance its fiscal responsibilities without sacrificing its families, and keep our social fabric as strong as our economy. The mission for tax reformers of the nineties is to apply the lessons and benefits of supply-side economics to the middle and working classes. The job ahead of us is not so much to reduce the total tax bill for average Americans, though we can and should reduce it for families with children; the important job is to eliminate the extra burdens of taxation that do little to raise revenue but discourage thrift and industry and throw up barriers to the pursuit of middle-class prosperity.

The income tax reached its political and economic limits in the 1970s as the nation began to feel the effects of levying rich people's tax rates on citizens of moderate means. The 1981 and 1986 reforms substantially rolled back those rates. Yet middle- and working-class taxpayers still bear burdens far greater than they have through most of the nation's history. If we do nothing in the way of positive reform, we may soon find ourselves again passing the limits of prudence and leaving the path of prosperity. With positive reform we can make the nation stronger and improve the lives of most Americans.

As we have broken down barriers to work, savings, and investment for the well-to-do, to the benefit of all, we must eliminate tax biases that raise the costs of housing and home ownership for average Americans, or discourage savings for college education, a home, or retirement. We must eliminate distortions that curtail investment in plant and equipment, or research, education, and training, forcing workers to work harder rather than smarter. We must stop pushing workers to take their pay in inefficient and often overpriced benefits rather than cash they can control. We must end provisions that punish families in which both parents must work outside the home to make ends meet, or that punish all families that do a responsible job of nurturing our most important resource, the next generation.

If we liberate working- and middle-class Americans from these and other extra and unnecessary burdens of taxation, the United States will be a happier, more industrious, and even better trained and educated nation in the next century, ready to take on all comers in the global competition. Before embarking on these reforms, however, we need a clear understanding of the very purpose of income taxation, and of what we can and cannot accomplish through the tax code.

If economic growth and international competitiveness, or the well-being of America's families, were the only objectives of government tax policy, we would probably dispense with the income tax entirely. The income tax invariably discourages maximum economic effort. And it can never be made painless, even for the middle and working classes, which no modern state could afford to exempt from taxation.

We levy taxes because the government must have revenue. Only when we keep that first priority clearly in mind can we design a tax code that also encourages industry and the happiness of the people. It turns out that keeping our eye on the revenue ball positively helps us design an income tax that encourages growth and does not overburden families.

The only reason the income tax is the dominant tax today is that it is a fabulously effective means of collecting revenue for the government. Though the personal income tax contributes but 45 percent of total federal tax revenues, the total for all income taxes, including social insurance taxes and the corporate income tax, is nearly 90 percent. The federal government now takes nearly 20 percent of GNP in total revenue, a figure undreamt of before the days of the income tax when most federal revenue was raised from tariffs and excise taxes. As we explained in chapter 2, these taxes were ineffective revenue producers because substitutes were often easy to come by—and so the tax base quickly narrowed as tax rates rose and people bought less of the taxed commodities, be they imported goods or alcoholic beverages. In other words, at high rates excise taxes and tariffs produce large excess burdens relative to the revenue they produce.

The excess burden of a tax is the result of two factors: the tax rate and the elasticity of the demand for the item or activity taxed.[1] Elasticity, though often tricky to measure in practice, is simple in theory. Recall one of our examples from chapter 2. A tax on cars would be much more effective than a tax on Fords because the demand for Fords is much more elastic than the demand for cars. Facing a tax on Fords, people quickly reduce their demand for Fords and buy Chevys. Faced with a tax on cars, people cannot so quickly reduce their demand and buy oxcarts instead. Of course, at some very high tax rate people will start finding substitutes for even so necessary an item as cars, greatly burdening both themselves and the economy in the process.

Thus the second factor in the excess burden story is the tax rate itself. Even if the demand for the item being taxed is very elastic, there will be little excess burden if the rate is low enough. And even if demand for the item is very inelastic, the excess burden can be heavy at very high rates. Economists have long known that at any given elasticity, the excess burden of a tax is proportional to the square of the tax rate. That means that a 20 percent tax will impose four times the excess burden of a 10 percent tax, not just twice the excess burden. A 50 percent tax will impose twenty-five times the excess burden of a 10 percent tax, not just five times as much. Raising tax rates increases excess burdens very quickly.

Note that this formula does not tell us the excess burden of a tax in any absolute sense. Though we know that a 50 percent tax on some item would produce twenty-five times the excess burden of a 10 percent tax, we cannot say exactly what that would be without knowing the excess burden of the 10 percent tax. To estimate the excess burden we would need a good estimate of elasticity of the demand for the item being taxed.

FIGURE 11.1 Excess Burden, 20 Percent Tax

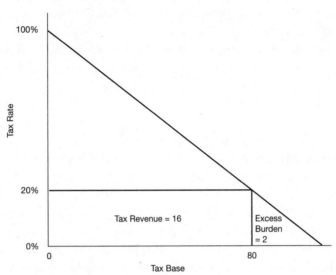

Still, the formula is useful in giving a sense of how dangerous high rates can be. Figures 11.1 and 11.2 show the progress of excess burden at high tax rates. The figures assume that for every percentage point increase in income tax rates the tax base—the amount of reported taxable income—declines by $1.00. (For the purposes of our example the base started at the modest total of $100.) That is our measure of elasticity and is shown in both figures by the "demand curve," line A, a straight 45-degree line. The demand curve governs the relationship between the tax rates and the tax base. On both figures the horizontal axis stands for the tax base and the vertical axis stands for tax rates. The rectangular box, which is a product of the tax rate and the tax base, stands for revenues. The triangle to the right of the box is the excess burden, that additional cost to society and taxpayers of rearrangements made to avoid taxes.

Note the differences between the two figures. For the first figure, the tax rate is 20 percent and the base is $80, or 80 percent of maximum. The excess burden triangle is rather small. In the second figure, the tax rate is 50 percent, 2.5 times higher than the 20 percent rate in the first

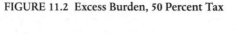

FIGURE 11.2 Excess Burden, 50 Percent Tax

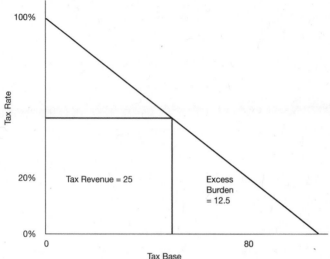

figure. But the excess burden triangle is 6.25 times larger. And because the base has been cut in half, the revenue box is not 2.5 times but only 56 percent larger.

These results vary greatly if the shape of the demand curve, line A, changes. In reality, line A need not slope at 45 degrees, nor need it be a straight line. The income tax is such a successful tax not only because its base is large—all reported taxable income—but also because in practice its demand curve is fairly forgiving. The demand for income is much less elastic than the demand for Fords, or imported steel. The only way to avoid paying the income tax is to not earn income. The evidence from the Kennedy and Reagan tax cuts suggests that people do exactly that when tax rates get too high. But at moderate rates of tax, which can still produce enormous amounts of revenue, this distorting effect of income taxation is manageable. Whereas a 20 percent tariff might all but eliminate many imported products, a 20 percent income tax rate, in recent practice, has had a much less drastic effect on the income tax base.

FIGURE 11.3 The Laffer Curve

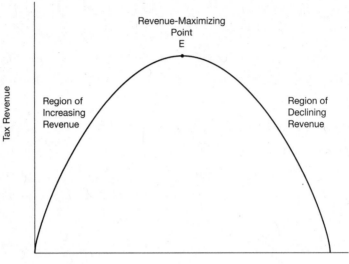

There is a direct relationship between a tax's excess burden and its ability to produce revenue. As rates rise, the excess burden mounts up more quickly, the tax base shrinks, and less additional revenue will be raised from a rate increase. For every tax there is a limit at which the most possible revenue is being produced and any additional increase in rates will lose revenue. But this revenue-maximizing tax rate is much higher for taxes with low excess burdens (such as the income tax) than taxes with high burdens (such as tariffs).

This relationship between low excess burdens and high revenue-maximizing rates led to a serious error among some early supply-siders. They argued that the revenue-maximizing rate, the famous point E on the Laffer curve (see figure 11.3), was the point at which the government *should* levy taxes. Jude Wanniski wrote in *The Public Interest* of point E:

It is the point at which the electorate desires to be taxed. At [lower rates] the electorate desires more goods and services and is willing— without reducing its productivity—to pay higher rates consistent with revenues [at the maximum point]. [At lower rates], the electorate de-sires more private goods and services in the money economy. . . . It is the task of the statesman to determine the location of [the revenue maximizing point] and follow its variations as closely as possible.[2]

Actually the revenue-maximizing point is far from being optimal. It is better described as the point at which the taxpayer is being soaked for as much money as possible. Under almost all conceivable circumstances (a war in which the survival of the nation is at stake being one excep-tion), the actual tax rate should be set well below the revenue-maximiz-ing level. To see this, consider further the scenario that produced figures 11.1 and 11.2. Imagine a tax base that involves $100 worth of economic activity. For every 1 percent at which the base is taxed, the tax base shrinks by $1. Table 11.1 shows the resulting tax revenue and excess bur-den at different tax rates. Note that the total tax revenue collected is sim-ply the product of the tax rate and the tax base. At first this figure rises very steeply, but the rate at which revenue increases slows as the tax rate goes up. At the 50 percent tax rate, revenue reaches its maximum point. At higher rates, revenue declines. The 50 percent tax rate is the revenue-maximizing rate, point E. On this tax base the government can collect no more than $25. Clearly, in this example, the government would never want to raise the tax rate above 50 percent, for it would lose revenue.[3] And none of this is to say that the government *should* set the rate at 50 percent so as to collect that $25.

Remember, tax revenue is no gain to society; it is simply a transfer from one part of society, the taxpayer, to another part of society, the gov-ernment. The cost of performing this transfer is the excess burden of the tax. At the revenue-maximizing rate in our example, taxpayers not only paid the government $25 but also changed their behavior to avoid addi-tional payments. The cost to them of this change in behavior—the excess burden of the tax—amounted to $12.50. So the total cost of the tax to the taxpayers was $37.50, the $25 in revenue plus the $12.50 excess burden. Note that the taxpayers would have been even worse off if they had not changed their behavior: If they had not reduced their taxable activities they would have been out $50 in taxes. It makes sense to the taxpayer to incur a $12.50 change in behavior in order to avoid an extra $25 in taxes.[4]

TABLE 11.1 Rate, Revenue, and Excess Burden of Hypothetical Tax

Tax Rate	Tax Base	Total Revenue	Total Excess Burden	Additional Revenue	Additional Excess Burden
0%	$100	$0	$ 0		
10	90	9	0.5	$9	$0.5
20	80	16	2.0	7	1.5
30	70	21	4.5	5	2.5
40	60	24	8.0	3	3.5
50	50	25	12.5	1	4.5
60	40	24	18.0	−1	5.5
70	30	21	24.5	−3	6.5

At a 50 percent tax rate the government gains $25 in revenue at a total cost to the taxpayer of $37.50. On average, the government imposes a cost on society of $1.50 for every $1.00 it collects in revenue. But this average cost is not a useful guide to policy. Rather the government should consider the marginal costs versus the marginal benefits of a change in rates. As table 11.1 shows, the additional, or marginal, revenue collected by increasing the rate from 40 percent to 50 percent was $1.00. But the additional, or marginal, excess burden imposed by that increase was $4.50. In order to collect the last dollar in revenue, the government imposed a total cost of $5.50 on its taxpayers. That was a very expensive dollar. By contrast, a change in the tax rate from 30 percent to 40 percent produces $3.00 extra in revenue with an added excess burden of only $3.50. Thus each dollar in revenue cost taxpayers a total of $2.17 ($1.00 in tax plus $1.17 in excess burden). As rates fall off from the revenue-maximizing level, the cost of raising revenue drops dramatically. The excess burden on the first $9.00 of revenue is only 50 cents, for a total cost to the taxpayer of less than $1.06 for every dollar collected.

Far from being optimal, then, the revenue-maximizing point indicates the point at which increased revenue is most expensive to society. At each step in the rate structure the government should ask itself whether it needs a dollar in revenue enough to impose a cost on the private economy equal to the revenue collected plus the excess burden. By this standard, a 20 percent rate is fairly easily justified and a 30 percent rate is probably acceptable. But a 40 percent rate, which involves an excess burden greater than the revenue collected, is almost certainly imprudent. A 50 percent rate, the revenue-maximizing level, would be acceptable only if the government were so desperate for revenue that its needs completely overwhelmed considerations of the health of the economy or the happiness of citizens.

Nor is there ordinarily any need to impose tax rates highly damaging to the economy or hurtful to individuals. The income tax's broad and relatively inelastic base allows it to collect enormous revenues at relatively harmless rates. The potential base of the personal income tax is the roughly 80 percent of national output that is received by individuals. Today the personal income tax takes in about 11 percent of all personal income in tax revenue. Because the base is so large, the government could raise this enormous sum, nearly $500 billion, at quite low rates. At present the income tax exempts over half of personal income from taxation, and still obtains its revenue with a maximum tax rate of only 33 percent. Most taxpayers pay only a 15 percent tax rate. From experience with the Kennedy and Reagan tax cuts we also know that the income tax becomes inefficient as rates rise, producing less additional revenue and greater burdens on the economy with every step up the scale.

These considerations suggest that if revenue and economic efficiency (that is, economic growth) were the only considerations in question, the best income tax would be a flat tax on a very broad tax base. For instance, if all deductions, allowances, credits, and exemptions whatsoever were eliminated, we could probably reap the same 11 percent of personal income now produced by the personal income tax with an excess burden of only 1 or 2 percent since such a low rate would do very little to erode the base.

Such a scheme, though on the right track, has drawbacks. Though such a flat rate would reduce rates for most taxpayers, it would raise taxes for some. A considerable number of Americans now pay less than 11 percent of their overall income in taxes. (Though most such people face a 15 percent marginal tax rate, much of their income is exempt from tax, making their average tax rate much lower.) Most of these are low- or moderate-income taxpayers with families. They could not afford the tax increase implied by our truly flat tax, in which marginal and average tax rates are always the same. In other words, efficiency bumps up squarely against fairness. Nearly everyone agrees that in some sense taxes ought to be based on the ability to pay and that the poor should not be more burdened than the rich. Adding fairness to our list of objectives for taxation, we now have a trinity: raise revenue, minimize the damage to the economy, be fair to the less fortunate. There is an old saying that it is not difficult to make a meal that is either cheap and easy, or cheap and good, or easy and good, but impossible to combine all three. The conflicts between raising revenue, encouraging the economy, and being fair are much less pronounced, but at the margin there are real conflicts that must be confronted and resolved.

To resolve those conflicts we first need a better grip on what we mean by fairness. We can certainly agree on some things that seem unfair. The income tax presently generates about $1,500 per person in the United States. But we know that fairness precludes sending everyone a bill for $1,500. No one would seriously propose that we ask a four-person family living on $20,000 to pay 30 percent of its income in taxes while a family earning $100,000 pay but 6 percent of its earnings. At a minimum, almost everyone would agree that the working-class family should be asked to pay no greater percentage of its income than the rich family. At a minimum, fairness requires proportionality. Most people would probably go even further and say that the low-income family in this example should pay less than their proportional share, that we should have a progressive tax in which the rich will pay somewhat more not only absolutely but as a percentage of income.

Here things get difficult. The economics profession has spent a good deal of effort trying to express this basic notion of fairness, or what in economic jargon is termed "equity," in a more scientific fashion. But attempts to formalize fairness quickly break down. Once progressivity is accepted, the obvious question is: How progressive is fair? No formally acceptable answer has ever been offered.[5]

Generally speaking, when economists, political scientists, or politicians advocate fair taxation they mean one of two things. First, they mean that revenue should be raised in a fair way, and specifically that taxes should be based on ability to pay. Let's call this type of fairness "being fair." They may also mean that taxes should reduce inequalities of wealth, redistributing the goods of society from the rich to the poor. Let us call this goal "creating fairness." Both turn out to be elusive when pursued in a systematic way.

Let's start with "being fair." Though it might seem the simpler of the two goals, through its long history as a goal of political scientists and economists it has failed of attainment.

John Stuart Mill, the nineteenth-century economist and political thinker, argued that taxes should be based on a prescription of equal sacrifice.[6] Taxpayers' ability to pay a tax should be judged by how much of their well-being the tax would cost them. In the example, the family making only $20,000 per year would end up sacrificing more of its well-being than the family making $100,000 per year on almost any practically conceivable tax schedule, however progressive. That is because the last dollar earned by the family making $100,000 is worth less to that family than the last dollar earned by the family earning $20,000. This is the principle of the declining marginal utility of income: Additional dollars of income make people happier, but at a decreasing rate. The ten-thousandth dollar is valued more than the twenty-thousandth dollar, which in turn is valued more than the thirty-thousandth dollar. Thus under Mill's prescription of equal sacrifice even if we had taxed the rich family $70,000 and the working-class family nothing, if it happened that the government needed one more dollar in revenue it still would be right to take it from the richer family. With $30,000 remaining they would be less pained by losing a dollar than the $20,000 family. Since the value of each dollar declines with income, the person most able to contribute is always the richest person in society. The richest person will continue to be the right person to tax until he or she ceases to be the richest person. At that point, someone else is richest and places the lowest value on each additional dollar taxed away.[7]

The logic seems flawless. On the other hand, if we tried to apply such a system in the United States today it would be necessary to confiscate all taxable income above $40,000 in order to raise as much money as the income tax now raises. Money, jobs, and talent would flee overseas, the economy would certainly collapse, and the $20,000 family, probably made up of hourly wage workers, certainly would be made worse off by the ensuing depression.

Such obvious difficulties led to an alternative formulation of Mill's basic insight: the principle of equal proportional sacrifice. Under this principle, the total "utility" value of each level of income would be determined, and each taxpayer would be asked to sacrifice the same percentage of his or her utility. In most cases, this will produce a progressive tax schedule. The value of dollars to very high income taxpayers is so low that they must sacrifice a lot of them to make up for the sacrifice of just a few dollars of the lower-income taxpayers. Still, problems emerge.

Consider, for example, two identical twins endowed with the same traits, who received identical upbringing and equal love and attention from their parents. One chooses the life of a college professor, which—if common opinion is true—involves teaching six to eight hours per week with a three-month break in the summer and long vacations at Christmas, Easter, and between semesters. The professor earns the usual rather modest salary that college professors are paid for this grueling regime. The other twin chooses to start his own business, works fourteen hours per day, six or seven days per week, and is amazingly successful, making lots of money.

Under a progressive tax scheme, not only must the businessman twin pay absolutely more taxes than his brother, he must also pay proportionately more. How does this square with the principle of equal proportional sacrifice? We might begin by assuming that since we are dealing with twins, their view of the utility of income is the same. Yet they chose professions with different incomes. Why? The obvious answer is that the college professor is paid not only in money but also in free time. In effect, the extra money the businessman earns compensates him for the extra hours he works.

By our reasoning, the twins are identically happy. Yet under a progressive income tax the businessman would be forced to pay a bigger percentage of his compensation in taxes than the professor. If we truly had a tax system based on the principle of equal sacrifice, these two equally happy twins should pay the same amount of tax. The problem is that money has become synonymous with happiness. The college professor should pay tax on the value of his time off, or the businessman should get a discount for extra hours worked, but the twins should pay the same number of dollars in taxes. Not only should the tax system not be progressive, it should be regressive, taking a bigger share of the money income of the college professor than of the businessman. Of course the twins may not have equal views of the opportunities they face. Perhaps some slight difference in their upbringing caused one to value time off and the other to value earning money. In this case the professor who does not value money should pay more than the businessman twin who values money very highly. By this reasoning, the professor should pay not only a higher percentage of his income in taxes, but a greater absolute amount as well!

Thus any strict notion of being fair fails in practice, because it requires destructive rates on the rich and even the upper-middle class, and in logic, because utility and happiness are so subjective. But what about creating fairness by redistributing wealth? Here we find no problem in logic. Once we have decided that economic equality, or some other standard, is what we mean by fairness, we need not worry that the twins see things differently. That is their problem. But any such scheme founders on the same practical difficulties as attempts to be fair. To create fairness and also fund the government at adequate levels we would have to establish even more draconian standards than confiscating all income above $40,000. The Trumps and the Rockefellers would still be vastly wealthy even if we allowed them additional income of only $40,000 per year, so we would have to start taxing wealth as well as income. The excess burden effect would be even more pronounced. Capital and jobs would flee the country even more quickly. The government would become desperate for money and would soon either give up the taxes on the rich or raise taxes on the middle class or surrender the scheme altogether. By that time wealth would have been considerably rearranged, but equality would be nowhere in sight. The country and the people would be much poorer and quite miserable.

By now, some readers who want to create fairness should be shouting "that isn't what we meant at all." No, of course not. We like to imagine that we can come up with a strict notion of fairness and then apply it moderately. Try it. Pick any tax rate for the rich low enough not to destroy the economy. (Or if you pick a high number like 91 percent, apply it high enough up the income scale, and with enough deductions and loopholes so that the damage is limited.) Now pick any tax rate for the middle class high enough to support the government. (We'll even eliminate the working poor from the tax rolls altogether, to make it easier for you.) No matter what reasonable numbers you chose, it is still going to be very much easier and less painful for the rich to pay their high taxes than for ordinary folks to pay their moderate taxes. The tax system is not going to "be fair." The same calculations apply if you try to "create fairness" without destroying the economy or bankrupting the government. As the lady said, "I've been rich and I've been poor, and rich is better."

These conundrums of fairness are almost enough to make one give up on progressivity altogether. As James McCullough wrote in the last century, the introduction of progressivity seems to leave the tax system "at sea without rudder or compass."[8] Proportional taxes at least unite the interests of the nation behind a specific standard, while progressive taxation, McCullough argued, invites political mischief.

Such has proved the case. In the seventy-five years of progressive income taxation in the United States, the top marginal tax rate has been 50 percent or greater for sixty-one years. The top rate has exceeded 60 percent for fifty-four years. It has been 70 percent or greater for forty-nine years, 80 percent or greater for thirty-one years, and 90 percent or more twenty-three years. And in nearly every case a rise in the top rates has been used to cover or excuse a rise in the tax rates and tax payments of poorer taxpayers. Perhaps it really would be better to draw a single line in the dirt and unite all citizens on one side of it.

What then becomes of fairness? We need not abandon it. But we do need to discover what we really mean by it. Our common concern that the working or middle class not be forced to pay what they cannot afford was not merely a rough-and-ready version of the more formal ideas of fairness suggested earlier. It was a different and better idea: Low- and moderate-income taxpayers must be allowed to obtain the necessities of life, by modern American standards, before we treat any significant portion of their income as discretionary and tax it away.

Lower-income taxpayers are less able to avoid income taxes than those with more income. In the first place, most of their income is from wages and is hard to hide. More important, their demand for income is less elastic than that of the well-to-do. They need every additional dollar they can get even if those dollars come at a high cost in taxes. More comfortable taxpayers pay taxes out of what is in some sense discretionary income: They can lower their tax bill by giving up some income (and taking more leisure) or by rearranging their finances (in a suboptimal way) to avoid taxation. These rearrangements will carry a price and burden the economy. Nevertheless, for people who have the option of making such rearrangements, taxes are, if in an attenuated sense, voluntary. For low-and moderate-income taxpayers, who lack such choice, taxes are hardly ever voluntary. Where there is no escape from the law, the law can quickly become oppressive. As we have seen, it often has. The government early discovered that moderate- and lower-income taxpayers produce lots of revenue. In large part this is because there are so many of them. But in part low- and moderate-income taxpayers have been good revenue producers because they have no escape.

Deciding what level of income enables people to obtain the necessities of American life is a judgment call. But democracy can make this judgment pretty well if it follows several important rules of designing a tax system. If we start with the number one rule that the purpose of a tax system is to raise revenue, and adhere also to the corollary that revenue should be raised in a way that produces the least possible additional burden on the economy, we can be sure the top rates will not be too high. Sticking rigorously to the first two principles and avoiding political posturing over defining the third, fairness, will make that last easier to achieve. Top rates have historically set the parameters for lower rates, so keeping top rates moderate should ensure that lower rates do not become oppressive.

The probable result of keeping our eye on the revenue ball would be a relatively flat, pro-growth tax rate that is nevertheless gentle to moderate- and lower-income taxpayers, especially those with families. In the final chapter I outline just such a tax code. It has only one rate. But it is progressive in the sense that it provides generous exemptions to remove many working-class families with children from the federal income tax rolls and greatly reduces the tax burden on middle-class families in the same situation.

Recall that a perfectly flat tax of 11 percent with no exemptions, deductions, etc. would produce enough revenue to fund today's federal government. A more "progressive" flat tax system would tax all income at a single rate of 19 percent. But it raises the current individual exemption to $6,000, or $12,000 for a married couple; raises the exemption for children to $3,000 each; and adds an extra $2,000 for each child under four years of age. A family of four with two young children would pay no taxes on its first $22,000 of income. These and several other adjustments push the rate up to 19 percent from the 11 percent of a pure flat tax, but these adjustments would do much to accomplish that goal we have been calling fairness.

Achieving fairness through exemptions rather than staggered rates has great advantages. It helps get us off the slippery slope of a steep tax rate structure. Politically and psychologically, if not logically, it should be easier to hold down tax rates if we establish the principle that all Americans pay the same rate. When the politicians play divide-and-conquer, we all stand to lose. Most important, a flat rate would never be allowed to rise to levels where it causes significant excess burdens to the economy.

There is one final advantage to a flat rate. Taxes are used not only to raise revenue but to control behavior. Our system has frequently imposed very high tax rates on top earners, but it has also allowed them to avoid taxes through meritorious expenditures such as contributing money to charitable organizations, purchasing city or state bonds, or spending money on a home rather than a vacation. These loopholes are sometimes useful and can be superior to direct government spending as a way to achieve certain goals. Tax subsidies can sometimes target individuals more precisely than government programs, and taxes are administratively less costly than new government programs because the IRS bureaucracy is already in place. Tax programs can avoid both duplication of services and the problem of people "falling through the cracks." In practice, however, tax loopholes are rarely as well designed or as cost effective as their proponents believe. It is good policy to be cautious in their use. A flat, low-rate tax blunts the government's ability to direct our behavior through the tax code, making politicians a little less quick on the draw with new behavior modification strategies. Moreover, a flat tax ensures that whenever the government does enact a new loophole, every taxpayer will be eligible for the same benefit. Since every taxpayer will be taxed at the same marginal rate, deductions for tax-favored activities will affect each the same. This was not the case under the sharply progressive codes of the past, which caused some conspicuous injustices.

Before the Reagan tax cuts, for example, rich homeowners in the 70 percent brackets received huge tax rewards from the home mortgage interest deduction and the deduction for state and local taxes. Though most taxpayers did not benefit at all from the interest deduction, every dollar the rich paid out in mortgage interest on lavish homes cost them only 30 cents after taxes. And while a dollar in local or state taxes cost most taxpayers a dollar in after-tax income, the after-tax cost to the rich was but 30 cents. In effect, the residents of poor towns with modest public services paid for the lavish public services the rich voted themselves in wealthier areas. The flat tax ends such anomalies. With a flat tax there would be no such thing as a loophole for the rich. Loopholes, for better or for ill, would be for everyone. All would have the same choices to spend their money on themselves or on tax-favored government-approved objects like charity and housing.

Some may argue that the old combination of high rates for the rich plus a generous schedule of loopholes for socially beneficial activities did channel the wealth of the rich away from conspicuous consumption and into more useful directions. But it was an enormously inefficient system, for it discouraged not only conspicuous consumption but work, savings, and investment as well. If we wish to limit conspicuous consumption we can do so directly through sumptuary taxes on luxury cars, boats, household servants, second homes, and the like instead of discouraging people from earning income in the first place.

The proper purpose of the income tax is to raise revenue in the way most painless to the people, the economy, and the nation. The most effective way of raising revenue would be by a flat-rate tax on as broad a tax base as possible. The rigorous pursuit of fairness through steeply progressive tax rates is too costly for all concerned; in designing a tax system to meet the needs of the next century we cannot afford wasteful digressions. But we can afford generous treatment of hard-pressed families and, the daily headlines to the contrary, another tax cut. But that is our next story.

$\begin{bmatrix} 12 \end{bmatrix}$

The Great Surplus of '99

"The Reagan Administration's economic policies are
neither careful nor protective of the nation's future. . . .
They have touched off a national borrowing and buying binge that will have to be paid for in the morning."
—EDITORS, *THE NEW REPUBLIC*[1]

Now for a short civics test. Answer "true" or
"false." To balance the budget in the 1990s the Congress must
either increase taxes or cut spending from current levels.

The right answer is "false." If you responded "true," however, I
won't take off too many points. There is probably no more widespread
myth about the US budget system than the supposed need to raise taxes
or cut spending.

Let's consider how the myth got started. We do have a budget
deficit of some $160 billion.[2] For the Congress to balance the budget in
a single year, it would have to enact some $160 billion in combined tax
increases or spending cuts. Since most of our budget is "uncontrol-
lable," in that it is composed of defense, Social Security, Medicare, and
interest on the debt, cutting $160 billion is impossible. So the pundits
say we need a major tax increase as well.

The fallacy in this analysis is that no responsible economist would suggest that the United States try to reduce its budget deficit by $160 billion in a single year. The result would almost inevitably be a very sharp recession, or even a depression, as the government desperately sucked spending power out of the economy. Most sensible people favor narrowing the gap by $30 billion to $40 billion per year, ridding ourselves of the deficit over four or five years. That requires neither raising taxes nor reducing spending below current real levels, for the current tax code will *automatically* provide $75 billion to $80 billion more in income tax revenue each year for as long as economic growth continues at its current rate. With an automatic $300 billion revenue increase already scheduled for the next four years, we could increase spending by $140 billion (roughly enough to keep up with inflation) and still bring the deficit down to zero in just four years.

This chapter began with a trick question. The Congress does not need to raise taxes because taxes are going up anyway. There is no voodoo involved. Both the real growth in the economy and continued inflation effectively increase average tax rates and tax revenues over time. In the 1960s Keynesians called this effect a "fiscal drag," or a "fiscal dividend,"[3] depending on whether they were advocating more stimulus or arguing that such stimulus was largely self-financing. Table 12.1 summarizes this relationship for each of the major types of taxes the government collects, in each case showing the effect on tax revenue of a 1 percent increase in the economy's real output as well as a 1 percent inflation.

Start with the personal income tax. We are all aware of the phenomenon known as bracket creep by which inflation pushes us into higher tax brackets without our real income increasing. As discussed in chapter 4, ERTA's indexing provisions curbed this highly destructive practice. With indexing, if both your income and prices rise 1 percent, your tax payments—not your tax rate—will also rise 1 percent, and taxes will take the same percentage of your income as before. As a general rule, therefore, 1 percent inflation will cause personal income tax revenue to rise only 1 percent. But because not all parts of the income tax are fully indexed, tax revenues do rise slightly faster than inflation, or a bit more than 1 percent for every 1 percent rise in prices.

TABLE 12.1 Tax Revenue and the Economy

Type of Tax	FY89 Revenue* Collections (in billions)	Percent Change in Revenue with	
		1% Real Growth	1% Inflation
Personal Income	$425	1.3–1.4%	1.0–1.1%
Corporate Income	107	1.4	1.4
Social Insurance	364	1.0	1.0
Other	80	0.4	0.0

*Estimates from the *Budget of the United States Government FY1990* for fiscal year 1989.

Of more importance is what happens when you get a real raise, not just an inflationary increase. Since indexing does not apply to changes in real income, you may be pushed into a higher tax bracket when your income rises. Even if your tax bracket does not change, your tax payments will go up because you will be paying on a bigger income. Moreover, your *average* tax rate will rise because a smaller percentage of your income will be protected by basic exemptions and deductions.

Consider the case of a four-person family earning $30,000 in 1989. In 1989 the family is allowed a deduction of $2,000 for each person plus a standard deduction of $5,000, for a total of $13,000. The family's taxable income is then $17,000. The tax rate on *taxable* income up to $31,000 is 15 percent, so this family pays a tax of $2,550, which is 8.5 percent of its *total* income, or an average tax rate of 8.5 percent. Now assume the family's real income increases by 10 percent to $33,000. Its deductions are unchanged, so its taxable income rises to $20,000. The tax on $20,000, at the standard 15 percent rate, is $3,000. The family's tax payments rise 17.6 percent ($450 on top of $2,550) though the family's income went up only 10 percent. On average, every 1 percent rise in the family's income caused a 1.76 percent rise in its tax payments. The family's average tax rate rose from 8.5 percent to slightly more than 9 percent. This increase occurred even though the family remained in the same 15 percent tax bracket. A greater fraction of the family's income was taxed at the 15 percent rate while a smaller percentage was in the "zero" rate. Note that unlike bracket creep, in which inflation increases the rate applied to the same real income, this family is paying a higher average rate because it really is making more money. This is fundamental to any progressive tax code. The family is still better off.

On average, if everyone in the United States got a 10 percent raise, tax revenues would rise about 15 percent. Ordinarily this would imply that every 1 percent of real growth would produce about 1.5 percent extra revenue. But not all real economic growth can be attributed to salary increases for those currently working; about one-third is due to new workers joining the labor force. New workers add to tax revenues, but they do not produce the same average increase per point of economic growth that occurs when existing workers get higher wages. The actual average effect is thus about 1.3 to 1.4 percent extra tax revenue per point of economic growth.

Corporate income tax revenues also rise much faster than the economy, as long as the economy is expanding.[4] Corporations pay a flat tax rate, and so are not subject to bracket creep. But corporate taxes are increased both by inflation and real growth because of the way that the tax system defines corporate profits.

Imagine the production process as a giant pipeline: Raw materials, labor, and capital enter one end and finished products come out the other. Corporate profits are the difference in value between what goes into the pipeline and what comes out, or the difference between costs and final sales. When the economy slows down, fewer finished products are purchased and items build up in the pipeline, a process known as inventory accumulation. Corporations thus incur the costs of producing the inventory without having any final sales, and corporate profits fall.

When, on the other hand, the economy speeds up, existing items in the pipeline, already largely paid for, are ready to move. Final sales increase faster than input costs, and corporate profits rise quickly.

This "pipeline effect" is most dramatic at turning points in the economy. When the economy turns up or down, corporate profits can easily change as much as 3 to 5 percent for every 1 percent change in the economy. As business expansion continues, the ratio drops to about 1.4 points of corporate profit for every 1 point of economic growth. As business expansion persists, rising demand for products can be met only by new investment: The pipeline itself must be expanded in order to accommodate the greater flow of products. This is where the tax system plays a part. Suppose a business invests in expanding the capacity of its pipeline by 10 percent. We might expect sales, profits, and costs, including capital costs, to rise together in proportion and the capital costs of a 10 percent bigger pipeline to be also 10 percent higher. But the tax system does not allow corporations to deduct the capital costs of the bigger pipeline right away; these added costs must be depreciated over many years. Because the costs of the expansion cannot be fully counted, profits appear to rise much more quickly than economic activity expands. Thus corporate profits, and therefore corporate taxes, increase more than point for point with economic activity during periods of real economic growth.

Inflation has a similar effect. Again, consider the goods moving through the pipeline. During periods of inflation, the value of the inventory in the pipeline rises with the general price level. The corporation does not really gain, because the cost of replacing the materials at the beginning of the pipeline also rises. But the tax system views the rising value of inventory as a source of corporate profit. This is particularly true for corporations that use the first in–first out (FIFO) method of accounting, under which the cost of products is based on the original cost of the materials that went into them, not their replacement or current costs. The last in–first out method (LIFO) uses replacement or current costs. A surprising number of firms use FIFO rather than LIFO, even though it overstates their corporate profits and therefore their corporate taxes.

The tax system also fails to take into account the effect of inflation on the capital costs of the pipeline itself. When inflation is high, the depreciation allowances for the cost of the pipeline are far less than the cost of actually replacing the pipeline at inflated prices. The result, since corporations cannot fully deduct the true capital costs of production from their profits, is an artificial rise in both profits and taxes. All these factors combine to increase corporate tax payments about 1.4 percent for every 1 percent increase in the price level.

Social Security tax payments tend to rise point for point with both real economic activity and inflation because they are indexed to the price level and have a proportional rather than progressive rate structure.

Unless social insurance tax rates change, these revenues will continue to grow almost exactly as fast as the economy.

Excise taxes, such as those on gasoline, alcohol, and cigarettes, included as "Other" in table 12.1, are generally levied on a "cents per unit" basis, and so are totally unresponsive to inflation. Sales of goods taxed in this way tend to increase more slowly than the expansion rate of the economy. As a result, revenue from these sources does not rise as fast as overall economic activity. All together, however, tax revenues will grow significantly faster than the economy, and this rapid expansion will balance the federal budget if we are at all sensible about spending. The only question is how fast we can expect the economy to grow.

Long-term economic projections are chancy, but let us consider two possibilities. The long-term growth of the US economy since the end of World War II, averaging out recessions and expansions, has been 3.2 percent per year. Though there is no reason to expect that we will do better in the future, there is also no reason to expect worse. We might reasonably project an average growth of 3.2 percent over the next twenty years. If we limit our base to more recent years, say from 1981, the peak of the last business cycle, through 1986, which includes the deepest recession we have experienced since the Great Depression, we get an average growth in the economy of only 2.7 percent per year. Projecting that figure forward would produce what we might call the bearish long-term forecast. Table 12.2 shows what would happen to revenues with these rates of growth over the next twenty years, assuming inflation continues at the average rate of the past several years, or about 4 percent. In both cases, revenues grow quickly over time, though an increase of just 0.5 percent in average real growth adds $530 billion per year by the twentieth year. This is an important indication of just how sensitive the US budget is to continued economic growth.

To reduce the deficit we do not need to cut spending. But we must show some self-control. After all, the Congress could spend every penny collected in revenue and then some. To illustrate the long-term budget needs of the country, the "spending" column in table 12.2 employs a five-year "flexible freeze" such as President Bush championed during his campaign. The flexible freeze limits spending growth to the level of inflation for five years, then allows real program growth of 2

TABLE 12.2

| | Revenue | | | Difference | |
Year	3.2%	2.7%	Spending*	3.2%	2.7%
1989	$976	$976	1137	–$161	–$161
1994	1425	1386	1382	+43	+4
1999	2100	1982	1752	+347	+230
2004	3115	2853	2142	+973	+711
2009	4649	4127	2880	+1769	+1246

*Data for 1989 from the FY1990 budget. It shows $971 billion in program spending and $167 billion in interest. Under this scenario the program spending grows with inflation until 1994 and at inflation plus 2 percent thereafter. Interest payments are calculated as 7.6 percent of the outstanding debt and are then added to program spending to get total spending.

percent per year. Thus program spending rises at a 4.0 percent annual rate through 1994 and at a 6.1 percent annual rate thereafter. We assume the interest rate on the national debt, which cannot be frozen, will be about 7.6 percent annually.[5]

Table 12.2 shows that a tax increase is completely unnecessary. If spending is limited to the growth of inflation until 1994, we will have either a balanced budget (with slow growth) or a $40 billion surplus (with average growth). After 1994, a large surplus arises and begins to grow even though spending is allowed to grow faster than inflation. By 2004 we will be showing annual surpluses of roughly $800 billion and will have paid off the existing national debt.

Of course, this will not happen. Given such enormous revenues, the Congress will try to increase spending. Assuming the freeze holds until 1994, both spending and taxes will be 19.5 percent of GNP in that year. Over the next fifteen years, taxes would automatically grow to between 22.3 and 22.9 percent of GNP. The Congress could drastically increase the size of government and the government's share of the economy if it appropriated all of the extra tax revenue for that purpose.

Instead, the country should insist on a series of tax cuts in the latter part of the 1990s. The $300 billion surpluses forecast for 1999 would easily finance a 15 percent reduction in tax rates across the board. If the entire surplus were applied to reducing the income tax rates in the current code, the bottom rate could be reduced from 15 percent to 10 percent and the top rate lowered from 28 percent to 20 percent.

All of this may seem magical given the headlines about the government's current fiscal crisis. Yet these calculations do not assume any behavioral changes on the part of the public, or any sharp drop in interest rates, or any unusual rate of economic growth. The only magic involved is the magic of normal economic growth compounded year after year, coupled with permanent restraint on the growth of government spending.

The current tax burden on American families remains too high. As with the Reagan tax cuts, Form 2000 rearranges the national tax burden to shift it further from lower- and moderate-income families. By exchanging lower rates for fewer loopholes, it reduces excess burdens, making the entire tax system more efficient and less disruptive to the economy. As time passes we can do even better: We can have not only more tax reform, such as Form 2000 proposes, but another round of tax cuts, particularly for the Americans who need them most.

Present-day pundits, stuck in their static analysis of a single year's budget, never calculate the effect of revenue growth on the prospects for the US budget. Hence the persistent calls for tax increases. But tax increases would tend to slow the rate of economic growth and reduce future revenue growth. Much better to keep taxes at current rates—or lower them—and assure continued economic growth not only for the treasury but for all Americans. It is to this task that the next chapters turn their attention.

PART II

UPDATING THE LESSONS: THE NEW CENTURY

$\begin{bmatrix} 13 \end{bmatrix}$

That Was Then,
This Is Now

I T IS EMINENTLY APPROPRIATE THAT THIS REPRINTING OF
the original version of *The Growth Experiment* concludes with the
chapter "The Great Surplus of '99." When the book was written it was
far from conventional wisdom that America would end the 1990s with a
fiscal surplus. Instead "deficits as far as the eye can see" was the mantra.
The role of tax policy in creating this surplus will be examined later in
great detail. Suffice it to say for now that contrary to conventional wisdom, changes in tax policy had very little to do with moving the government from deficit to surplus during the 1990s.

Instead the strategy that was actually pursued was remarkably similar to the one outlined in chapter 12. First, immediately following the
1994 elections the incoming Congress acted to limit the growth rate of
spending, going to the brink—including temporarily shutting down portions of the government—to force spending cuts. That election produced the biggest one-month rally in the government bond market in
history, pushing down interest costs and cutting interest expense. Second, the economy grew. There was a slight slowdown in 1993 relative to
1992, but the real growth in the American economy averaged 3.2 percent between 1989 and 1999. This real growth produced the "real
bracket creep," higher average rates for all taxpayers as their real income

increases, described in chapter 12. The average tax rate on personal income rose from 10 percent in 1996, when the cuts the Congress enacted in 1995 took effect, to 11.6 percent in 1999 and then to 12 percent in 2000.[1] A good portion of this growth was due to revenue from the stock market bubble, and this growth proved temporary once the bubble collapsed. These revenue increases had nothing to do with the 1993 rate increases, which had taken effect years before. As will be shown later, statutory changes in tax policy had remarkably little effect on the overall move from deficit to surplus.

This experience raises a crucial question: Why can't we do it again? Certainly the issue of government deficits is far more pressing today than it was a quarter century ago when *The Growth Experiment* was first written. In the 1980s the country ran an average fiscal deficit of 3.9 percent of GDP.* In the past five fiscal years it has averaged 7.9 percent of GDP. Moreover, under current policies, the deficit will average 5.0 percent over the next ten years even if the economy returns to a solid growth path.[2] So the need is there.

The laws of mathematics haven't changed either. Real tax revenue will still rise faster than real GDP. If real government spending growth is held below the rate of real GDP growth, then by definition the deficit will shrink over time. Economic growth is still the single most powerful force in creating deficit reduction.

The Hole Is Deeper,
Making Growth Necessary but Not Sufficient

Unfortunately, the country has dug its hole a lot deeper this time than ever before and has a lot of structural impediments in place that it didn't have before. Some of these are policy changes that must be reversed, including a confused and growth-reducing mis-regulation of our financial system, ill-conceived changes to health care financing, an inefficient tort system, and a costly yet failing education system. Others

---

*The consensus of the economic profession on how best to measure economic activity changed from gross national product (GNP) to gross domestic product (GDP) between the time the original *Growth Experiment* was written and this revisitation. The concepts are quite similar and the differences have no significant impact on the calculations done here. But to both preserve the original book and to keep with the prevailing convention, the GNP concept is retained in the original twelve chapters, while the new chapters use GDP.

are demographic; the baby boomers are about to retire and put ever-increasing demands on the existing system. So, even though the laws of budgetary math haven't changed, the politics that lies behind the numbers has, and in a way that will make closing the government deficit more politically painful.

That does not mean that a combination of sensible taxation, careful budgeting, sensible regulation, and economic growth won't go a long way toward solving the problem. But because real program spending has increased to a record share of GDP in peacetime in the past few years even without accounting for baby boom retirement, real cuts in government spending will likely be necessary in a way they were not in the 1990s. In addition, changes in our tax laws are likely to make it *politically* more difficult to achieve the kind of budgetary math needed to close our deficit. These issues center on distributional questions. Not only has the share of income going to higher-end households risen since *The Growth Experiment* was written, so has the share of income taxes paid by higher-end households. Moreover, the share of income taxes paid by the well-to-do has risen faster than their income. These three factors come together to make the politics of gathering additional revenue a challenge. Back in the 1960s and 1970s, when the top tax rate was 70 percent, the top 5 percent of households paid 36 percent of all federal income tax. In 2012, they paid 59 percent—that is, before the tax hike just passed on taxpayers making more than $400,000. Over the same time period, the Census Bureau reports, their share of income rose from 16.8 percent to 21.5 percent. So while their share of income rose by 5 points, their share of taxes rose by 23 points!

Spending Has Become Politically Tougher to Cut

First, consider spending. When the math was done for "The Great Surplus of '99," program spending (including everything spent on defense, social programs, and general government functions but excluding interest) in 1989 was $971 billion or 18 percent of GDP. In 2011 program spending was $3,373 billion, or 22.5 percent of GDP. Contrast this level of program spending with the average level from 1970 to 2010, which was just 18.6 percent. So program spending is roughly 25 percent higher as a share of GDP than its historical average. This rise has happened in just the past few years. As recently as 2007, program spending was just 18.1 percent of GDP. Other things equal, one would need either a 21 percent increase in all taxes (including income and Social Security taxes) or a return to the 2007 levels of program spending just to get back on track.[3] While 2007 was hardly the dark ages in terms of government services, the rise in government spending since that time has been taken as a "given" by those who benefit from it. Many now think of it as a permanent part of their income, not as an emergency measure. Undoing this will be politically difficult.

The composition of spending makes this even more difficult. Table 13.1 shows the share of GDP being spent on defense, entitlements, and non-defense programs. Note that a major portion of the decline in program spending during the 1990s occurred in the defense arena. This was accomplished fairly painlessly due to the collapse of the Soviet empire. Defense spending fell from 5.6 percent of GDP in 1989 when the Soviet Union collapsed to just 3 percent of GDP ten years later. The 3 percent figure proved to be unsustainably low, as defense spending is about 4.75 percent of GDP currently. So unless China were to suddenly reverse its military expansion and peace were to break out in the Middle East (probably for the first time in several thousand years), it seems unlikely that a "peace dividend" of the kind we enjoyed after the fall of the Soviet empire will be available.

We have also rapidly expanded entitlement spending—Social Security, Medicare, and Medicaid, along with other programs, such as food stamps.

TABLE 13.1 Federal Spending by Category

% of GDP	1989	1999	2011
Defense	5.6%	3.0%	4.7%
Entitlements	8.4%	8.9%	12.1%
Domestic Discretionary	4.0%	4.1%	5.7%
Interest	3.1%	2.5%	1.5%
Total	21.2%	18.5%	24.1%

SOURCE: White House Office of the Management and Budget.

At the end of the Clinton administration, entitlements were just under 9 percent of GDP. Now they are roughly 12.1 percent. Some of this is demographic, but a good portion is simply program expansion. Again, as recently as 2007 entitlement spending was just 9.5 percent of GDP.

But the really difficult part of the budget picture is in the non-program area. Back in 2000, when the country last had a balanced budget, interest payments composed 2.3 percent of GDP. In 2011, despite a massive deficit, interest was just 1.5 percent of GDP. The reason for the drop, of course, was a very rapid decline in interest rates as the Federal Reserve sought to stimulate the economy. In 2011 the average interest rate on federal borrowing was just 2.5 percent. The average rate over the previous twenty years was 5.7 percent. Should we get back to "normal" when it comes to interest rates and economic growth, those extra 3.2 percentage points of interest would be applied to all the existing debt owed to the public. As of this writing, that measure of debt stood at around $12.5 trillion. So, just the *extra* interest cost of a return to normal interest rates would amount to $400 billion—the equivalent of half of our defense budget or more than a third of our total income tax collections.

So, the first part of the challenge we face is that the spending situation has worsened. We have greatly expanded entitlement programs—which will be politically painful to cut. We have already enjoyed the "peace dividend" of rapid cuts in defense spending, and so will not be able to enjoy those benefits again. And we have drastically pared our interest costs by adopting temporarily low interest rates. Normalization of those interest rates will only worsen our fiscal problem.

Tax Revenue Has Become More Difficult to Raise

The second part of the challenge is that much of the politically "easy" part of the deficit reduction from taxation has already taken place and, like further cuts in defense, will be difficult to repeat. What do we mean by easy? By far the easiest way to raise revenue in a politically easy way is to exploit the famous Laffer Curve and cut rates from above the revenue-maximizing level to below it. Rates go down, revenue goes up. Chapter 5 made clear that this is exactly what the reduction in the top tax rates did in the 1981 Reagan tax cut. The revenue-maximizing rate was somewhat under 50 percent, and cutting the top rate from 70 percent to 50 percent was a clear revenue gainer. But Chapter 4 showed that this "easiest" way of raising revenue did not apply to the entire tax cut, but only to the reduction in the top rate. Still, achieving lower rates and more revenue is an unambiguous win, with no one made worse off. Suffice it to say that this is no longer the case. Cutting rates from current levels will not produce more revenue, even if it might produce more economic growth.

The next most politically easy way to raise revenue is to leave the rate structure of a tax in place but to have people "move" automatically from a lower rate bracket to a higher one. The most obvious way is outlined in chapter 12. When incomes go up faster than inflation, people are pushed into higher tax rate brackets even if those brackets are indexed to the inflation rate. The taxpayers (voters) still feel better off because their real incomes have gone up, and the government is better off because its tax collections have also increased. This also seems like a win-win situation politically. That is the essence of growth and we all hope it will occur. But this kind of growth is already built into the government's budgetary projections. So, although this is an attractive option, it is already fully exploited in the budgetary arithmetic.

One variant of this "movement" into higher rates is somewhat less attractive, but politicians, cynical creatures that they are, have managed to find it politically acceptable. This is a movement of *aggregate income* into higher tax brackets without having the majority of taxpayers be any better off. Specifically, when the distribution of income becomes more unequal and skewed to higher-income individuals, the average tax rate applied to the income in the economy rises. Higher-income individuals pay higher average tax rates, so increased income inequality means more money for the government. This is true even if some very high-profile people lower their tax liability by exploiting the complexity of the tax code. So while Warren Buffett and Mitt Romney may pay only a 15 percent average rate, the average rate paid by taxpayers in the top 1 percent is twice as much. And of course even their 15 percent rate is far higher than for most people, half of whom pay no income taxes at all.

Now of course the majority of voters are unhappy with this development. So politicians have found a very good coping mechanism. They give speeches attacking the rise in inequality and demand that something be done about it while they pocket and spend the extra real tax revenue the government gets from the less equal distribution of income. It is as if the two facts are totally unconnected in the politicians' minds, even though they are directly connected mathematically. This somewhat cynical approach to inequality and taxation reached its pinnacle in the 1990s when the country had the greatest decadal increase in income inequality since records have been kept but the higher revenue allowed politicians to talk about how they had balanced the budget. So the "easy way out" of letting rising inequality raise revenue, as it did in the 1990s, is no longer an option.

According to the Census Bureau, the share of income going to the top 5 percent of households rose from 18.1 percent in 1991 to 22.4 percent in 2001.[4] To put those numbers into perspective, it means that over 36 percent of the total rise in personal income during that decade went to the top 5 percent. The real incomes of the top 5 percent rose 61 percent, nearly three times as much as everyone else's income. As we will see in chapter 15, this rising inequality, not any change in the tax law, was the principal reason income tax receipts rose during the 1990s. It produced an extra 1.3 percentage points of GDP in income taxes, which when coupled with the 2.6 percentage-point drop in defense spending explains the federal deficit's movement into surplus.

The problem is that income inequality has already reached fairly high levels. The share of income going to the top 5 percent of American households has been stable at about 21.5 percent for the past decade. Producing a similar surge in tax revenue from rising inequality would mean pushing the share of income going to the top 5 percent to truly unprecedented levels, ones that would only cause more social unhappiness.

On top of this is a long-standing economic factor known as "regression toward the mean." When discussing "shares" we have a maximum of 100 percent and a minimum of zero percent, so trends can't go on forever. Moreover, when one share goes up, another share must go down, and economic forces tend to resist this. Therefore, it is a safe bet that the share of income going to the top 5 percent is at least as likely to fall over the next ten to twenty years as it is to rise. Other things equal, this means that income tax collections are at least as likely to fall in that period as rise due to changes in income distribution. Though politically relatively painless, a changing income distribution is certainly not something we should be counting on to solve our nation's fiscal problems.

The next most politically acceptable way to raise revenue is an old standby: "soak the rich." Many politicians actually consider this a real winner. First, most voters aren't rich, so the political cost is small. For those friends and large donors of the politicians who are rich, often very narrowly tailored exemptions are placed in the law to allow those particular individuals to escape at least some of the higher taxes. Second, many politicians consider the rich to be a politically unpopular group. So, based on the theory of reflected glory, calling for higher taxes on the rich not only solves a revenue problem, it also makes politicians more popular in some quarters.

If this sounds like an overly cynical view, consider the facts behind the so-called Buffett Rule, which would impose a second alternative minimum calculation on all taxpayers making more than $1 million. Under this rule they would have to pay at least 30 percent of their income in taxes. It was advanced as a way of dealing with the nation's fiscal crisis. Yet, according to the Congressional Budget Office, the tax would raise just $1.4 billion in its first year in the midst of a deficit that was $1.4 trillion, or 1,000 times as large.[5] As a fiscal measure, the Buffett Rule was a joke. Worse, although it would add yet another complication to the tax code, it is estimated that only one in 1,000 taxpayers would actually be affected by the tax.[6]

But if we move beyond the merely cynical and into the realm of substantive solutions to our deficit problem from soak-the-rich taxation, the problem becomes much more difficult. The unpopular truth is that the rich are already being "soaked," at least relative to everyone else. The data on this subject will be explored in detail in chapter 15, but the top 5 percent of the households ranked by income currently pay 59 percent of all income tax, even though according to the Census

Bureau they receive just 21.5 percent of all income. Stated differently, the effective tax rate on the top 5 percent is five times what it is on the other 95 percent of the income distribution. Moreover, half of all adults actually pay no income taxes at all.

Of course, the effective tax rate on higher-income individuals can be more than five times that of the rest of the population. But some simple math suggests that this may not work very well as a means of raising revenue. For example, let's imagine that the *average* tax rate on the top 5 percent (people making over $150,000) increases to 30 percent.[7] For context, this is the rate that the Buffett Rule's supporters should apply only to people making more than $1 million. Moreover, it was the same average tax rate on the high end as prevailed back in the Carter administration, when the top tax rate was 70 percent. As *The Growth Experiment* pointed out, that puts the tax system in the "prohibitive" zone on the Laffer Curve—that is, the point at which higher rates actually produce less revenue. So, most would consider that to be the maximum possible *average* tax rate.

But if that is true, and someone wanted to keep the ratio of high-end effective rates at five times those on everyone else, then the rate on everyone else would be limited to just 6 percent. These rates would limit the share of personal income taken in taxes at just over 10 percent, the equivalent of about 6.7 percent of GDP. The only problem is that this is almost a full point below the share of GDP generated in income taxes during the George H. W. Bush administration—a period some denounced as a low-tax era. That is far too low a tax share to make any progress on the deficit through higher income taxes.

Therefore, the math leads to one unmistakable conclusion that most politicians—and most voters—do not want to hear. If the country is going to make progress on its deficit problems through higher income taxes, the effective tax rate on the "bottom 95 percent" will have to go up. That means higher taxes on the vast majority of voters. Moreover, given the effective limitations on upper-end taxes described above, it also means that the income tax will have to become *less* progressive. That is not the message people want to hear and therefore not the message that politicians want to deliver. But this is a matter of math, not politics.

A less progressive income tax does not necessarily mean we are going back to the dark ages. Lyndon Johnson was generally considered a progressive president, yet the ratio of the effective rate on the top 5 percent was only 2.6 times that on the remainder of the population, far lower than the 5.3 of today. The same was true under Jimmy Carter, when the ratio of effective tax rates was just 3. And under Bill Clinton the ratio was 4.[8]

The reason for this, of course, is political choice. Typically it has been Republican presidents, especially tax-cutting Republican presidents, raising the ratio of taxes on top relative to those on the bottom. To make tax cuts politically popular, everyone's taxes had to be cut. But because both the actual level of taxes and the effective tax rate were higher on upper-income people, it became necessary to cut taxes proportionately more for people who were not at the top. But if taxes are cut proportionately more at the bottom and in the middle than at the top, then over time the ratio of the effective rate at the bottom relative to the effective rate at the top must drop. Again, the laws of math necessarily overcome the narratives of politicians.

The Job Is Tougher;
The Response Must Be Smarter

The above analysis is not a font of cheer. There is no sugarcoating. As difficult as the challenges of 1980 might have seemed, the hole in which America found itself was not as deep as the one we are now in. Our debt-to-GDP ratio was only 26 percent in 1980; today it is 67 percent. The American economy was 25 percent of the global economy. Today it is just 20 percent. The dollar was unmistakably the king of the world. One dollar could buy 250 Japanese yen; today it buys just 100. More debt, more money created, a weaker role for the dollar, and a smaller global economic footprint—not a great starting point.

Nor are the trends moving in our direction. In 1980 baby boomers were entering the years in which skills and experience led to maximum productivity gains—typically one's thirties. Today that huge segment of the population is entering retirement, a period of life when many will place ever greater strains on the government's finances. Defense spending consumes far less of our national output and global challenges seem more likely to grow in the decades ahead rather than to shrink. All of these issues are interesting in their own right but frankly are outside the scope of this book.

Instead the focus here, as in the original version of *The Growth Experiment,* is on tax policy and its connection to economic growth. That remains a central link in dealing with our fiscal and other economic challenges. Without growth, we will not be able to generate the resources needed to meet our challenges. Without a sensible tax policy we will not be able to achieve the needed growth. And without a tax policy that generates at least as much revenue as taxes have historically produced in America—about 18 percent of GDP—we will never be able to finance our government. This means that taxes must go up as a share of GDP from current levels, where they take just 15.4 percent of GDP. But they must do so in a way that does not hinder the prospects for long-term economic growth.

So, the answers that Ronald Reagan adopted in the early 1980s, as successful as they proved to be, are not the ones we must adopt today. That was then, this is now. But the lessons he taught the country, the lessons of his Growth Experiment, remain. Rates should be as low as possible, sufficient only to produce the revenue the government needs. The base should be as broad as possible. The primary purpose of taxation must be to raise revenue, not to achieve other social objectives, as important as they might be.

The chapters ahead will explore how to apply those lessons to our current predicament. But first we must carefully examine the "conventional wisdom" that now drives much of the thinking on tax policy. The original version of *The Growth Experiment* avoided the ideological prejudices of the time. On the one hand, it showed that the prevailing prejudices against supply-side economics were incorrect. Taxpayers did respond to lower rates in ways that produced more revenue above a certain level of tax rates. On the other hand, it also showed that *on balance* across-the-board tax cuts did not "pay for themselves." Moreover, the original version showed that Keynesian-style demand-side forces were roughly as important as supply-side forces in making the tax cuts successful.

The next chapter looks at the misinterpretations that have been applied to the tax policies of the 1990s. We will examine in detail the real causes for the Great Surplus of '99. We then pivot to look at the first decade of the twenty-first century, at the purpose behind the George W. Bush tax cuts, and the extent to which those cuts served their purpose. We then take a detailed look at our economic morass and the political domination of economic policy. This leads to an obvious dead end, so we must find new options. We conclude by suggesting what would seem, given all these lessons, to be the best way forward.

[14]

The Roaring Nineties

WHO DIDN'T LOVE THE NINETIES? IT WAS AN AGE OF incredible freedom, before 9/11, airport searches, and the worries about homeland security. The 1980s ended in ways that gave us some incredible gifts. America had just won the Cold War. We had cleaned up our banks and they could begin lending again. New inventions kept hitting the market and companies whose names ended with "dot-com" became the rage. The stock market surged, as did employment and personal wealth. Stock prices and even home prices went up while the cost of many goods and services actually fell. The price of gasoline dropped back under a dollar for a time!

Our justifiable fondness for the nineties allows us to forget some of the fine details. Tax policy in particular becomes part of the blurring of fact and fiction into an era of generalized economic good feeling. And when it suits the speaker's purposes, tax policy, particularly the tax hike of 1993, isn't just blurred into the generalized fond remembrance of the decade, it actually is alleged to be the *cause* of all the happiness.

The human mind tends to resist looking for the real cause of happiness (as well as sadness) because uncovering the cause might make it go away. Best to sit back and enjoy the fond memories. But this can lead to all kinds of superstitious, and even counterproductive, behavior. For example, if I see the number seven several times one morning and later that day my boss gives me a raise, I could ascribe the raise to a year of hard work, but that might mean I would have to work hard again this year to get another raise. It is much easier to believe that seven is my lucky number, a decision that might induce all kinds of strange behaviors. Some might be harmless, such as chanting a prayer seven times, or I might start playing number seven at the horse races, or if the superstition got really bad, move my house to 777 Seventh Ave.

Economic historians began to develop quantitative analytic tools so that rather than learning the wrong lessons from history, we might more carefully analyze what actually occurred, and this developed into a branch of economic history known as cliometrics. *The Growth Experiment* applied the principles of cliometrics to the tax policy of the 1980s.[1] In this chapter we use the same type of quantitative analysis to examine what happened in the 1990s.

For those interested in the Cliffs Notes version, all of the tax changes of the 1990s, including the 1993 tax hike, were relatively insignificant compared to other events. For example, the American victory in the Cold War led to the addition of over 300 million industrial workers in the global economy. This pushed down production costs globally and allowed a huge monetary expansion to occur without causing inflation. The signing of the North American Free Trade Agreement (NAFTA) further enhanced the disinflationary pressure from free trade. The development of the Internet led to a revolution in both information and commerce. All of this, coupled with a very accommodative monetary policy, combined to create one of the largest stock market bubbles in history.

Cliometrics allows at least a modicum of analytic power for teasing out how important tax policy actually was. It is based on the principles of the scientific method, where you form a hypothesis, design and run a test of that hypothesis, and analyze the results. When something happens that either your hypothesis or established scientific principles say shouldn't have, you look for other factors that might have affected your experiment. It is important that your search for other factors be consistent with underlying scientific theory. Then you can use your revised experiment to test that theory.

The Growth Experiment showed the incoming tax return data for the period 1981–1984 to be inconsistent with the consensus belief, which held that the Reagan tax cuts would sharply reduce revenue. Revenue proved to be higher, and it was much higher at the top of the income distribution, where rates had been cut the most. This led to the need for a revised hypothesis that was consistent with both the data and broader economic theory: that individuals might respond to higher after-tax compensation, work harder or at higher-paying endeavors, take more risks, and invest more. In addition, they might take advantage of purely pecuniary gains by changing their behavior to reflect changes in tax law, as in the case of someone who changes his portfolio to take advantage of lower capital gains tax rates. In all cases, the new hypotheses were consistent with the established theory about how individuals respond to incentives. As the data showed, not only did individuals respond to changed incentives, the bigger the change in the incentives, the bigger the change in taxpayer behavior.

In considering the effects of the 1993 tax changes, which raised the top rate from 31 percent to 39.6 percent, we begin with the basic hypothesis that was laid out by those who proposed the changes in the law. The Joint Committee on Taxation, which is the arm of Congress that estimates the effect of tax law changes, estimated that the tax rate hikes, the stiffening of the alternative minimum tax, and limitations on personal exemptions and itemized deductions for high-income taxpayers would produce annual revenue gains of between $23 billion and $26 billion over the first four years they were fully in effect,[2] and slightly more byt the end of the decade.

Now, consider the claim that the 1993 tax hikes on high-income individuals caused the government to go from a budget deficit to a surplus. That would have involved an increase in tax revenue of roughly $500 billion. In 1992 the deficit hit a record $269 billion. In 2000 the government ran a record surplus of $236 billion, or a net swing of half a trillion dollars.[3] But that change in the deficit was nearly *twenty* times what the law's authors projected to be collected from the high-end personal tax rate increases when the law was enacted.

So the claim that the high-end tax changes *caused* the deficit to go away is nothing more than a fanciful rewriting of history, completely ignoring the scientific method. The tax law certainly contributed to the reduction in the deficit, but not even its authors projected that it would cause the size of deficit reduction that actually occurred. Something else, far more important, must have happened.

The fact is, other economic changes occurred that had nothing to do with the tax law that produced a much faster growth in the economy. Those changes interacted with the higher rates to produce a large increase in tax revenue. So, this static calculation of the effect of the upper-end tax increases on the budget deficit suggests that only about 5 percent of the deficit reduction was due to the tax law changes. This is what the authors of the 1993 tax increase expected at the time, so it is important to keep in mind since it forms the baseline for considering what happened in the 1990s. But due to this interaction with economic events, the actual increase in tax revenue was larger than expected. One of the tasks of this chapter is to provide a range for the contribution of the higher-end tax cuts to the conversion of the deficit into a surplus.

But more was involved in deficit reduction than taxes. Another key was lowering the rate of growth of spending. Two factors contributed. One, already mentioned, was the tremendous reduction in defense spending made possible by the American victories in the Cold War and in Operation Desert Storm in 1990–91. The former eliminated the main strategic competition that America had faced for the preceding half century; the latter established American dominance in the single critical region for which America had become global policeman, the Arabian (or Persian) Gulf. The other factor that slowed growth was what is often called the "Gingrich Revolution," which led to some drastic reductions in the rate of growth of federal spending, the elimination of some programs, and even some modest tax cuts.

Spending Restraint and Deficits During the 1990s

So, the first step in deciding what caused the government deficit to change into a surplus is to consider how much was due to spending changes and how much was due to tax changes. As in *The Growth Experiment*, we can construct a counterfactual for this purpose. In this case, to consider the spending side of the equation, we consider what would have happened if the Gingrich Revolution had not occurred.

The Gingrich Revolution was a discrete political event. It radically altered the composition of Congress from what had been total control of both houses by large Democratic majorities into Republican control of both houses. The counterfactual question to ask is, "What would have happened to spending had the 1994 elections not produced this change in Congress?" Then, by comparing what would have happened with what actually happened, we can separate out the contribution of the Gingrich Revolution in controlling spending and getting the deficit under control from other factors.

The Gingrich Revolution not only changed the majority party, it also changed Washington's ideology. Eight years before, in another discrete political event, Democrats took control of the Senate and widened their majority in the House to such an extent that the party's liberal wing could pass legislation without help from the diminished conservative wing. In the subsequent eight years, domestic outlays (excluding defense spending and interest on the debt) rose from $583 billion to $1,011 billion, or at a compound annual rate of 7.1 percent. In the next six budgets, passed by the Republican-controlled, post–Gingrich Revolution Congress, domestic outlays rose just 4.9 percent. Had domestic outlays grown at the pre–Gingrich Revolution pace, total spending would have been $176 billion higher.

A similar counterfactual analysis can be applied to defense. The rate of growth of defense spending dropped from 10 percent per year in the decade *before* the fall of the Berlin Wall to minus 1 percent in the decade after. Again, had defense spending grown at the previous pace, it would have been $655 billion higher in 2001 than it actually was. Even if defense spending had grown only as fast as GDP—that is, the defense share of GDP was kept at its 1989 level—defense spending would have been $264 billion higher.

Figure 14.1 presents these alternative scenarios to give an idea of how important the spending cuts were as a result of the Gingrich Revolution and the American victory in the Cold War. In addition, reduced spending meant that there was less cumulative debt than there otherwise would have been. This lowered the net interest the government had to pay on the debt in 2001. We calculate this by taking the spending reduction and multiplying it by the prevailing treasury borrowing costs in 2001, neglecting any additional second-round savings because the lower deficit from the spending restraint also probably contributed to lower interest rates. These results suggest that spending restraint during

FIGURE 14.1 Effects of Spending Restraint on
2001 Spending (in Billions of Current Dollars)

Spending Growth	Defense	Nondefense	Interest	Total
Historic Trend	959	1,528	525	3,013
Increase with GDP	573	1,407	364	2,344
Actual	305	1.352	206	1,863
Cut Relative to Historic Trend	655	176	319	1,150 *(11.2% of GDP)*
Cut Relative to GDP Trend	268	55	158	481 *(4.7% of GDP)*

the 1990s lowered the fiscal 2001 level of the deficit by between 4.7 and 11.2 percent of GDP.

The importance of spending restraint, and of the Gingrich Revolution in particular, is not just a hypothetical academic exercise. It is borne out in the behavior of the bond market through the 1990s. Figure 14.2 shows the difference between the ten-year treasury bond and the Federal Reserve's target Fed Funds rate. The Fed Funds rate is set by the Federal Open Market Committee and is the base lending rate over which all other rates are measured. It is the cost for banks to borrow from each other on an overnight basis. Markets usually demand a higher rate to lend to the government because they are often uncertain about what future policy may bring. The ten-year bond rate is the most frequently cited measure of the market's assessment of this longer term risk. If, for example, markets think inflation is going to rise in the years ahead, investors will likely demand an extra premium over the current overnight rate to compensate for that risk. Similarly, if markets think that government spending is going to rise in a way that will put more demand on the credit markets in the years ahead, they will bid up the price of the ten-year bond to compensate for that risk. Conversely, if markets think that inflation or government spending is going to fall in a way that lowers these risks, the ten-year rate will fall relative to the overnight Fed Funds rate.

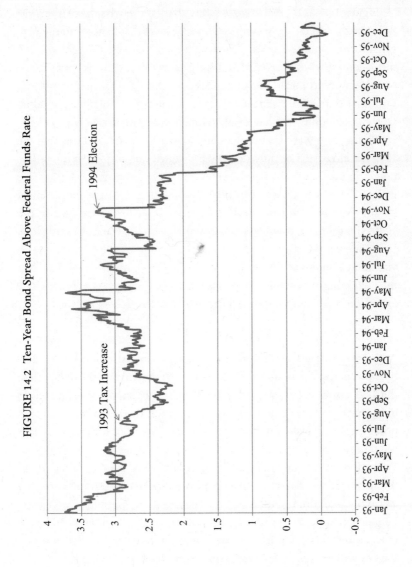

FIGURE 14.2 Ten-Year Bond Spread Above Federal Funds Rate

Figure 14.2 also labels two discrete events: the passage of the 1993 tax increase and the 1994 congressional election that ushered in the Gingrich Revolution. It is quite clear which event markets thought was the most consequential for reducing long-term interest rates. In fact, the 1994 election produced the biggest single monthly bond market rally up until that time. The political change it produced completely altered investor perceptions of what would happen to federal fiscal policy.

The same figure also provides an eloquent test of the thesis that the 1993 tax increases not only reduced the deficit but also led to the reduction in interest rates that let the economy expand during the 1990s. This is the "Tax Hikes Caused the 1990s Boom" thesis. And even the most cursory examination of the bond market's performance during the 1990s shows that this was essentially a nonevent. To the extent that lowering interest rates was the key to the expansion of the 1990s (and this was at best one of several causes of the decade's growth), it is clear that the 1994 congressional election was a far more important event and, by extension, a far more important cause of the decade's expansion.

The Effect of Taxes

At the macro level, therefore, the data clearly indicate that the 1994 election was perceived as far more consequential in reducing the deficit than the 1993 tax increases. There can be no question that those tax increases did contribute to reducing the deficit, but even by the analysis of those proposing the legislation, it was only a small fraction of the total deficit reduction.

A more careful and detailed analysis of the tax changes of the 1990s requires that we dissect the events into tax-related and non-tax-related issues. In addition, it requires us to separate the responses of non–capital gains income from capital gains income, not only in estimating the revenue response, but also in carefully examining the central thesis of the Growth Experiment—that taxpayers respond to changes in tax rates. A large school of conventional wisdom holds that taxpayers did not respond to rate changes in the 1990s, and that thesis needs to be examined in some detail. Obviously the tax changes in the 1990s were small compared to those of the 1980s, and the original analysis in *The Growth Experiment* held that, in general, tax rates under 40 percent were likely to cause only moderate effects on taxpayer behavior. That general thesis had broad support in academic studies. It is no coincidence that the top rate in the 1993 tax hike was 39.6 percent or that Nigel Lawson, Margaret Thatcher's Chancellor of the Exchequer, picked a 40 percent top rate for Britain.[4]

The rubric for analyzing the 1990s is to break the analysis into changes over time, between income groups, and between capital gains and non–capital gains income. The analysis uses two time periods: 1992–1994 and 1994–2000. The year 1992 was the last before the tax hikes began, and 1994 was the year they became fully effective. As 1992 and 1994 are only two years apart, relatively little changed outside of tax policy to allow a straightforward comparison of the effects of the tax hike. On the other hand, the boom of the 1990s took place largely after 1994. We can therefore compare the effects of the boom period with a more simplified time in which only taxes changed. There is also a natural division of the analysis between income groups, since marginal rate increases affected only higher-income taxpayers. A 36 percent bracket was created for taxpayers reporting taxable income of $140,000 and another 39.6 percent rate bracket was created for taxpayers reporting more than $250,000 of taxable income. The $140,000 taxable income level corresponds to adjusted gross income (AGI) of roughly $200,000, which also happens to be one of the breaks in the income classification in the tax return data the IRS provides. This allows us to compare the behavioral response of taxpayers above and below this income threshold, since the former group had an increase in tax rates while the latter group did not. The $200,000 income threshold also provides a good analytic breakpoint because there were essentially the same number of taxpayers above that income level in both 1992 and 1994: 846,000 in 1992 and 866,000 in 1994. This permits a like-for-like comparison of the top taxpayers.

Finally, separating the data into capital gains and non–capital gains income is important because the rate on non–capital gains income increased over the decade, while the rate on capital gains income was actually lower at the end of the decade than at the beginning: the capital gains rate being 28 percent in 1992 and 1994 and only 20 percent in 2000. The rate was cut to encourage investment in the stock market and because a 28 percent rate was considered to be high enough that it might adversely affect tax revenue. The analysis of the behavioral response of taxpayers to the capital gains tax rate depends on not only the level of the capital gains rate, but also the differential between the capital gains tax rate and the ordinary income tax rate. The differential affects how individuals structure their investment and business behavior. Even at an unchanged capital gains rate, one might expect to see higher capital gains realizations (or growth in those realizations relative to other income) if the ordinary income tax rate were increased.

The Immediate Response to the Tax Cuts

Figure 14.3 shows the changes between 1992 and 1994 in capital gains and non–capital gains income for taxpayers in different income classes. The first part of the figure presents the percentage changes in AGI, capital gains, and non–capital gains income for taxpayers, sorted by whether they made more or less than $200,000. As mentioned previously, there were essentially the same number of taxpayers in each group in both years, so this is a like-for-like comparison. The second part of the table shows the *per-return* changes for taxpayers earning between $200,000 and $500,000 and those earning over $500,000. The reason for showing data on a per-return basis is that, thanks to the

FIGURE 14.3 Percent Change in Real Income 1992–1994

	AGI	Capital Gains	Other Income
Real Income Group			
All Taxpayers	1.9%	14.1%	1.4%
Under $200,000	2.3%	8.7%	2.2%
Over $200,000	–1.2%	19.0%	–4.5%
Per Return Changes			
$200,000–$500,000 (36% Bracket)	–1.6%	1.9%	–2.0%
$500,000+ (39.6% Bracket)	3.8%	15.4%	–2.7%

behavioral response of taxpayers, the incomes of high-end taxpayers dropped. As a result, some taxpayers who earned more than $500,000 in 1992 earned less in 1994, and the number of returns with incomes over $500,000 dropped 8.2 percent between the two years despite the overall improvement in the economy. Presenting data on a per-return basis helps adjust for this. The $500,000 breakpoint is also a rough estimation of the break between taxpayers facing the new 36 percent rate and those in the higher 39.6 percent bracket.[5]

All of these data help confirm that when tax rates were increased between 1992 and 1994, people responded by changing their behavior. First, note that AGI rose for taxpayers overall between the two years in question. This is consistent with the overall improvement in the economy. The IRS data behind the table are for real, inflation-adjusted income. So the overall 1.9 percent growth in AGI reflects real income growth of approximately 1 percent per year. Note, however, that income grew much faster for taxpayers reporting income under $200,000 than for taxpayers reporting income over $200,000, and moderately for all groups under $500,000 between 1992 and 1994. But the distribution of that income growth, as reported on tax returns, was skewed toward people making under $200,000.

One possible explanation is that overall economic trends were leading to a more equal distribution of income. But careful analysis of income distribution trends throughout this period by the US Census Bureau suggests the opposite was true.[6] Overall income was becoming more skewed toward the top of the income distribution throughout the 1990s and was particularly sharp in the early part of the decade. So, that thesis has to be rejected.

Though the data are not consistent with Census Bureau information on overall income distribution trends, they are quite consistent with the thesis that taxpayers responded behaviorally to changes in tax rates. This is true both overall and given the decomposition of income into capital gains and non–capital gains sources. While all income groups experienced increases in their capital gains realizations during this period as the stock market revived, the percentage gains among higher-income taxpayers was more than twice that for taxpayers earning less than $200,000. So, when capital gains are excluded from income, the percent change in reported income shows an even greater disparity than for overall AGI. Taxpayers earning less than $200,000 reported a 2.2 percent increase in their non–capital gains income while taxpayers earning over $200,000 reported a 4.5 percent decline in that income. Again, the former group did not see their marginal tax rates increase between the two years, while the latter group saw an increase of either 8 percentage points or 11.6 percentage points, depending on whether they were going into the 36 percent bracket or the 39.6 percent bracket.

It is also important to bear in mind why capital gains realizations rose so much for the higher income group even though the capital gains tax rate was unchanged. The data confirm the hypothesis that the realization of capital gains depends not only on the level of the capital gains tax rate, but also on the differential between the tax rate on capital gains and the rate on ordinary income. In 1992 the capital gains and ordinary income tax rates were an identical 28 percent for taxpayers in these top two income classifications. In 1994 the ordinary income tax rate was raised by 11.6 percentage points for these taxpayers. The effect was to encourage taxpayers to rearrange their investment portfolio in ways that increased the realization of capital gains and reduced the realization of other forms of income, such as dividends and interest. The reverse effect happened after the 1986 tax reform, when the differential between capital gains and ordinary income was eliminated after having been 30 percentage points.[7]

The second part of figure 14.3 looks at the top income group in a little more detail. Here, the over $200,000 income classification is broken down between those earning between $200,000 and $500,000 and those earning more than $500,000. The data are provided on a per-return basis to correct for the overall decline in income at the top part of the income distribution, which pushed taxpayers into lower income classifications. The over $500,000 income classification is generally consistent with taxpayers in the 39.6 percent bracket while the $200,000 to $500,000 group is composed primarily of taxpayers in the 36 percent bracket.[8]

At first pass, it may seem surprising that the average AGI rose in the higher income group, subject to the 39.6 percent bracket, while falling for the lower income group, subject only to the 36 percent bracket. But, as above, it is important to separate out capital gains income for which the tax rate did not change for either group from non–capital gains income. When we do this, the data show that the average reported non–capital gains income fell for both groups, as one would expect from higher rates, and also fell more for the group with the greatest increase in its tax rate. Thus, all of the evidence is consistent with the hypothesis that there was a continued behavioral response by taxpayers to the higher rates.

Further evidence of this strong behavioral response is provided by what happened to business and professional income between 1992 and 1994. This income classification is known as Schedule C income, named after the schedule on which it is reported on IRS Form 1040. This is income received by individual sole proprietors. They are the boss. They get to control the wages and fringe benefits of their employees and how much to invest in the business as well as other current expenses. The original work done on *The Growth Experiment* showed that after capital gains, this type of income was most responsive to changes in tax rates.[9] In addition, many higher-income individuals derive much of their income from partnerships, LLCs, and Subchapter S corporations. These have become increasingly popular vehicles since the 1980s as the law has developed and knowledge of this option for business organization has become more widespread. But because the individual taxpayer is not the sole owner, there is less control over the details of how these firms are run and these firms typically show less tax rate sensitivity than do sole proprietorships in reporting income. But they do show some sensitivity, nonetheless.

As the economy expanded between 1992 and 1994, the profitability of businesses rose across the board. The National Income and Product Accounts compiled by the Commerce Department reported that corporate profits surged 25 percent, from $479 billion to $600 billion. The same non-tax measure of profit growth for the unincorporated business sector rose from $427 billion to $473 billion, or 11 percent. The overall tax data also showed growth in reporting profits for the unincorporated business sector. The overall income of proprietorships grew 2.1 percent between 1992 and 1994 while the profits reported by partnerships, LLCs, and Subchapter S corporations expanded 24.4 percent. The combined profits of both forms of unincorporated business organization rose 10.3 percent, very much in line with the data compiled by the Commerce Department's Bureau of Economic Analysis for the National Income and Product Accounts.

But when these data are decomposed into the same income classifications described above, the tax sensitivity becomes clear. The income of sole proprietorships rose $6 billion or 5 percent on tax returns with AGI under $200,000 but *fell* nearly $3 billion or 12 percent on tax returns with AGI over $200,000. We would have to conclude either that well-to-do proprietors suddenly became incompetent and less profitable at a time when all other businesses suddenly got more profitable, or that the same kind of tax responsiveness that was exhibited to other, earlier tax changes was still in play. As expected, the tax responsiveness at the partnership and Subchapter S level was less than at the proprietorship level, but was still present. Upper-income taxpayers reported a 17 percent rise in their income from these companies while tax returns with AGI under $200,000 saw a stunning 57 percent growth in such income. Again, it seems implausible that firms owned by higher-income individuals were only one-third as successful as those of lower-income individuals at raising profits during this time period.

The Effect of the Behavioral Response on 1994 Tax Collections

In sum, the data from 1992 to 1994 clearly indicate that taxpayers' tax responsiveness was still very much in existence. Because the tax rate changes were less than in the 1990s, the behavioral response was much less. This raises an important empirical question about just how big the response was and what effect that response had on overall tax revenue. As in *The Growth Experiment*, the key step is to compute a counterfactual of what would have happened had the tax rate changes not occurred. Then we can compare what actually occurred with what would have happened to estimate the total net impact of the tax changes.

To compute the counterfactual, we used the published data compiled by the Statistics of Income division of the Internal Revenue Service in its annual report on individual income tax returns. These data are unadjusted for inflation, and so differ somewhat from those of the previous analysis. But they do offer a detailed examination of how the taxes were computed, separating out the calculation of capital gains tax from other taxes. The IRS reports that the taxable income of taxpayers earning less than $200,000 (and thus largely unaffected by the tax rate changes) rose 8.3 percent between 1992 and 1994 and that the number of returns reporting taxable income rose by 2 percent. This provides a baseline growth of per-return taxable income of 6.3 percent between 1992 and 1994, the key figure in computing a counterfactual. The IRS also provides the number of taxpayers in each income class. There were 935,530 taxpayers reporting income of over $200,000 in 1992, so the baseline for 1994 represents the income that would have been reported by the same number of taxpayers at the top of the reporting scale in that year.[10] Finally, the IRS data separate out capital gains from non–capital gains income and provide information on how taxpayers computed their taxes in 1994 when the capital gains and ordinary income tax rates were different.

Figure 14.4 presents these data for the three major income groups most affected by the tax rate increases: taxpayers with AGI between $200,000 and $500,000, between $500,000 and $1 million, and over $1 million. The first column shows the amount of non–capital gains taxable income that would be predicted for each group using the counterfactual analysis. The level of non–capital gains income for each group in 1992 was increased by 6.3 percent, the per-return increase in taxable income for taxpayers not affected by the tax rate changes to get the counterfactual level for 1994. The second column shows the actual non–capital gains taxable income reported for each group in 1994. The difference between these two columns represents the estimated behavioral response of taxpayers (in terms of taxable income) to the higher tax rates they faced. This calculation suggests that non–capital gains taxable income was about 7 percent, or $24.8 billion, lower than it would have been without the tax rate hike.

Before we proceed, it is useful to consider the plausibility of that figure in light of previous research on the behavioral response of taxpayers to changes in tax rates. For example, the work behind *The Growth Experiment* estimated that the elasticity of taxable income with respect to the after-tax share kept by the taxpayer was about 0.7. Stated in plain English, that means that if you let a taxpayer keep 10 percent more of his

FIGURE 14.4 Expected Versus Actual
Non–Capital Gains Taxable Income in 1994

Income Group	Expected Non-CG Income	Actual Non-CG	Taxable Income at 36%	Taxable Income at 39.6%	Extra Tax at 36%	Extra Tax at 39.6%	Foregone 31% Tax	Revenue Raised
$200k-$500k	181.6	177.0	61.9	21.9	3.1	1.9	1.4	3.6
$500k-$1,000k	71.1	67.3	15.2	45.2	0.8	3.9	1.2	3.5
Over 1 million	117.3	101.0	7.1	100.7	0.4	8.7	5.1	3.9
Total	370.1	345.3	84.1	167.8	4.2	14.4	7.7	11.0

income after-tax, he or she will report 7 percent more income. Conversely, if you cut the taxpayer's after-tax share of the marginal income earned, he or she will report 7 percent less income. The higher-income taxpayers saw their marginal income tax rate rise from 31 percent to 39.6 percent. About 30 percent of the taxpayers in the $200,000 to $500,000 bracket saw their marginal rate rise to this higher figure while the remainder saw a 5 percentage point rise, from 31 to 36 percent. On net, therefore, about 30 percent of the taxable income in these three groups saw a 5-point rise while 70 percent saw an 8.6 percent rise in the marginal rate.

The increase in the top rate from 31 to 39.6 percent lowered the share of income these taxpayers could keep at the margin from 69 cents on every dollar to 60.4 cents. Using the standard arc elasticity formula, this is a 13.3 percent drop in the share of income taxpayers could keep after-tax. (The same calculation for those taxpayers seeing an increase in their marginal tax rate to just 36 percent was a 7.5 percent drop in the after-tax share.) An elasticity of 0.7 would predict a decline in reported income of about 9.3 percent for those in the 39.6 percent bracket and about 5.3 percent for those who now found themselves in the 36 percent bracket. This suggests that the estimated $25 billion, or 7 percent, decline in the reporting of non–capital gains taxable income is quite consistent with earlier estimates of the behavioral response of taxpayers to changes in tax rates.

Figure 14.4 extends this analysis of the shortfall in taxable income to tax revenue. The third column presents the Internal Revenue Service's computation of the taxable income that was taxed at the new 36 and 39.6 percent rates. The fourth column simply extends this analysis to compute the *extra* revenue that was collected by taxing this income at 36 percent and 39.6 percent instead of at the old 31 percent rate. As the figure shows, the 36 percent bracket collected an additional $4.2 billion compared to what would have been collected on that income had the top rate remained at 31 percent. The 39.6 percent tax bracket produced an extra $14.4 billion compared to having had that income taxed at 31 percent.

But those numbers reflect only the higher rate on income that was realized despite the rate being higher. The behavioral response of taxpayers lowered the amount of income that was reported and the IRS would have collected taxes on that revenue at a 31 percent rate. This calculation is provided in the final column. The difference between the counterfactual level of non–capital gains taxable income and the actual level of non–capital gains income is multiplied by the 31 percent tax rate to produce this measure of forgone revenue. By this calculation, the true *net* increase in revenue collected by the IRS was only $11 billion, the difference between the extra revenue collected at the higher rate and the revenue that would have been collected at the lower rate on the income that was not produced.

A good reality check on this computation can be obtained by considering what the Joint Committee on Taxation (JCT) thought it would collect from the higher rates and what it actually collected. At that time the JCT used a largely static model to estimate the revenue effect of tax rate changes. That is, it assumed in most cases that taxpayers did not respond to tax rate changes, instead simply paying the higher tax rates on the income they would have reported anyway. At the time the legislation was passed, the JCT estimated that the higher rates and alternative minimum tax adjustment would produce an extra $22.8 billion in FY95—essentially the taxes that would be collected on income reported on the returns filed on April 15, 1995, on 1994 income.[11] The alternative minimum tax changes produced roughly $800 million in extra revenue from higher-income taxpayers that year, so the target amount of extra revenue collections from the higher income tax rates should have been roughly $22 billion.

Note that by the IRS's own calculations those higher rates produced only $18.37 billion in extra revenue. The source of the other revenue they expected to receive can be found in the counterfactual. The original

JCT estimation of taxable income for that year actually came very close to the counterfactual estimate in figure 14.4. One can see this by multiplying the "extra" income—$24.8 billion—by the 8.6 percentage points of higher rates that would have been collected on this income had it been reported. The extra $2.1 billion on top of the $18.37 billion produces total collections of just under $21 billion, almost exactly the static JCT estimate.

But note, not only did the IRS fail to collect the "extra"·8.6 percentage points of tax on this income that did not appear due to the behavioral response of taxpayers, it also failed to collect the 31 percentage points of tax it would have collected had rates not been raised. Thus, the original JCT estimates done at the time the bill was passed actually confirm that the behavioral response of taxpayers was as large as estimated in figure 14.4. On net, therefore, the total effect of the higher rates was to add only $11 billion to federal coffers, only about half of what was originally estimated, leaving the behavioral response of taxpayers to offset roughly half of the static revenue gain from higher rates.

Some supply-siders might be disappointed by these figures. They do confirm that the tax rate hikes of 1993 produced more revenue for the federal government. But rates were raised only to 39.6 percent—below the revenue-maximizing level. The more important point is that the dislocating effects of the higher rates were large relative to the extra revenue collected. As pointed out in chapter 11, the revenue-maximizing tax rate is not a good target for tax policy to shoot at. Instead, it is the rate at which further tax hikes are totally counterproductive, making both the government and the taxpayer worse off. The key question is how much worse off is it fair to make the private sector in order to improve the government's budget balance. As this analysis makes clear, as policy approaches the 40 percent rate, the extra burden high rates put on the private sector becomes serious enough to be taken into proper policy analysis.

$$\left[\, 15 \,\right]$$

The Bubble Years

THE PREVIOUS CHAPTER EXAMINED THE EFFECT OF THE 1993 tax rate increases on taxpayer behavior by comparing two fairly similar years, 1992 and 1994. But the world—and the US economy—really began to change after 1994. Some of Washington's changes, such as budget consolidation, which affected interest rates and therefore moved markets, had long-run implications. But the biggest changes happened outside of the Beltway, in two widely different parts of America: Silicon Valley and the canyons of Wall Street.

The economic transformation that happened in America is a story unto itself, but its ramifications for tax policy provide an important lesson about how government finances are related to the boom-bust cycles in the economy. Between 1994 and 2000 there were no additional tax hikes—in fact, there were two important tax cuts passed as part of the Contract with America. The Contract was the campaign platform on which Republican congressional candidates ran in 1994. It was the first time a party used this for a midterm election, an innovation of Newt Gingrich, who subsequently became Speaker after the Republican victory. Middle-class and lower-income American families got a major tax cut from the Contract with America in the form of a $500 per child credit. Upper-income Americans saw a cut in the capital gains tax rate from 28 percent to 20 percent. Although both of these were consequential, they paled in comparison to the more sweeping economic changes of the period.

The best way to show this is with a parlor game of sorts that you, the reader, can try out on your friends, family, guests, and coworkers. It is one of the classic paradoxes of statistics and is shown in figure 15.1 below. The figure shows the *average* tax rate for various groups across the entire income spectrum—from the top 1 percent to the bottom 50 percent. First, note that the average rate for all taxpayers rose by 1.76 percentage points, from 13.5 percent to 15.26 percent—this in an age when no tax rates were increased and some were cut. The reason for this should be familiar to anyone who read chapter 12: When there is real growth in per capita income, taxpayers are pushed into ever higher tax brackets due to income growth, not due to higher tax rates.

The second point, and the great parlor-game paradox, is that the average rate for all taxpayers increased more than for every single taxpayer group. At the top and the bottom of the income distribution, average tax rates actually fell. They dropped about three-quarters of a percentage point for the top percentile, largely due to the cut in the capital gains tax rate from 28 to 20 percent. Bracket creep had its big effect on the middle and upper-middle classes, where rates increased as people saw more of their income pushed into higher tax brackets. In 2000 the adjusted gross income (AGI) for the top quartile of the income distribution started at about $55,000, and for the top percentile (where average rates dropped) the threshold was $313,000. But even for each and every one of these groups, the increase in the average tax rate was less than for the population as a whole.

So, the great paradox is: How can groups—some of which saw their tax rates fall, and others of which saw their tax rates rise by a *maximum*

FIGURE 15.1 Average Tax Rate

	1994	2000	Difference
All Taxpayers	13.50	15.26	1.76
Top 1%	28.23	27.45	-0.78
Top 5%	23.04	24.42	1.38
Next 5%	14.20	15.48	1.27
Next 15%	11.57	12.04	0.47
Next 25%	9.42	9.28	-0.13
Bottom 50%	4.32	4.60	0.27

of 1.38 percentage points—be lumped together and produce a tax rate hike of 1.76 percentage points? It is like having the average of a group of numbers be higher than every single number in the group!

The answer to the paradox is a huge rise in income inequality between the two years. The top 1 percent of taxpayers was still just 1 percent of taxpayers in both 1994 and 2000 but their share of the income reported on tax returns skyrocketed from 13.8 percent to 20.8 percent. Since there is only 100 percent to be allocated, this gain in share at the top came at the expense of someone else. In this case, nearly all of that 7 percentage points of income came from a decline in the share of income received by the bottom 90 percent of the population. The group between the 75th and 90th percentiles (incomes between $55,000 and $92,000) saw its share of income drop by 2.3 percentage points or about 10 percent. The group between the 50th and 75th percentiles (incomes between $28,000 and $55,000) saw its share of income drop 2.6 percentage points, or 12 percent. And the bottom 50 percent of taxpayers, with incomes under $28,000, saw their incomes drop by 1.9 percentage points or 13 percent.

These three lower groups that lost 7 percentage points of the overall reported income had average tax rates in 2000 of between 4 and 12 percent. Those extra 7 points of income were moved up the income distribution into an average tax rate of 27.45 percent—an increase of almost 20 points. Taxing 7 percentage points of income at an average rate that is almost 20 points higher raises the average tax rate for the entire group by 1.4 percentage points—accounting for about 80 percent of the entire increase in taxes. Thus, the real reason for the surge in tax revenues during the late 1990s (over and above the normal bracket creep) was an enormous increase in income inequality.

Figure 15.2 presents the breakdown in all of the tax changes that occurred during the 1990s and the effect they had on revenue. Overall, the average tax rate on AGI rose 2.32 percentage points from 1992 to 2000. This was the equivalent of a tax increase of $149 billion. But as the figure shows, this extra revenue had little to do with legislated events in Washington over this period and much more to do with other economic trends. For starters, the overall economic base expanded smartly. AGI rose almost 75 percent between 1992 and 2000, 23 percent of which was

FIGURE 15.2 Contributions to Higher Revenue 1992–2000

	Change in Average Tax Rate	Contribution to Increased Revenue	Percent of Revenue Increase
Growth in Tax Base	0	354.9	71%
Real Bracket Creep	1.51	96.1	19%
Rising Inequality	1.43	91	18%
1993 Tax Increase	0.56	35.6	7%
Static Capital Gains Cu	−0.77	−49	−10%
Child Credit	−0.41	−26.1	−5%
Total Tax Change	2.32	502.5	100%

due to inflation, the rest to real growth both in income per return and in the number of returns.

Even if the average tax rate from 1992 had remained unchanged, income tax receipts would have risen by $354.9 billion over that period. That's $246 billion more than would have been required to keep income tax receipts level with inflation. So, government is a major beneficiary of real growth even if the overall tax rate remains unchanged. But, as previously mentioned and discussed in detail in chapter 12, the tax code has a way of automatically increasing the average tax rate even as the economy grows. This is true even with a tax rate system that is indexed to inflation, as is the current tax code. The process known as "real bracket creep" occurs because the real, inflation-adjusted incomes of taxpayers rise. As it does, these taxpayers are pushed into higher tax brackets. The effect of real bracket creep during this period created a rise in the average tax rate of 1.51 percentage points, equivalent to a 16.7 percent tax rate hike. That was worth $96 billion in tax revenue in 2000.

Real bracket creep assumes that the income distribution doesn't change, but that all taxpayers enjoy the same increase in their real incomes. When income becomes more unequal, more of it is received by people in higher tax brackets and so the average tax rate rises. This was the case during the 1990s as income massively moved up the distribution scale, with the share of income received by the top 1 percent of taxpayers rising from 13 to 20 percent. The effect of this on the average tax rate can be computed by taking the average tax rates on income in 2000 and applying them to the 1994 income distribution. This would produce the average tax rate in 2000 if the income distribution were the same as in 1994, thereby isolating the income distribution's effect on the average tax rate. This rise in inequality added 1.43 percentage points to the average tax rate, the equivalent of $91 billion in 2000.

At this point a careful examination of the table shows that these economic effects on tax revenue produced a greater combined increase in taxes than the overall increase in income tax receipts over these eight years. Stated plainly, more revenue would have been collected had Washington done nothing.

The effect of the 1993 tax hike can be put into perspective. It added 0.56 percentage points to the average tax rate, the equivalent of $35.6 billion in 2000. This pales in comparison to the effect of economic factors on tax revenues. Moreover, it was offset by the static estimate of two other tax changes: the reduction in the capital gains tax rate from 28 percent to 20 percent and the child credit. These cut taxes by $49 billion and $26 billion, respectively. On net, therefore, simple economic growth accounted for about 71 percent of the rise in nominal revenue during this period, and the effect of real income accounted for 63 percent of the total rise in real tax revenue during this period. The automatic effect of bracket creep accounted for about 19 percent of total revenue growth and rising inequality for an additional 18 percent. The 1993 tax rate hikes contributed only 7 percent of the total rise in revenue, while the capital gains rate cut and the child credit lowered revenue by a combined 15 percent.

Is This a Model for the Future?

Figure 15.2 is important because it shows how relatively minor legislative changes were in affecting tax revenue during the 1990s. As the table shows, on balance they actually contributed negatively to the growth in revenue between 1992 and 2000. But even if we look solely at the 1993 tax rate hikes, it is clear that their effect was swamped by other economic factors. The largest of these was the growth in the tax base, which is a natural part of a growing economy and involves no change in either tax rates or on the real burden felt by the taxpayer. It does, however, increase real revenue to the government, sufficient to keep government revenue at a constant share of GDP. As a matter of tax policy, concern instead should focus on the two major *unlegislated* tax changes that occurred during this period: "real" bracket creep and the inequality issue.

Real bracket creep is an inevitable consequence of a progressive tax structure. If people with higher incomes are going to be subjected to higher rates, it is inevitable that as real incomes rise in the country, all taxpayers will be treated as if they were richer. That means their tax rates go up. But the concept of a progressive tax structure is justified not by some idea about the absolute amount of taxes someone at a given income should pay, but by the relative amount of taxes that person should pay compared to someone else. A look at the rate structure of the income tax since the end of World War II suggests a consensus notion that the elasticity of taxes with respect to income should, on average, be about 1.4. That means that someone earning 10 percent more than someone else should pay about 14 percent more in taxes. Someone earning twice as much as someone else should pay 180 percent more in taxes (just a little less than three times as much).

There are two mathematical exceptions to this rule: one at the top of the income distribution, and one at the bottom. At the top must be a maximum rate. Once incomes start to rise well above the income threshold for that maximum rate, the old elasticity relationship has to break down. Say the top rate of income tax is 40 percent and starts at an income of $400,000 and at that income level tax liability is $100,000. (Aside from some rounding, this is approximately what the current tax structure looks like.) That means that someone making $800,000 would pay $260,000 in taxes: $100,000 on his first $400,000 and $160,000 on his next $400,000. This gives an elasticity of 1.3, where a taxpayer at twice the income pays 160 percent more in taxes. But when the income doubles again to $1.6 million, taxes go up by $320,000 to $580,000, an increase of only 123 percent, or an elasticity of just 1.12. When income doubles again, taxes go up only 110 percent. In the extreme, when income doubles from $100 million to $200 million, taxes only double. That is because virtually all income is taxed at the very top rate, so no "bracket creep" can occur.

The other mathematical exception is at the bottom of the income distribution, where individuals are essentially exempted from paying taxes. The zero-tax threshold for a family of four today is about $40,000. So, below that threshold the taxes don't go up at all—the average tax rate at $40,000 is the same as it is at $20,000 and at $10,000: zero. On the other hand, the average tax rate starts to rise very rapidly over $40,000, as taxpayers go from a zero rate to paying something. So, the percentage increase in taxes is infinite at first and then very high. With a 15 percent bracket, a taxpayer making $60,000 pays $3,000 in tax while one making $80,000 pays $6,000. Between those two numbers taxes doubled—a 100 percent increase—while income went up by only 33 percent. That is an elasticity of 3, not 1.4. Again, this distortion is a mathematical inevitability.

The reason this is important is that bracket creep is *not* a distributionally neutral tax increase. It is focused on the middle class, and particularly on the upper-middle class, because this is where the tax bracket increases are the steepest. Consider a married couple with two children earning $56,000 in 1992. Like most middle-income taxpayers, this family takes 20 percent of their income in itemized deductions and they get a further subtraction of $9,200 for their four personal exemptions, giving them a taxable income of $35,600, all of which is taxed at the 15 percent bracket. They pay $5,340 in taxes. Between 1992 and 2000 their income rises by the average of all taxpayers, a total of 74.5 percent. Of this, 22.5 percent is inflation and is covered by the indexation of brackets. So in 2000 they have an income of $97,720. They take 20 percent in itemized deductions and $11,200 in personal exemptions, leaving a taxable income of $66,976. The 15 percent bracket got indexed up to $43,850, leaving $23,126 of income to be taxed at the 28 percent bracket. They pay a total tax of $13,053, or 13.4 percent of their income compared to an average tax rate of just 9.5 percent in 1992. If their average tax rate had stayed the same they would have paid $3,770 less in taxes—a real bracket creep tax increase of 40 percent!

That particular family had an income in 1992 right at the point where the 15 percent bracket turns into the 28 percent bracket. This is where the tax rate schedule has its steepest jump. It is not surprising, therefore, that this is also the point with the biggest percent increases in taxes from real bracket creep. By our estimates, the group earning $92,000 to $128,000 in 2000, taxpayers in the 90th to 95th percentile of tax filers, had an average real bracket-creep tax increase of 21 percent between 1992 and 2000. That is a substantial increase in effective tax rates on a particular part of the income distribution that was totally unlegislated.

The second part of this issue is the more generic problem of unlegislated tax increases. Even though real bracket creep was the fundamental predictive element in the extra revenue projected in chapter 12 and even though it did contribute substantially to the overall reduction in the deficit, real bracket creep is not necessarily something that can be counted on as an appropriate public policy tool for the long run. In the most extreme case, consider the situation where real bracket creep went on unchecked for decades. Nearly all taxpayers would find themselves in the very top tax bracket!

Suppose, for example, we made no changes in the tax law or adjustments in the tax brackets to account for real bracket creep until the children being born today were ready to retire. Moreover, assume that each year real incomes rise by 2 percent. In terms of today's dollars, real bracket creep would produce $1.5 trillion in extra revenue, enough to eliminate the current deficit. Of course, average tax rates would be much higher. Someone who now has an average rate of 15 percent would have an average rate of 34 percent, for example. So, the unlegislated nature of real bracket creep is not something that a democratic political process can, or should, sustain over an extended period of time even though it might prove useful at ameliorating a deficit problem for a shorter period of time, as it did during the 1990s. While that decade is remembered fondly in the popular imagination, particularly the reduction in the deficit, it is usually forgotten that unlegislated rising tax rates on the middle and upper-middle classes due to bracket creep were a major contributor to this progress. And while plenty of credit is given to the 1993 legislated tax hikes, it is almost never mentioned that the unlegislated tax hikes through bracket creep were nearly three times as important in revenue terms than the legislated tax changes that get the credit.

Rising Income Inequality

The rise in income inequality is also never mentioned in popular re-membrances of the 1990s and the resulting deficit reduction. But higher income inequality was two and a half times as important as a revenue raiser as the legislated tax hikes of 1993 at producing extra tax revenue during the decade. This is probably due to the improved economic con-ditions in the 1990s. When a rising tide is lifting all boats, focus tends to be on one's own improving conditions and not on the fact that the largest yachts in the harbor are rising faster.

Today, by contrast, with stagnant or declining economic conditions, rising income inequality is on everyone's mind. The first thing to realize about it is that *everyone across the political spectrum* is against it. For exam-ple, in 2012 the left-wing publication *Mother Jones* ran an article titled "It's the Inequality, Stupid" with a subhead saying "Plutocracy Now,"[1] while *Forbes* (with the decidedly right-leaning advertising slogan "Capi-talist Tool") editorialized that income inequality was hurting economic growth.[2] And the headlines can get ahead of the facts. The *Huffington Post* breathlessly said, "Income Inequality Worse than in 1774," appar-ently implying that a second American Revolution was on the way. However, the article the publication cited, by Lindert and Williamson, actually ended its analysis in 1860 (making comparison to 2012 difficult), but also found that America was a remarkably equal place in 1774 even when accounting for the presence of slavery.[3]

The second fact about income inequality is that although no one likes it, few have any really effective ways of doing something about it. This stands out most clearly in the decade now under review, the sup-posedly fabulous 1990s. Surely the Clintons would be the first to opine that they opposed income inequality. And yet income inequality rose more during the Clinton presidency than in any other since the Census Bureau has kept records.

Two of the measures the Census Bureau has used to gauge income inequality are compared in figure 15.3, showing that although statistical quirks might affect one measure, the story told is essentially the same. The Gini coefficient is an eponymous measure developed in 1912 and is the most often used in the public literature. The mean-log coefficient is an alternative statistical measure that in many ways better captures the dispersion of incomes at the extremes. In either case, the numbers range between zero and one; the higher the number, the greater the measure of inequality. Over the time period presented, the Gini coefficient rose from 0.386 to 0.469 and the mean-log measure rose from 0.356 to 0.572. In either case, it would be fair to conclude that the forty-two-year time span showed a significant rise in income inequality.

But the question at hand is an essentially political one: the effect of rising inequality on taxes. So, the most relevant observation is that income inequality has been rising continuously since the late 1960s, regardless of who was in office. Although income inequality is often used as a political rallying cry, particularly by the Left, even the most casual observer of these data would have to conclude that income equality is like the weather—everyone complains about it but no one can do anything.

FIGURE 15.3 Presidency/Change in Gini Coefficient/Change in Mean-Log Coefficient

Presidency	Change in Gini Coefficient	Change in Mean-Log Coefficient
Nixon/Ford	+.012	+.005
Carter	+.005	+.014
Reagan	+.023	+.026
Bush elder (41)	+.007	+.015
Clinton	+.029	+.074
Bush younger (43)	+.004	+.051
Obama (first 2 years)	+.003	+.031

If in fact "progressives" could implement policies that would reduce income inequality, would the rise in income inequality have been greatest during the Clinton presidency? Would those eight years really have produced as much of a rise in income inequality as sixteen years of the two presidents progressives revile the most, Ronald Reagan and George W. Bush? Would the first two years of an Obama presidency and an overwhelming Democratic Congress have increased inequality almost as much as eight years of Bush? A fair reading of the actual performance of the Left is that they generally are more effective at redistributing economic activity to the public sector from the private sector than from rich to poor. On the other hand, the Right has tended to view inequality as a nonissue.

This political paradox regarding inequality is made even more complicated by examining state data. The US Census Bureau estimates the level of inequality within particular states in the country as well as for the country as a whole. In 2009 the five most equal states were, in order: Utah, Alaska, Wyoming, New Hampshire, and Iowa. The first three are among the most Republican states in the country. The latter two are currently politically "purple," considered swing states, but historically both Iowa and New Hampshire have voted Republican. Most notable culturally is that all five have a strong sense of rugged individualism and self-reliance built into their cultures. The state motto of New Hampshire, for example, is "Live Free or Die." It is one of the few states without a state sales tax or a state income tax and is well known for being the most conservative state in the Northeast. The individualism of Iowa was well captured in the song "Iowa Stubborn" in the musical *The Music Man*, as the townspeople sing a song to their guests allowing them to "eat all of the food you bring yourself."

By contrast, the five most unequal states in the country are, in order, the nation's capital, the District of Columbia, New York, Connecticut, Massachusetts, and Louisiana. The first four are among the most liberal and Democratic in the country. Louisiana has a complex state political history that includes Huey Long, known for his demagogic attacks on the rich and a corrupt political machine known for lining its own pockets. The political cultures of these states could not be more different from those of the most equal. It certainly reinforces the notion from the national political scene that having a left-of-center tilt in the government does not lead to a more equal distribution of income.

But as social scientists often say, correlation does not mean cause and effect. What the data do is raise the classic chicken-and-egg question: Does liberalism cause inequality or does inequality cause liberalism? Conservatives might argue that liberalism fosters dependency and a culture of dependency will never produce a more equal outcome. Self-reliance and self-improvement, not dependency, are the best ways to advance one's own position. In general those on the Left do not want to acknowledge their failure at addressing inequality when they hold political office, preferring instead to say we just need more of those policies—the same kind of redistribution policies channeled through an even larger government.

But a better social scientific retort might be that it is the inherent inequality in those states that creates a demand for left-of-center government. All of those states have powerful elites in charge of most of the local economy. In the District of Columbia it is the government itself that produces a large lobbying class at the top of the income distribution. In New York and Connecticut it is the financial industry. In Louisiana the energy industry plays this role.

But even more striking about all of these industries is how prone they are to bubbles. Certainly all of these states have seen them. Bubbles create the get-rich-quick mentality that undermines success, among both the successful and those who are not. If one can get rich quickly through a process only tangentially related to hard work, then one can be psychologically prone to believing that it is undeserved. Support for high taxes is one way of alleviating the guilt this must produce. On the other hand, if one is not successful and sees others get rich through what appears to be luck rather than skill or hard work, then the politics of envy becomes an attractive belief system. If this is the case, then conservatives might do well to pay attention to the root causes of the demand for left-of-center policies. And there is nothing more pernicious to undermining faith in self-reliance and hard work than a bubble economy.

Political theories aside, we are left with the ramifications of the bubble economy of the 1990s and particularly its effect on tax revenue. The hard fact is that a major source of extra tax revenue during the 1990s was the result of something no one likes and no one can do anything about: rising income inequality. When this, coupled with unlegislated bracket creep, has an effect on tax receipts that is five times as great as the legislated tax changes of 1993, it is time for serious policy makers to conclude that a rerun of the 1990s is simply not in the cards as a way out of America's deficit dilemma.

Income inequality is really driven by two important factors that policy makers talk about but really can't influence: one generally good for society, and one reflecting social disintegration. On the positive side, the rise in incomes at the top of the income distribution is largely the result of the emergence of new industries and entrepreneurship. A scan of the Forbes 400, for example, shows that only twenty-five of the one hundred richest people in America inherited their wealth, and even of those, most are the children of entrepreneurs who have recently passed away.[4] The rest are founders of technology companies or of retailing firms, or are financial innovators.

On the negative side, rising income inequality is often the result of divorce and family breakup. A simple thought experiment indicates why. Imagine a society in which everyone is part of a two-earner married couple and everyone earns the same amount. Then half of the married couples get divorced but no one's income changes. All of a sudden, the number of households has risen by 50 percent, and the bottom two-thirds of households (those with a single adult) now earn only half as much as the top one-third. Any examination of the Census Bureau data shows that income inequality among families with a given demographic profile has risen far less than the overall inequality in society. Just as with innovation, there is probably little that policy makers can do about this (and society probably doesn't want our politicians legislating in this area). That means politicians are likely to talk about the rising tide of inequality, but unlikely to be able to do anything about it.

Mean Reversion

This also raises an intriguing possibility that those looking for a magic solution to our tax and debt situation should consider: that income inequality is mean reverting. This is a fancy way of saying that history tends to run in cycles. For example, a common measure of income inequality, the Gini coefficient, rose from 0.386 in 1968 to 0.469 in 2010. Does this mean that it will rise a similar amount, to 0.552 in 2052? "Mean reversion" would suggest that income inequality is more likely to drop back to its 1968 level of 0.386.

This concept is particularly true of indicators that run between zero and one, such as income inequality. If the trend were to continue for a couple of centuries, all of the income in society eventually would be collected by one individual. This obviously is not going to happen, and the famous economist Herb Stein had a memorable saying for this: "If a trend is unsustainable it will stop."

Innovation clearly runs in cycles, and so does its economic aftermath. For example, the last great period of innovation in America occurred in the late nineteenth and early twentieth centuries. It became known as the age of the robber barons. New industries and new ideas tend to agglomerate around a single driving individual. This may occur because technology requires that only one approach prevail. Those of a certain age may remember that Betamax competed with VHS as a way of delivering video. Now both are in the museum, replaced by DVDs, which in turn are being replaced by purely electronic delivery. At any point in time, only one technology dominates, and the inventor of that technology prospers. But if innovation slows for some reason, there are no new prosperous billionaires to come in on top—and the wealth accumulated by the old innovators gets dissipated by charitable contributions or the behavior of ne'er-do-well, spoiled future generations. In fact, unless the returns to invention and innovation continuously rise over time as a percent of the overall economy (also mathematically impossible), then at most income inequality from this source will peak and begin to decline.

The same is true for the dissolution of the family. There are mathematical limits to the divorce rate. Moreover, in times of economic distress, family bonds tend to become more important as a means of survival. The family, like the tribe, is a way for individuals to self-insure their economic condition, relying on the successful members of the family or tribe with the knowledge that at some point those members may in turn become reliant on others.

FIGURE 15.4 Income Group/Taxes/Share of Income

Income Group	2008 Taxes Actual	2008 Shares of Income	1980 Share of Income	Hypothetical Taxes
Top 5 Percent	606	34.7	21.0	366
Next 5 Percent	116	11.0	11.1	117
Next 10 Percent	169	21.6	24.6	192
Next 25 Percent	113	19.9	25.6	145
Bottom 50 Percent	28	12.8	17.7	39
Total	1032	100.0	100.0	859

This digression into the causes of inequality is important because of its impact on the prospects for tax revenue from the existing tax system if mean reversion happens to be the case. Figure 15.4 presents just such a thought experiment by considering what would happen to tax revenue if 2008 average tax rates still applied but the distribution of adjusted gross income returned to its 1980 level.

If the distribution of 1980 share of Adjusted Gross Income for each income class was applied to the average tax rate that prevailed in 2008, total taxes collected would drop by $173 billion. The drop would be particularly acute at the top of the income distribution where the share of income and taxes would drop by 40 percent—with a revenue loss of $240 billion. The income "lost" by the top 5 percent would be made up elsewhere, but because the average tax rate in each of those other income classes is less than one-third what it is for the top 5 percent, only $67 billion of the $240 billion in taxes is recouped.

One way of looking at this effect of income distribution on tax revenue is to consider how much taxes would have to be raised just to make up the difference. One approach would be to have a 20 percent across-the-board increase in income tax rates. So, the 15 percent tax bracket would become 18 percent, the 28 percent tax bracket would rise to 33.6 percent, and the 35 percent tax bracket would rise to 42 percent. Of course, this would only restore the 2008 level of tax revenue. The distribution of taxes would be less at the top, as the share of income was lower there as well. If one wanted to restore the 2008 share of taxes paid by the top 5 percent but keep his or her share of income at the 1980 level, the top 35 percent tax bracket would have to be raised to a staggering 57.8 percent. Moreover, one would have to assume that there would be no adverse behavioral response to this much higher tax rate.

So, the story on the income distribution and tax revenue is even worse than the weather. Everyone talks about it. No one can do anything about it. But if politicians actually succeeded in doing the kinds of things about it that they say they would do, it would make the income tax situation much worse. The next time a politician talks about how bad the income distribution is and how he is going to "fix it," he might be asked if he is also willing to raise income taxes 20 percent across the board to make up for the resulting loss in revenue.

[16]

The Bubble Bursts:
Patching It Using
Keynesian Policies with
a Supply-Side Twist

I DEAS MATTER. THAT HAPPENS TO BE PARTICULARLY TRUE over time as lessons learned in a particular circumstance become applicable to an entirely different situation. The key idea presented in the original version of *The Growth Experiment* was that tax policy should be evaluated not just in a traditional Keynesian context or exclusively in the terms of the supply-side theories of the time, but in both contexts. Chapter 4, "The Great Experiment," laid out a rubric for this analysis. It showed that the success of the Reagan tax cuts involved both traditional Keynesian changes to the size of the economy thanks to increased demand and spending power as well as incentive-based changes to the supply side of the economy that increased its productive power.

In January 2001 the economy was in free fall. That was the message to President-elect Bush at a closed-door meeting with more than three dozen corporate CEOs in Austin, Texas. As if to punctuate the importance of their message, the Federal Open Market Committee announced a surprise intra-meeting cut in interest rates. It was to be the

first of many. The equity bubble that had been the single most important economic and fiscal feature of the 1990s had begun to crash. The
NASDAQ, where the bubble had been most pronounced, had peaked on
March 10 with a midday high known as a "blow off top" of 5,132 but
closed at a much lower 5,048. By the end of 2000 the index's value had
been cut in half, closing at 2,470 on its way to a low in October 2002 of
just 1,114. All told, the index would lose nearly 80 percent of its value.
Similar, albeit smaller declines occurred in all of the major indices. The
wealth loss for American households would be nearly $4 trillion.

The effects of the equity market crash were beginning to show up in
the real economy. Growth had slowed to just a 1.4 percent annual
growth rate in the second half of 2000 and was declining at a 1.3 percent
annual rate in the first quarter of 2001. Although no one knew it at the
time, the economy would be hit with another shock later that year—on
September 11—and the economy would have another negative quarter
as a result.

But what to do about the bursting of the bubble of the 1990s was the
salient point of economic decision-making in early 2001. The resulting
wealth loss was the largest since the 1930s. No one knew it at the time,
but the 2000 crash was a precursor to a far larger multimarket crash
eight years later. In hindsight, that second crash resulted in part from
the ease with which fiscal and monetary policy handled the bursting of
the 1990s bubble. Amazingly, despite the crash, the economy never had
two consecutive quarters of negative growth, the usual benchmark for
defining a recession. It created a sense of hubris among policy makers
about their ability to control events. It also led them to forget the lesson
that those very fiscal and monetary policy measures had not been spon-
taneous reactions to events, but had been planned long in advance.

The story of the 2001 and 2003 tax cuts and the accompanying monetary policy response to the crash of the 1990s bubble began more than
four years earlier in the meeting room of the Board of Governors of the
Federal Reserve System on Constitution Avenue. The simple fact is that
the Federal Reserve board knew in 1996 that what was happening in
America was nothing more than a financial market bubble. They also
knew that the economic and financial "party" caused by the bubble

would produce a lot of near-term benefits but incur long-term costs. The economy of the 1990s, and the resulting surge in tax revenue, was not some miracle conjured up with a relatively minor tax change in 1993. It was the result of a decade-long policy of accommodation of a major financial bubble.

At the September 24, 1996, meeting of the Federal Open Market Committee, I unambiguously confronted what was going on for the first time:

> What worries me more is that our luck is about to run out in the financial markets because of what I would consider a gambler's curse: We have won this long, let us keep the money on the table. . . . The IBES earnings expectations survey for five-year projected earnings hit a twelve-year high in August. It indicated that earnings are expected to grow at a rate of a little over 11.5 percent per year. . . . Readers of this transcript five years from now can check this fearless prediction: Profits will fall short of this expectation. Unfortunately, optimism is ripe in the markets. . . . The long-term costs of a bubble to the economy and to society are potentially great. They include a reduction in the long-term saving rate, a seemingly random redistribution of wealth and the diversion of scarce financial human capital into the acquisition of wealth.[1]

Just for the record, corporate profits did not grow 11.5 percent per year over the next five years. In fact, they grew at only a 3 percent annual rate, with the total earnings of the S&P 500, the largest publicly traded companies in America, going from $36 in 1996 to $42 in 2001. The long-term saving rate plummeted. Personal saving dropped from $281 billion in 1996 to $205 billion five years later. Total private saving fell from $557 billion to a low of $389 billion in 2000. The "seemingly random redistribution of wealth" led to the record-setting rise in income inequality during the Clinton years, as discussed in the last chapter, and the political demands we hear today to "do something about it."

Though a review of the transcripts suggests that I may have been the first to raise it, all of this was not some great eye-opening insight to the Federal Open Market Committee. Chairman Alan Greenspan's response indicated as much:

> I recognize that there is a stock market bubble problem at this point, and I agree with Governor Lindsey that this is a problem that we should keep our eye on. We have very great difficulty in monetary policy when we confront stock market bubbles. That is because, to the extent that we are successful in keeping product price inflation down, history tells us that price-earnings ratios in those conditions go through the roof.[2]

Three months later, in December, Greenspan gave his famous "Irrational Exuberance" speech at the annual dinner of the American Enterprise Institute in Washington. This speech was an official warning that a bubble was brewing. The speech took markets by surprise but had only a temporary effect. At the committee meeting a few weeks later I announced my intention to leave the Board of Governors in February and predicted that, despite the speech, "1997 is going to be a very good year for irrational exuberance," to which Greenspan retorted, "Then I will give another speech." I responded, "Don't wait another year."[3]

The irrational exuberance was to continue through not only 1997, but 1998 and 1999 as well and into the spring of 2000. But the nature of the bubble was becoming more and more evident to the world at large. In April 1998 Greenspan and I were meeting in his office at the Fed to discuss my upcoming book *Economic Puppetmasters*, in which he features prominently. The latest issue of the British publication *The Economist* was on the coffee table with the cover story "America's Bubble Economy." The bubble had gotten to a size where it was likely going to end not merely with some minor adjustment in economic conditions, but quite badly.

So the question at hand was really: What do we do now? Greenspan had a wonderful answer. He said, "1929 did not cause 1933; it depends on what you do in 1930 and 1931."[4] Of course in the real-life 1930 and 1931 what the Fed and the Congress did was not exactly something to emulate. The Fed kept credit conditions tight and the Congress raised income taxes as well as tariffs. More important, Greenspan had been making a very important point in his speeches and one that he reiterated at our meeting. During times of technological innovation, the wise thing to do was to allow easy financing to embed the new technology into the economy faster. Doing so would accelerate economic growth sooner, and output would rise. The role of policy, therefore, was not to preempt a bubble, but to be there afterward to clean up the mess.

From that analysis, the idea behind the 2001 tax cuts was born. I had been meeting regularly with then-Governor George W. Bush and discussing the state of the world. Having been an oil man in Texas, he had seen booms and he had seen busts. There was no need to educate him on the adverse consequences of a boom-bust cycle. His question was what to do about it should he become president when the bubble burst. The economic textbooks reiterated what Greenspan had said about 1929 not causing 1933—essentially do the opposite of what happened in 1930 and 1931. So while monetary policy would be in the hands of the Fed, the Bush campaign began putting together a tax cut program that would be ready to be implemented in 2001 to clean up the mess.

Bush formally proposed the tax cut on December 1, 1999, in Des Moines, Iowa. It was an awkward time to do so. The bubble was continuing to balloon; in fact, it was only a few months from its very peak and optimism was at a high. Bush said, "Yet I also believe in tax cuts for another practical reason: because they provide insurance against economic recession. Sometimes economists are wrong. I can remember recoveries that were supposed to end but didn't. And recessions that weren't supposed to happen but did. I hope for continued growth—but it is not guaranteed." This became known as the "Insurance Policy" speech.

During the 2000 presidential campaign Bush's "insurance policy" came under attack as "blowing a hole in the budget." The budget that was actually proposed was calibrated to come in just under the Clinton administration's estimated surpluses for the next five years. But the very idea of an "insurance policy" came under attack from Vice President Al Gore. Asked what he would do if the economy slowed and deficits returned, he said he would raise taxes to balance the budget. My good friend former Fed Vice Chairman Alan Blinder assured me in a debate we had during the 2004 campaign that his economic advisers would never have allowed Gore to raise taxes in those circumstances, but the juxtaposition of those two views is an important one for considering tax policy.

Essentially Bush was proposing a standard Keynesian remedy for a recession—quite literally to do the opposite of what was done in 1930 and 1931, to use Greenspan's formulation. But the proposal had a supply-side twist. In the final tax cut bill the top rate of tax would be cut to 35 percent along with significant cuts to the bottom rate and a doubling of the child tax credit. The idea was two-pronged. The bulk of the revenue reduction would go to lower taxes on middle-class families with children. For example, a married couple with two children earning $50,000 would receive a $1,600 tax cut—equivalent to well over half of what they had been paying. The zero-tax threshold at which such a family would start paying income taxes would rise from $27,000 to nearly $41,000.

The second part of the 2001 tax cut was to improve the cash flow of the small-business sector. The implosion of the equity market had an adverse effect on the ability of businesses to access capital. The bubble had seen the emergence of a variety of new financing mechanisms, such as venture funds and angel funds, designed to help small and medium-size businesses get the capital they needed to expand. These funds were one of the big casualties of the collapse of the bubble. Since 95 percent of all businesses pay taxes at the personal level and over half of all upper-income taxpayers have income from such businesses, a reduction in the top rate of tax was a means of directly improving the after-tax cash flow of those firms.[5] It is important to remember that what is typically considered "owner's draw" in partnerships and proprietorships does not go primarily into consumption, but to pay income taxes. By lowering the amount needed to pay taxes, the draw is lessened, leaving more cash in the company.

What is stunning is how this fairly straightforward, textbook response has been characterized. Two criticisms stand out: first, that this tax cut "turned the Clinton surpluses into Bush's deficits"; second, that this was a "tax cut for the rich." Neither of these criticisms stands up to factual scrutiny.

Consider first the proposition that the tax cut turned surpluses into deficits. According to the Congressional Budget Office, the revenue loss from the 2001 tax cut amounted to $70 billion in 2001 and $31 billion in 2002. Yet taxes fell by $143 billion between 2000 and 2001, and by $382. billion between 2001 and 2002 to just $797 billion.

The reason for the decline in tax revenues was therefore not the tax cuts, but the collapse of the bubble and the resulting economic damage. As noted previously, this preceded the enactment of the tax cuts by four-teen months and even preceded Bush's election by eight months. So blaming it on the tax cuts really strains credulity.

Moreover, a close examination of tax return data shows the powerful effect of the bursting bubble on key types of revenue—particularly capi-tal gains and the incentive portions of salary income, typically stock op-tions. These types of income were, and still are, received largely by higher-income individuals. The bubble was an important part of the "seemingly random redistribution of income" toward these individuals, and the collapse of the bubble put that process into reverse.

Consider, for example, what happened to overall income reported on tax returns between 2000 and 2002. Even though the economy ex-panded modestly over these years, adjusted gross income fell in the ag-gregate from $6.365 trillion in 2000 to $6.170 trillion in 2001 and $6.034 trillion in 2002.[6] The decline in adjusted gross income (AGI) was partic-ularly pronounced at the high end. Among taxpayers reporting at least $1 million in AGI, total AGI reported fell from $817 billion in 2000 to $579 billion in 2001 and $476 billion in 2002. Some of this decline was due to the drop in the number of taxpayers reporting at least $1 million in income. But a similar group, the notorious "top 1 percent," also saw a sharp drop—from $1.337 trillion in 2000 to $1.004 trillion in 2001 and just $986 billion in 2002.[7]

Declining capital gains was one of the main reasons for the drop in reported income. Overall capital gains for all taxpayers dropped from $628 billion in 2000 to $348 billion in 2001 and just $268 billion in 2002. The decline in reported gains was greatest at the top of the income dis-tribution with millionaires, those with total income over $1 million, re-porting a drop in capital gains from $348 billion in 2000 to $185 billion in 2001 and just $129 billion in 2002.[8]

Another manifestation of the bubble was to compensate key em-ployees with stock options. Under prevailing law, the option value of this compensation was taxed as wage and salary income. If the option was sufficiently "out of the money," or above the current market price, this might have been a small number relative to the potential value of the option if the security rose in value. The appreciation in the option would then be taxed at capital gains rates if the option were sold rather than exercised, or the employee could potentially acquire a large number of shares of stock.

Wage and salary income reported on tax returns was essentially flat between 2000 and 2002 for all taxpayers. But for highly compensated employees the figure dropped substantially. Taxpayers with AGI over $1 million reported $271 billion in wage and salary income in 2000. This dropped to $207 billion in 2001 and just $167 billion in 2002. Again the "seemingly random redistribution of income" that accompanies a bubble went into reverse.[9]

But the effect on tax revenue was dramatic. Just the decline in wages and salaries reported by millionaires between 2000 and 2002 would have meant a roughly $40 billion drop in income tax revenue. The overall decline in capital gains realizations between 2000 and 2002 produced a roughly $75 billion decline in tax revenue. These were the overt and direct manifestations of the bubble collapse on revenue. But other taxes fell as well. Corporate tax receipts, unaffected by the changes in the 2001 tax law, fell from $207 billion in 2000 to $148 billion in 2002. In sum, there is no evidence that the legislated tax cuts caused the major portion of the revenue decline at the beginning of the decade. It was the collapse of the bubble of the 1990s that "blew a hole in the budget."

The other common claim that the 2001 tax cut was a "tax cut for the rich" is similarly unsupported by the data. In fact, the tax cut was designed to be progressive at first—giving the largest percentage tax cuts to middle-income families and roughly proportional in terms of tax cuts over the long haul. In addition, the tax cut was designed to favor middle-income families with children since it was presumed that they needed the tax relief the most and that any money they received would be most likely to enter the spending stream. To illustrate, figures 16.1 and 16.2 are reproduced from the Tax Policy Center, sponsored by the Urban Institute and the Brookings Institution.

FIGURE 16.1 Distribution of Income Tax Changes by Percentiles, 2002

| AGI Class | Income Tax Change | | Average Tax Change($) | Percent Change in Total |
	Dollars (millions)	Percent of Total		
Lowest Quintile	−668	0.9	−26	0.5
Second Quintile	−7,489	10.6	−283	1.8
Middle Quintile	−12,385	17.6	−469	1.7
Fourth Quintile	−15,870	22.5	−601	1.3
Next 10 Percent	−11,508	16.3	−871	1.2
Next 5 Percent	−7,143	10.1	−1,081	1.1
Next 4 Percent	−7,491	10.6	−1,418	0.9
Next 1 Percent	−7,860	11.2	−5,950	0.9
All	−70,489	100.0	−534	1.2

SOURCE: Tax Policy Center, table T02-0022, www.taxpolicycenter.org/numbers/content/pdf/T02-0022.pdf

Figure 16.1 presents the magnitude of the tax cut for different income groups in the population, ranging from the lowest quintile, up to the top 1 percent for 2002. The last column shows the tax cut as a percent of after-tax income. As figure 16.1 shows, the tax cut is clearly oriented toward the middle class. Families in the middle three quintiles of the population received tax cuts equal to between 1.3 and 1.8 percent of their after-tax income. By contrast, families in the top 1 percent of the population received tax cuts of nine-tenths of 1 percent of after-tax income. In short, middle-income families got roughly twice as much of a tax cut relative to their incomes as upper-income families.

Figure 16.1 also presents the size of the tax cut relative to the overall tax burden on each group. It shows, for example, that the middle three quintiles of the population received 10.6, 17.6, and 22.5 percent of the tax cut, respectively. These three quintiles got 50.7 percent of the total tax cut. By contrast, these same income groups paid 2.4, 8.2, and 17.6 percent of the taxes, or a total of 28.2 percent of the taxes. In sum, these three middle-income quintiles got roughly twice as big a share of the tax cut as was the share of taxes that they paid.

The reverse was true for the top 1 percent of taxpayers. They received 11.2 percent of the tax cut in 2002 but paid 25.3 percent of the

FIGURE 16.2 Current Law Distribution of
Federal Tax Change by Cash Income Percentile, 2011

Cash Income Percentile	Percent Change in Taxes Ex-AMT
Lowest Quintile	−9.2%
Second Quintile	−17.2%
Middle Quintile	−10.0%
Fourth Quintile	−8.2%
Top Quintile	−9.4%
All	−9.5%
Addendum	
80–90	−8.9%
90–95	−8.3%
95–99	−7.0%
Top 1 Percent	−11.6%
Top 0.1 Percent	−12.5%

taxes. Thus, their share of the tax cut was less than half their share of the tax burden. Since the share of the tax cut was twice as great as their share of the burden for middle-income families and only half as great as their share of the burden for the top 1 percent, it could be said that the distribution of the tax cut was four times as favorable for middle-income families as for the top 1 percent.

Figure 16.2 shows the Urban Institute–Brookings Institution estimates of the 2001 and 2003 tax cuts' long-term distribution (excluding the alternative minimum tax). The figure shows the percent reduction in taxes for each of the major income groups. Note that the figures are essentially even throughout. The lowest percentage tax cut was for the 95th through 99th percentile of the income distribution at 7 percent of taxes paid. The highest percentage tax cut was for the second quintile (21st through 40th percentile) of the population with a 17.2 percent reduction in taxes. A fair characterization of an equal percentage reduction in taxes for all income groups is that it was a "tax cut for everybody." It was only a "tax cut for the rich" in that most taxes were paid by the rich.

The figure also shows the strong bias in the tax changes toward families with children. For example, families with children in the bottom two quintiles of the income distribution received tax cuts equal to 40 percent of the taxes they had paid. Families in the second and third quintiles received tax cuts of 13 and 17 percent, respectively. This compares with the roughly 10 percent tax cuts received by the top 10 percent of the income distribution.

The figure also provides a good segue into a discussion of the second round of the Bush tax cuts, enacted in 2003. During 2002 it became obvious that the knock-on effects of the collapse of the 1990s bubble were beginning to show up in some unanticipated places. The most important was in the pension arena. There, the easy gains of the bubble period had persuaded companies and state and local governments that it was not necessary to continue to contribute to employee pension programs. Appreciation in the stock portfolios of these pension funds was providing sufficient income to cover the actuarially required level of funding in the plans. Of course, the bubble's collapse exposed the underlying problems these funds had. Not only had new money not been invested in the funds during much of the preceding decade, but the appreciation on which the funds had relied had been more than wiped out.

A number of regulatory changes were made, particularly with regard to the interest rate used in calculating the present discounted value of future benefits that bought the funds some time. But without a significant appreciation in the stock market, it would be very difficult for these funds to return to an actuarially sound position in an acceptable period of time. Instead, so much money from corporate plan sponsors would have to be added to the funds that it would impair the free cash flow of many companies. The result would be a negative for the economy since these funds might have gone into business plant and equipment investment instead. This would both retard the economic recovery that was beginning and impair the long-term health of the economy by diminishing corporate investment.

But fundamentally the pension funds would recover only with a recovery in asset prices. The most straightforward means of doing so would be to raise the after-tax return to holding equities. Cutting the tax rate on dividends and capital gains would do this. While this provided a traditional Keynesian-style justification for the 2003 tax cuts, there were also ample supply-side reasons to cut the capital gains and dividend tax rates. Corporate income is doubly taxed—at the corporate rate, 35 percent at the margin, and again when the shareholders receive the profits, either directly through dividend payments or indirectly through share price appreciation and capital gains taxation.

The capital gains tax rate impacts two key economic drivers—the return on capital and the return on entrepreneurship—but is only part of the calculation on both. Consider first the taxation of the return on corporate capital in its most straightforward form. When a corporation earns a dollar in profits domestically, it pays a 35 percent corporate rate. The remaining 65 cents is then either retained by the corporation or paid in a dividend. Typically a dollar retained by the corporation raises the company's value by a dollar, which would then be realized and taxed at the capital gains tax rate when the shareholder liquidated his position in the company. At a 15 percent tax rate, this would imply a *total* tax rate of 44.75 percent on the dollar the company earned.

Now, the shareholder might not sell the stock immediately, thus deferring the capital gains tax. But if he or she makes that choice, the dollar remains in the corporation, where it produces a rate of return that is taxed at the corporate rate of 35 percent. Internal compounding of returns by deferring capital gains tax is not particularly tax efficient, so tax calculations that emphasize deferral as a tax preference miss the point.

On the other hand, if the dollar is paid out in dividends, it is taxed at the dividend tax rate, which currently is the same as the capital gains tax rate, producing a total rate of tax, again, at 44.75 percent. Some are now advocating raising the dividend tax rate. At the 44 percent rate that would prevail if the Bush tax cuts lapsed totally, the effective tax rate on corporate profits paid to shareholders would rise to 63.6 percent.

From an economic point of view, such a tax rate is preposterously high. It would not only not make America the best place in the world in which to invest, start a business, and create jobs, it would make it one of the worst. Even a 44.75 percent effective tax rate is far higher than is economically optimal if the objective is to promote growth in America in a very competitive world economy.

The capital gains and dividend tax rates will be reflected in share prices. In preparing for the 2003 tax bill, we estimated that the reduction in the capital gains and dividend taxes would produce a minimum 8 percent rise in the level of share prices. A recent study by Allen Sinai, one of the leading macroeconomic modelers of the past forty years, estimated that the elimination of the capital gains since the mid-1990s would lead to a 20 percent reduction in the S&P 500 index.[10] Such a change would not only adversely affect the wealth of American consumers, it would also severely damage the already impaired position of America's pension funds. So even though the direct effects of the capital gains and dividend tax cuts of 2003 were skewed toward the top of the income distribution, the macroeconomic motivation for them was that they really were also a tax break for everyone.

Economic Performance

Admittedly it is hard to be fully objective about the effectiveness of a policy action with which one is involved. This is particularly true in this case because it involves both fiscal and monetary policy changes, and I was involved in both. But as this narrative makes clear, the intent from the beginning was that those changes should be combined and coordinated in a way designed to clean up the mess from the bursting of the bubble.

The 2001 and 2003 tax cuts achieved the narrow mission for which they were designed. The economy stabilized and began to recover despite the surprise attack on September 11, 2001, and the exposure of the corporate scandals that had developed during the bubble years. On the other hand, the tax cuts were designed to tackle a specific set of problems, ones that no longer are salient. One of the advantages of time is that it allows the unintended consequences of the policy action to manifest themselves, and it is tackling these unintended consequences to which policy should now turn.

As to the narrow mission, the economy quickly stabilized as soon as the tax cuts hit the economy in July 2001. The economy had expanded at an anemic 0.6 percent in the previous four quarters and promptly expanded to a 2.25 percent growth rate in the four quarters after that. In fact, the first quarter after the tax cuts hit led to the fastest drawdown in business inventories then on record as consumers went to the stores with their refund checks to buy big-ticket items, according to the government's official economic accounts, known as the National Income and Product Accounts. This was encouraged by a wave of patriotic fervor and interest rate cuts after 9/11 in what was admittedly a public relations push by the White House to get the economy moving again after the attacks.

With the passage of the 2003 tax cuts the economy began a trajectory of continuous growth of around 3 percent. There were some supply-side improvements in the economy as well. During the decade 2000–2010, non-farm business productivity grew 28 percent, which favorably compares with the 23 percent productivity gains in the supposedly miraculous 1990s. The unemployment rate peaked at just over 6 percent in 2003 and began a continuous decline to 4.4 percent by 2007. Despite the recession and the tax cuts, federal receipts expanded 25 percent between 2000 and 2008. The federal deficit shrank to $161 billion in 2007 before expanding in 2008 to $459 billion as a consequence of the financial crisis of that year. The cumulative deficits of the eight fiscal years during which Bush was president amounted to $2 trillion, or $250 billion per year, the equivalent of 2 percent of GDP over this period.[11]

But as stated at the outset, monetary and fiscal policies were both geared toward cleaning up the mess of the collapsed bubble as quickly as possible. A key thesis for the accommodation of the 1990s bubble was that it was far easier—and better for the economy—for the authorities to clean up the mess after the bubble burst than to interrupt the bubble. Greenspan described the two constraints on action, one political and one practical, during our April 1998 meeting.

Politically, he said,

> We are constrained by an unwritten set of rules. From where I sit, one of the toughest jobs is to know exactly where we cross the line. We are a central bank in a democratic society that functions under an existing set of laws. We have technical independence in the sense that

there is no body that has the legal capability of rescinding an action we take in the monetary area. But we cannot do things that are totally alien to the conventional wisdom of the professional community.[12]

On the practical side,

There is a fundamental problem with market intervention to prick a bubble. It presumes that you know more than the market. There is also a problem of timing. You might prick it too soon, in which case it comes back, and you may just make it larger the next time. There is also the very interesting question as to whether the central bank is intervening appropriately in the markets. This raises some fascinating questions about what our authority is and who makes the judgment that there actually is a bubble.[13]

Of course, we all now know what happened during the first decade of the twenty-first century. The efforts of the authorities to "clean up" the mess from the 1990s bubble created a new bubble, this time in housing. And if bursting the equity market bubble of the 1990s would have been a politically contrarian thing for the Fed to do, bursting a bubble in an asset owned by the overwhelming majority of American voters would have been even more difficult.

Historically the relationship between household wealth and income has been very stable, for a sound economic reason. If wealth gets "too high" relative to income, then the sales and production that drive the economy become a smaller and smaller fraction of the valuation of the firms and capital that produce the goods and services people buy. This makes stocks and other forms of capital relatively unattractive and they decline in value. When wealth gets "too low" relative to income, the reverse process sets in. Of course all of this is set on the assumption that the central bank is not creating too much money—money that has to find its way into either asset prices or goods prices. We call figure 16.3 the "Double Bubble" chart because it shows exactly what happened over the past two decades to the ratio of household wealth to income. ,

FIGURE 16.3 Double Bubble Chart

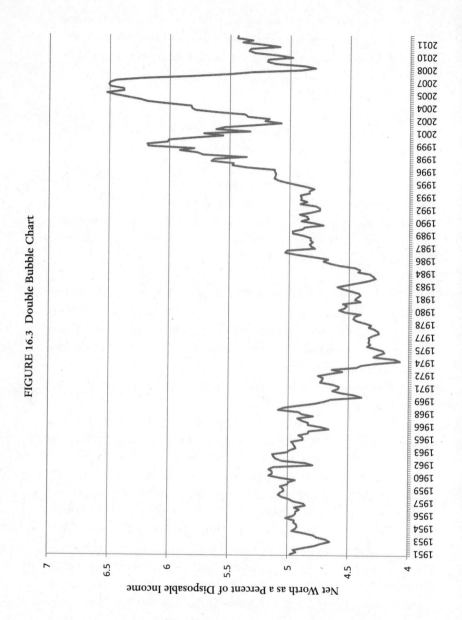

During the 1990s and again during the first decade of the twenty-first century, the excess money creation of the central bank found its way into asset prices, driving up the historic relationship between wealth and income. Fiscal stimulus doesn't cause this bubble directly. It often acts as a catalyst for an economic expansion. But the quality of fiscal policy and of regulatory policy can and probably should not encourage bubble formation.

Therefore, my main concern about the 2001 and 2003 tax changes was that they were not accompanied by, or perhaps later followed by, tax reforms that made a housing bubble less likely. Capping or rolling back the home mortgage interest deduction might have been one such reform. The same might be said of the state and local tax deduction. Regulatory policy constantly worked toward increasing the rate of home ownership and encouraged lenders to provide mortgages to individuals who might have been, at best, marginally qualified. Of course, this is all in the past. The real challenge is what to do about the current problems in which we find ourselves, and how to do so in a way that doesn't simply turn the "Double Bubble" chart into a "Triple Bubble" chart. That is the real challenge of tax policy going forward.

$$\left[\, 17 \,\right]$$

Forward: Deeper
into the Morass

THERE IS NO DOUBT THAT THE AMERICAN ECONOMY IS IN deep crisis. Our nation's deficits are running at a record share of the economy in peacetime and have continued to despite the end of the recession. We are paying for those deficits out of money creation, with the balance sheet of the nation's central bank, the Federal Reserve, having quadrupled in size since 2008. Despite record fiscal and monetary expansion, growth continues to be anemic. This has been the slowest economic recovery since we began collecting economic data, and this is despite the fact that deep recessions are usually followed by robust recoveries.

But there is an equally profound crisis in economic thinking about what to do about it. The models that have driven our economic policy for two generations seem not to work anymore. The issue goes well beyond tax policy. America faces a very fundamental decision about whether economic growth should still be the central goal of America's economic goals. To many, redistribution has become the central goal instead. This is certainly not the first time this issue has come up in human history. While couched in terms of moving money from rich to poor, history suggests that the main redistribution that occurs in practice when political economy shifts its focus away from growth is from the private market economy to government.

Government is not a neutral observer in this debate, and neither are those who make their living directly or indirectly from the government. The legal profession benefits from more complex laws and regulations in terms of billable hours, redistributing money toward the legally well-connected. A market-based world where "your word is your bond" just isn't as good for fee income. Journalists also benefit from the growth in government power; "media" literally means "come between," and the role of journalism is to translate, according to their own worldview, what is happening in politics and why it is important to you. When it comes to redistribution, big government redistributes both money and power to all those who are connected to the Leviathan and away from those who try to live their lives independent of the state. But of course the biggest beneficiaries are the politicians themselves since the coin of their realm isn't profit but power. The more of the nation's resources that flow through their hands, the more they and not the market or the population at large decide what, how, and for whom goods are produced. In economic terms this is the essence of redistribution.

Related to this focus on redistributing the economic pie is the question about just what "economic growth" involves. To many economists, growth is a mathematical concept that simply comes out of a model. You turn a dial and ramp up government spending or money creation and growth is supposed to result—only it isn't happening. American economic policy is now generating a record amount of fiscal and monetary stimulus, yet growth is simply not taking off. This has happened before, as chapter 3 made clear. But it never happened quite to this extent. When a model fails, we can do one of two things. The smart thing to do would be to search for a new model. But that is not always possible while in the midst of conducting policy. So the alternative, which is now being practiced, is to assume that the model works but that the parameters in the model were too low. If we expected to get X dollars of extra GDP from each dollar of fiscal stimulus and instead got only one-third as much, the "solution" is to do three times as much stimulus.

But consider what the word "stimulus" really means in economic terms. It means moving demand forward, from "tomorrow," when things are supposedly back to normal, to "today," when things aren't so great. Consider fiscal stimulus. The government borrows money from the private sector to run a deficit and spends it today. The thought is that the private sector wasn't spending that money right now anyway, so demand is stimulated by borrowing from nonspenders and putting the money into the hands of folks who are all too happy to spend it—the government.

So far, so good. But the government now has that bond on its books. At some point it presumably has to be paid off, which will mean cutting government spending or raising taxes. That will mean cutting demand. In this sense "stimulus" really is just moving demand from the time when the bond will be paid off to the present, when the bond is issued.

In the meantime, there is interest to be paid on the bond. That will mean still more tax collections in the future. That does not mean that borrowing is necessarily bad. It depends on whether the "stimulus" actually "stimulates" the economy. If it does and growth and tax revenue surge, then there are more than enough proceeds to service the debt. If it does not, then all you have left at the end of the stimulus program is a country deeper in debt.

Consider the Reagan cuts in the top income tax brackets. In 1980 the top 1 percent of taxpayers paid $47 billion in income taxes. In 1988 they paid $114 billion. That is a 142 percent growth in income tax collection, or an 11.6 percent annual rate of growth. It beat inflation by 82 percent over the same period. Looked at differently, the extra $67 billion collected from the top 1 percent was able to service 44 percent of all the net interest payments by the federal government. This was clearly a success. The Bush tax cuts had a similar effect. In 2002, the year before the top bracket was reduced to 35 percent and the capital gains and dividend rates were reduced to 15 percent, federal income tax collections from the top 1 percent of taxpayers were $269 billion. By 2008, despite the year's economic crisis, the top 1 percent paid $392 billion, and that figure was down from $451 billion the year before. But even accounting for the crisis, the top 1 percent was paying 46 percent more income taxes than they had just five years before. The extra $122 billion would service 48 percent of total federal interest payments in 2008, and more than cover the $105 billion increase in total interest costs over that five-year period. The key point about both of these examples is that the policy change helped to induce an improvement in the efficiency of the economy that more than covered the debt service involved, but also helped pay for the debt run up by other government programs.

Perhaps surprisingly, the overall thrust of fiscal policy had been essentially neutral since 1965, when Lyndon Johnson delivered his famous "Guns and Butter" speech, through 2008. In 1965 federal debt in the hands of the public stood at 38 percent of GDP while in 2008 it was 40.5 percent. This suggests that, on average, fiscal policy over that period was neutral. Part of the reason was that a good portion of the debt was inflated away during the 1970s. Debt peaked in the mid-1990s, just before the 1995 Clinton-Gingrich budget deal, at 49 percent of GDP. It declined modestly in the late 1990s and then rose back to 40 percent.

Since 2008 the federal debt–to–GDP ratio has grown from 40 percent to 75 percent. That represents an addition of roughly $5.6 trillion of debt from 2009 through 2012. At the end of this period, nominal GDP (according to the Federal Open Market Committee projection) will be less than $1.4 trillion larger than it was in 2008—not a very compelling payoff for $5.6 trillion in deficits. In fact, even if we add up the *cumulative* amount by which nominal GDP exceeded its 2008 level in all four years between 2009 and 2012, it amounts to only $2.1 trillion. So even if we assumed there was no permanent "multiplier" effect of government spending, in which the extra GDP generated by one year's spending carried through into the next year, government *deficits in the past five years have been $3.5 trillion more in total than the amount by which GDP has beaten its 2008 level. This means that the government's spending may have been well intentioned, but it was hardly cost-effective. On the net, the cost of the bailout was more than the forgone GDP.*

But remember, all of that "extra" GDP was merely borrowed from the future. In effect, government has borrowed $5.6 trillion to bring forward future demand to the present and yet has managed to increase GDP by only a third as much. *That means we are sacrificing roughly $3 of future demand for every $1 of demand we are getting today, even if we credit the deficits for the entirety of the growth in nominal GDP.*

Bringing Forward Demand with Monetary Policy

Having examined fiscal policy and its limits, we turn our attention to the other popular form of policy stimulus, monetary policy. Central banks, which are usually quasi-independent portions of the government, affect economic activity by controlling the quantity of money in circulation and by setting the short-term price of that money. The latter is the most normal form of stimulus and involves a reduction in interest rates.

Interest rates are thought to induce current activity by influencing how private individuals and firms contemplate the choice between buying something today and buying something tomorrow. Say I have some money saved up to buy a car. If the interest rate is high, I could leave the money in the bank, earn a lot of interest, and buy my car next year, thereby leaving myself the extra interest I earned to buy something else. On the other hand, if the interest rate is low, there may be very little point in waiting. The more sophisticated choice involves comparing how much interest I will collect with how much the price of the car will rise. If the car is going to go up more than the interest I will earn, it makes sense to buy the car now. The reverse is true if I expect the car to go up very little in comparison to the interest I will earn.

This difference between the interest rate and the expected rise in prices is known as "expected real interest rates," the real rate being how much the interest rate exceeds the rate at which prices rise. Obviously, how much the price will increase is unknown, so what is key to my decision is how much I expect them to rise. Monetary policy stimulus therefore means trying to make the expected real rate of interest negative—making it far more sensible for me to buy the car today rather than wait until tomorrow.

There are two ways to lower the expected real rate of interest. The first, most sensibly, is to lower the current interest rate. When I cut the interest rate a point, the real rate of interest also drops by a point. The second is to change my expectations about future price increases. If I expect prices to rise sharply next year, then it makes sense to buy the car now and beat the price increase. This is known as "raising inflation expectations." Lowering the rate of interest and trying to raise inflation expectations are simply ways of getting me to buy today what I would have bought tomorrow.

Now, let's say the central bank is successful and I buy my car today. What happens tomorrow? The car is already purchased. That means economic activity—or demand—will be lower tomorrow than it otherwise would have been because I have already bought my car. This means that monetary policy stimulus is not a free lunch—the current demand that is obtained through lower interest rates comes at the price of future demand. This is known as the paradox of policy. It really means that from a commonsense perspective, monetary policy cannot be a permanent form of stimulus.

The best exposition of this point was made in October 2012 by then-Governor of the Bank of England Mervyn King. King noted,

> Monetary policy supports demand and output by encouraging households and businesses to switch demand from tomorrow to today. But when tomorrow becomes today, an even larger stimulus is required to bring forward more spending from the future. Since the paradox of policy has been evident for almost four years, tomorrow has become not just today but yesterday. When the factors leading to a downturn are long-lasting, only continual injections of stimulus will suffice to sustain the level of real activity. Obviously, this cannot continue indefinitely. Policy can only smooth, not prevent, the ultimate adjustment.[1]

Thus, the point of "stimulus" of either the fiscal or monetary variety is to smooth out the growth of output over the business cycle. But our current challenges are not the outgrowth of a business cycle. Business cycles typically involve about eleven months of downturn and about five years of expansion.[2] America, and much of the world, has been in a soggy patch now for roughly five years with no end in sight. In economic lingo, this is a structural problem, not a cyclical one. Structural problems must be solved with structural reforms—making the economy more efficient. Monetary and fiscal policy can buy time to make those reforms, and such stimulative policies were certainly sensible as the downturn began in 2008 and 2009. But at this writing we have already "bought" five years with no end in sight. Each year economic growth has turned out to be less than the government forecast it would be. Rather than making the needed structural reforms in education, health care, entitlements, and legal complexity, the president and other policy makers continue to implement more of the same policy changes because they do not want to take the unpopular measures needed to bring about structural reform. Instead their strategy appears to be to take us even deeper into our economic morass by adding one more totally bizarre twist to this fiscal and monetary policy mix: print the money to buy the bonds.

Fiscal Capture and Its Ultimate Dominance over Monetary Policy

Sit back for a moment and empathize a bit with policy makers. Some are blissfully ignorant of the long-term consequences of their actions and are merely doing what politicians always do—take the path of least resistance in policy terms and prepare to lay the blame on their opponents should something go wrong. They are merely doing their jobs as their colleagues always have. Others are very much aware of the long-term consequences of what they are doing but hope to delay that long term as much as possible. Keynes's famous quip that "in the long run we're all dead" comes to mind. It actually has two quite different meanings, both valid in their respective time periods. The first is that when things are bad, we should focus on getting through the short run. After all, it is most controllable and, done right, things may just get better. The second meaning is more literal and is the root of the Paradox of Policy—these policies carried out for an indefinite period will in fact be self-defeating.

The rational policy maker in the latter position has two choices: either resign or try to buy as much time as possible and hope that something positive turns up. So, how does one avoid the short-term nature of fiscal policy when, as Governor King said, tomorrow becomes today and ultimately becomes yesterday? The most direct way is to find a mechanism by which the bonds issued to finance current demand "never" have to be paid off and, ideally, involve no debt-service cost either. There really is only one way to do this: have the government sell the bonds to itself.

That notion may seem a bit bizarre, but it can be done. The purchaser of the bonds is the central bank; in the case of the United States that is the Federal Reserve's System Open Market Account (SOMA). The Federal Reserve generates a liability on its balance sheet—in its simplest form this is "cash"—or a Federal Reserve note. Look at money in your wallet. The promise printed on the bill is that "this note is legal tender for all debts public and private." That means that the government or any private individual *must* accept it by law. Of course, what they must accept it for in payment of is a matter of negotiation. It could take a $1 bill to buy a hamburger at McDonald's or a $5 bill or a $100 bill. McDonald's decides. And if there is too much money around and their costs of labor, hamburger patties, special sauce, and sesame seed buns go up, so will the cost of the product they sell. All we know for sure in terms of value is that the money the Fed issues can settle a *past debt* for the amount specified. (As we shall see, this could be quite an important point.)

What does the Fed's SOMA get in return? It gets a government bond, which is a solemn legal obligation of the US government to repay the holder of the bond the face value of the bond at the date specified, and pay interest at the rate printed on the bond in the meantime. Here's where it gets quite elegant, really. When the SOMA buys the bond, the US Treasury sends it a check for the amount of interest it owes. That interest is the income to the SOMA, and since the Fed's expenses are essentially fixed, this additional income is almost all profit. That whole profit is returned to the treasury at the end of the year. So, in effect, the treasury is paying itself the interest, meaning that the cost of borrowing that money is effectively zero. Therefore, none of the problems discussed above about the need to service the debt come into play.

Then, when the bond comes due, something similar happens with respect to the principal amount. The treasury sends a check, backed up by those Federal Reserve notes that are legal tender for all debts public and private, right back to the Fed! Where do they get those Federal Reserve notes? They could raise them by increasing taxes on the private sector—but that involves the very reduction in demand that is at the heart of the Paradox of Policy. The alternative is that they could issue a new bond, sell it to the SOMA, and use the proceeds to retire the maturing bond. This is known as "rolling" the debt.

Note that the SOMA could roll the debt indefinitely. Moreover, the government could always issue new debt and send it to the SOMA to buy. Thus, in theory, the current practice of running government deficits could go on for quite some time without actually forcing the private sector to come up with the extra tax revenue to pay off that debt. That would mean that there is no real Paradox of Policy; new demand can be created now without ever paying a price for it in terms of a reduction in later demand.

But if that's true, why don't we simply print money? Moreover, why didn't we discover this trick decades ago and save ourselves a lot of anguish about economic policy, not to mention the recessions that happen when there is not enough demand around? Like all seemingly magical ideas, this trick has been tried before. The Roman emperors used to clip some of the gold or silver off of their coins and pretend the coin was worth the same as it always was. The Ming dynasty in China ran a series of experiments with printing paper money to cover government expenses, all of which failed. The most famous example was Weimar Germany where the central bank was actually covering more than 90 percent of all government expenditures with money created to buy the government's bonds.

The truth is, even though money creation buys policy makers time, it is not an indefinite solution. Consider a simple thought experiment. Imagine you are at an auction with dozens of other people just like you, except one of the people at the auction can print money with which to buy the goods for sale. Maybe there are so many goods for sale and the fellow with the money-printing press isn't too greedy, so no one notices. But there will undoubtedly be some goods that everyone wants to buy (think health care, for example). Will this really be a fair auction? Usually what happens at an auction is that if someone bids too much for one item, he or she will have less to spend on other items. But if that participant can simply print money, it will always be, "going once, going twice, sold to the fellow with the printing press."

This is just another way of saying that sooner or later money creation leads to inflation. And if you listen to policy makers, they will tell you that is exactly what they are hoping to do. It goes back to that basic idea of the expected real rate of interest. Japan, mired in a decade-long deflation, has overwhelmingly elected a formerly disgraced prime minister campaigning on a platform of raising inflation to 2 percent. By doing so, he is trying to induce the Japanese to buy today instead of tomorrow and thereby stimulate current demand. The Federal Reserve has made it amply clear that it will resist any deflationary expectation with every tool imaginable.

Why Isn't It Working?

Let's give the general public more credit than it may deserve, and assume that people really understand what is going on. Suppose I am fifty-five years old, plan to retire in ten years, and expect to live for twenty years after that. I've been saving all my life with that plan in mind. Trouble is, the current low interest rates mean that my nest egg isn't growing the way I thought it would. That means that to get to the amount of money I will need to retire at sixty-five and finance my twenty remaining years, I need to save more now out of my current income. But that means I will consume less today. So, the effort to bring demand forward from tomorrow to today may actually work in reverse and cause me to demand less today so that I will have enough money to live the way I want tomorrow.

Take that one step further and consider the implications of that auction discussed above from the perspective of the same individual. He says to himself, "I have read in the newspaper that the Affordable Health Care Act (Obamacare) will begin in 2014 with the government now insuring tens of millions of people more than they otherwise would, and the government has the printing press. Who do I think will win the auction for doctor hours when I am seventy-five and want some medical service that the decision makers in Washington have decided they won't let Medicare cover? My need for health care twenty years from now is not a purchase I can move forward in time. I may even be convinced that the expected real interest rate for health care spending is very negative because the government has fueled medical inflation while the Fed is suppressing interest rates. But because I can't buy future medical care today, the only way I can respond to the negative expected real interest rate is to save even more now!"

The policy of pushing expected real interest rates negative may therefore work well in the classroom or an academic seminar, but it may not work well in the real world for people who are planning their lives. In fact, the effects may be the reverse of what policy makers actually want to happen. Instead of inducing the rational individual to demand real goods and services in the present, this policy may instead reduce this individual's purchases of those items and buy real assets that she expects to hold their value in the face of rising expected inflation. This may be common stocks, it might be real estate, or it might be precious metals. But the resources used to buy incremental amounts of these assets will all be generated by forgoing current consumption of regular goods and services. An economy might therefore witness asset price inflation without ever seeing inflation in goods and services.

There is one more consequence of this policy approach that will have important long-term consequences for American economic growth: the destruction of those institutions whose mission is to provide funds for long-term investments, such as pension funds and life insurers. The business model of these institutions is based on demography, and with the age structure of the population generally known and life expectancy relatively predictable, they can ignore short-term fluctuations in market conditions and target historically average returns over long periods of time. So, for example, most pension funds base their models on a long-term return of 7 to 8 percent. This generally assumes that the economy will have 2 to 3 percent inflation and that real returns will run in the 4 to 6 percent range. For example, during the 1990s the average yield on a ten-year government bond was 6.65 percent. This was viewed as riskless and therefore on the "low end" of the yield structure. Life insurers base their policy premiums on a similar, though generally slightly lower, expected long-term return.

What happens if the country goes through an extended period where riskless returns aren't 6 percent, but are 2 percent? For example, the ten-year government bond yield ranged between 1.5 and 2 percent during most of 2012. Under current fiscal and monetary policies these yields can be expected to continue for a number of years in the future. But the economic assumptions of the long-term saving institutions haven't changed. Therefore, they must take on enormously more risk than they have been accustomed to in order to generate their expected returns, or they will slowly go bankrupt. During the next ten years we are likely to see a pension and life insurance crisis develop where these institutions—on which individuals like the one described above depend—will be unable to deliver on their promises. Will this be handled by a government bailout? And if so, will the government get the funds it needs for the bailout by selling bonds to the SOMA?

This fact may also be helping to reduce demand today—and thereby making supposedly "stimulative" policies not work out the way they were intended. If you are a corporation with a long-term pension plan, this math hits you with the same impact as it hits the fifty-five-year-old worried about financing his health care twenty years from now. The low current returns are forcing prudent corporations to *not* spend today to offset their inability to earn returns on the money they have because they will need even more of it in the future to cover their liabilities.

Fiscal Capture and Dominance

Under current fiscal and monetary policy, there will be about $16 trillion of federal debt outstanding by the end of 2015. The country will still be running deficits on the order of $1 trillion per year. Let's assume for the sake of argument that the fiscal and monetary policy dials that have been turned to full speed ahead begin to affect demand and the auction described above begins to show signs that prices are rising. Under normal practice, the Fed would have to begin to tighten monetary policy. Expected long-term real interest rates, which would be very negative at that point, would have to rise. This would require the Fed to raise the rates it set. When this last happened, beginning in 2004, the Fed raised rates 0.25 point at each of its eight annual meetings. In retrospect, this turned out to be too slow a pace, but it is a good benchmark for what we might expect.

Under this assumption, short-term rates would rise by about 4 percent by the end of 2017, and history suggests that from their current low level, long-term rates would have to rise just as much. Not all of this would be incorporated immediately into current federal outlays for interest since some of that debt is long term. But based on an average maturity structure of four years, we would expect that interest costs would rise from about $111 billion in 2016 to $404 billion by 2020 and $626 billion by 2022.[3] Presumably the Fed would also have to sell its bond portfolio back to the public during this time to facilitate the smooth functioning of its interest rate policy.

Could this be done? Unfortunately, the math is not auspicious. Federal tax receipts might be expected to rise by $1 trillion between 2016 and 2022 even with the faster pace of growth. This means that 30 percent of the entire growth of federal tax receipts would be consumed just to pay higher interest costs. Government spending generally grows about as fast as the economy, meaning that it would grow at least as much as tax receipts in nominal terms. Accordingly, the deficit would expand modestly in nominal terms even though it might drop as a share of GDP. But with interest eating up 30 percent of the revenue, the deficit would have to rise faster than GDP, or taxes would have to be raised even more than is now contemplated, or spending would have to be cut more drastically than is now envisioned.

At first, the central bank would be pressured to continue to buy government bonds to stop the rise in yields. This happened in Europe during 2011 and got worse in 2012. But this signals to markets that the fiscal, monetary, and inflationary situations are simultaneously spinning out of control. When a country literally can't pay both its expenses and its interest bill, relies on its central bank to cover the difference, and is doing so in a period of rising inflation, history suggests that a bond market and currency crisis will follow soon after.

The Bizarre Case of the Fiscal Cliff

This is the morass into which America will find itself as the decade progresses. The context is important as we return to the immediate issue at hand: tax policy. At the end of 2012 the country hung on news about what Congress would do about a series of tax cuts that were about to expire. Chief among them were the so-called Bush tax cuts of 2001 and 2003, discussed in chapter 16. For a decade they had been decried as tax cuts for the rich. But when the time came to extend them for one more year, Democrats joined Republicans in supporting the extension of the vast majority of them.

It was not easy to see why. The president was demanding that the Bush tax cuts for the rich be ended. The total cost of extending the top two rates at their Bush levels was $31 billion. In addition, two other provisions that primarily benefited upper-income tax payers that cost the treasury an estimated $10 billion had been allowed to lapse. Finally, the estimated revenue cost of holding the capital gains and dividend tax rates at 20 percent was a further $18 billion. The total one-year "tax cut for the rich," a group that paid more than half of all federal income taxes, was $59 billion. On the other hand, extending the Bush tax cuts for those making less than $250,000 had a revenue impact of $63 billion. The Bush tax cuts doubled the child credit, a provision that went exclusively to people making less than $100,000. This had a revenue impact of another $63 billion. Additionally, the Bush tax cut also eliminated the marriage penalty, a middle-class benefit worth $9 billion. So, the total one-year revenue impact of the Bush tax cuts on the middle class was $135 billion, more than twice what it was for the rich. Moreover, a one-year extension of the so-called AMT patch, to make up for a failure to index this part of the code back in 1993, primarily of benefit to upper-middle income taxpayers, was a staggering $92 billion. Thus, the benefits to the rich amounted to just 21 percent of the revenue cost of the package of expiring provisions.

With so little factual basis to the "tax cuts for the rich" argument, it is not surprising that the issue was primarily one of power politics, with little real relevance to the debt morass in which the country found itself. The debate got started in earnest immediately after the election and it became clear that the president was not interested in a deal, but he was interested in a triumph. As a result, he shifted his negotiating position dramatically so as to make a deal virtually impossible to obtain. Three issues were involved in the debate: the amount of revenue to be collected, how it was to be raised, and how much spending restraint would accompany the revenue increase.

During the summer of 2011 John Boehner, Republican Speaker of the House of Representatives, met with President Obama to try to fashion a long-term deficit reduction package. The *Washington Post* reported that the two had tentatively agreed upon a figure of $800 billion over ten years.[4] The story goes that when Obama met with the legislative leaders of his party, House Minority Leader Nancy Pelosi and Senate Majority Leader Harry Reid, they told him that their respective caucuses did not support such a deal. Obama went back to Boehner and demanded that the revenue figure be $1.2 trillion over ten years. Boehner refused to agree to this figure and the talks broke down. But the parameters of a deal were established. The bottom figure was $800 billion, and the top figure was $1.2 trillion.

During the 2012 election campaign, the president and congressional Democrats campaigned on a platform of ending the Bush "tax cuts for the rich"—defined as couples making more than $250,000 and single individuals making more than $200,000. The Joint Committee on Taxation estimated the revenue cost to be $840 billion over ten years, within the agreed-upon bounds of the negotiations of the previous summer. In addition, estate tax relief would involve an additional ten-year revenue cost of $130 billion, putting the entire package of "tax cuts for the rich" at $970 billion, right in the middle of the figure from the previous summer's negotiations.

So far, it looked like everything might be in order for a deal on the amount of revenue needed. Then right after the election Speaker Boehner proposed that the government obtain the desired revenue from high-income taxpayers in a way that did not raise tax rates, but broadened the base instead. The White House was caught off guard. Their immediate response was to move the revenue goalpost: $800 billion was no longer enough, nor was the $970 billion that they had campaigned on. Nor was the $1.2 trillion counter offer that had been rejected the previous summer. The new demand was $1.6 trillion in revenue. The point was clear: The president did not want a deal.

Then the issue turned to how to obtain the revenue. Speaker Boehner had suggested broadening the tax base. During the campaign Republican candidate Mitt Romney had suggested ways of doing that to *lower* tax rates. Boehner was offering to broaden the base as a way to get the desired revenue and keep rates the same. The White House adopted a new position—tax rates had to go up. In fact, in early December the president announced that he would not even continue negotiations with Speaker Boehner unless Boehner agreed in advance to end the lower Bush "tax rates on the rich."

This provided a second piece of evidence that the president was not interested in a deal. What was particularly strange was that his position flew in the face of conventional wisdom about the least-cost means of obtaining revenue. I remember my first visit to treasury in January 2001. Scrawled on a whiteboard in one of the offices was the phrase "broader base, lower rates." The incoming Bush appointees told me that the Clinton folks had left the phrase scrawled on the board for their benefit. It was a sign of bipartisan agreement on the obvious least-cost means of obtaining additional tax revenue. But the agreement went even further. A bipartisan group chaired by Clinton Budget Director Erskine Bowles and former Wyoming Senator Alan Simpson studied how to make the budget more sustainable through tax and other fiscal reforms. The Bowles-Simpson Commission had come up with a plan that broadened the tax base and lowered rates, all while increasing tax revenue. In fact, the Bowles-Simpson plan lowered the top tax rate to a 26 to 28 percent range while increasing the progressivity of tax collections. The president rejected the Bowles-Simpson plan when it was presented to him, refusing even to meet with the leaders of the commission when they visited the White House, even though he had appointed the commission. Now he was going in the opposite direction of that commission—and of the opinion of the overwhelming majority of the economics profession—by rejecting a plan to broaden the base while insisting that rates go up.

The final point regarding a deal over the fiscal cliff involved the amount of spending cuts to accompany the rate reductions. The general consensus, including from the Bowles-Simpson Commission, was that there would be about $2.50 of spending cuts for every dollar of tax revenue. More than half of the spending restraint would come from reforming the nation's entitlement programs. The Obama-Boehner negotiations had a similar ratio of spending cuts to revenue increases as their baseline. The president not only didn't propose anything close to $2.50 of spending cuts per dollar of revenue, he didn't even propose dollar-for-dollar. He suggested just $30 billion in spending cuts in comparison to a desired revenue package in the hundreds of billions. Again, there was little evidence that a deal was desired.

How might a deal have been reached that raised $900 billion or so from high-income taxpayers without raising rates? The easiest solution would have been to simply cap itemized deductions at $40,000. The overwhelming tax effect would have been from higher-end households, although possibly one million taxpayers earning less than $250,000 might have seen their taxes rise slightly. A $40,000 deduction cap would allow a taxpayer making $200,000 a $10,000 deduction for a 5 percent state income tax, a $9,000 deduction for the property taxes on a $600,000 home, where the tax rate was 1.5 percent of the home's value, and an $18,000 mortgage interest deduction for a 4.5 percent mortgage on a $400,000 outstanding mortgage on that home, and still leave $3,000 for a deduction for charitable giving. So, even families quite comfortably in the upper-middle class would either not be impacted, or have seen only a very small effect, at most, on their taxes. But such a cap proved to be politically impossible.

The lesson from the bizarre story of the fiscal cliff is that fundamental tax reform for the income tax is going to be very difficult to achieve. Moreover, with the top tax rate now already back up to 39.6 percent, augmented by a 1.2 percentage-point surcharge from the itemized deduction floor and a 3.8 percent tax to finance "Obamacare," the effective tax rate on upper-income taxpayers is already at 44.6 percent. This means that there is very little additional room for revenue to be collected from high-end taxpayers. An additional 4.6 percent increase in the top tax rate, bringing it to 49.2 percent, would yield only an additional $75 billion or so in revenue, even assuming no behavioral response from taxpayers. That would finance government spending at current rates for about eight days. Alternatively, it might be thought to cover just one month of the deficit.

The morass in which we find ourselves comes at a time when it appears that America may be finding the limits of income taxation. Either taxes will have to go up substantially on the middle class, or benefits will have to be cut, or we will need to pursue another path to find the revenue to cover our fiscal profligacy. The bizarre case of the fiscal cliff also suggests that the Growth Experiment may well be over politically, as the political coalition that suggested growth as a path to cover the economic problems of 1980 may have given way to a coalition with different economic objectives: namely to increase the size of government and to redistribute income. If this is actually the case, then we will move further into the morass. As the story of the Great Surplus of '99 showed, economic growth coupled with spending restraint and sensible tax policy can produce fiscal miracles. But the economic growth is needed. This suggests that we would be wise to turn our attention to a different tax formulation to engineer a twenty-first-century growth experiment.

[18]

Pro-Growth Tax Policy for the Twenty-First Century

SOCIAL SCIENCE EXPERIMENTS, UNLIKE THOSE IN THE laboratory, are done in the midst of the ongoing evolution of society. That was certainly true of the original Growth Experiment, which took place along with a fairly revolutionary change in the conduct of monetary policy. As radical as the Reagan Revolution was, it still left in place the same basic structure of income-based taxation that had been set up in 1913. It updated that tax to deal with the problems that had emerged over time that made the old structure obsolete: disincentives caused by extremely high marginal tax rates on an increasingly entrepreneurial society, high inflation and bracket creep, a marriage penalty on a newly emerging demographic—the two-earner middle- or upper-middle-class family—and the need to encourage retirement saving for the baby boom generation.

As we move deeper into the morass, it may be that merely modifying our income-based tax structure is not enough. The debate over the fiscal cliff showed just how difficult those changes are politically. It is also unclear whether any changes will be sufficient to meet the revenue needs we face. As was pointed out in chapter 17, a further hike in the top effective tax rate to almost 50 percent would cover just one month of our current deficit spending. Or consider itemized deductions. Putting on a cap of $40,000 covered roughly another month of deficit spending. We could, in theory, eliminate those deductions altogether and cover less than four months of the deficit, but the political impossibility of doing so within the current income tax structure is manifest. Moreover, by 2020 the government is likely to have about $18 trillion of debt in the hands of the public. Just the added interest cost of having rates be normal, rather than at their current artificially low level of about 2 percent, would add at least $500 billion to our annual interest bill. One would have to both take the top rate to 50 percent and eliminate itemized deductions just to cover that extra interest tab while making no progress on reducing the deficit.

This highlights a well-known political problem. Tax reform—broadening the base coupled with rate reductions—is difficult enough to accomplish in a revenue-neutral fashion. It is likely impossible to achieve politically in a way that increases revenue. The reason comes down to vote counting. Even in a revenue-neutral construct, there are some winners and some losers. The losers tend to fight the reform tooth and nail. Careful political construction of the reform requires producing a far larger—and more powerful—group of winners than of losers to get the package through. But as difficult as this is to pull off in a revenue-neutral reform, it is virtually impossible to achieve in a reform that increases revenue. The reason is simple—the extra revenue means more losers and fewer winners. Achieving critical mass for a coalition to pass the reform therefore becomes more difficult.

The art of political craftsmanship generally tends to handle this through complexity. Key groups that block legislative deal-making get narrowly crafted arrangements to buy their support. The result is that "the base will be broadened except for this special group." An examination of the 1986 tax reform legislation—which did broaden the base in return for lower rates—shows hundreds of side deals, essentially special exemptions for particular pet projects. In general this may well be worth it in order to pass the bill, but it hardly helps the long-term process. The 1986 bill was actually like waving a red flag before a bull—in this case K Street lobbyists and their clients—about the importance of access.

The most obvious example—and not exactly a small exception—was an effort on both sides to undo the lower rates–broader base deal. By

1991 an ill-designed compromise known as the bubble, during which the benefits of lower rates on some income were phased out, led to a new, higher rate—31 percent rather than 28 percent. But this was above the consensus view of the revenue-maximizing capital gains tax rate, which was 28 percent. So, the capital gains differential was restored. President Bush and the Republicans quickly began working, unsuccessfully, for a lower capital gains rate and a larger differential, since the key compromise and simplification of the code—equal treatment of capital gains and ordinary income—had been breached. President Clinton and the Democrats, upon winning the 1992 election, moved the code in the other way, taking the broadened tax base as a given and raising the top rate from 31 percent to 39.6 percent. This ultimately reopened the capital gains debate and led to an even larger differential, with the rate lowered to 20 percent in 1996.

So, the Growth Experiment did not lead to a permanent framework for a sustainable and predictable tax policy. But nearly all businesspeople say that predictability is what they need in order to plan. Thinking outside the box, a reasonable conclusion is that this endless battle over the details of the tax code needs to be truncated if we are to achieve the benefits of continuity and predictability. The only way to do this is to move away from income-based taxation, which invites differing interpretations about what is income, and whether one particular form of income should be taxed more or less than another, to a broader cash-flow-based system in which the "income" concept becomes moot. As they say on Wall Street, "Cash is a fact, income is an opinion."

An income-based tax system inherently produces constant debate, unpredictability, and code complexity. All of these are tied to economic problems that retard America's growth capabilities. Cutting the Gordian Knot of our current income-based tax code might therefore allow an even broader and open-minded look at what our economy actually requires in terms of tax policy to restore growth, employment, and fiscal sustainability.

Three interrelated problems plague the current code: excessive complexity, a widespread and justifiable perception of unfairness, and a bias against the supply side of the American economy. These are in fact interrelated. Complexity is the root cause of unfairness because much of the complexity in the current code is designed to favor one type of income (or group of taxpayers) over another. Complexity also tilts the code against the supply side of the American economy and therefore inhibits growth because, by favoring one type of income over another, the code biases the type and means of production or financial arrangements based on tax considerations rather than on underlying economics.

The political response to unfairness has actually been to increase complexity. Multiple rate structures are instituted to make sure that "the rich pay their fair share." But multiple rate structures mean that the tax-paying unit becomes a challenge to define. This invites all kind of mischief in defining the "family" as well as a need to separate "business income" and "personal income." A steeply graduated rate structure also has invited different income classifications—notably the creation of separate taxation of capital gains and an effort to turn income into that more tax-favored category. This then required still more complexity to define what is a capital gain and what is ordinary income in a way that minimized abuse. Needless to say, none of this is helpful to rationally allocating capital and making decisions about the financial structure of businesses. These are all keys to the smooth and efficient functioning of the supply-side of the American economy. In turn, the need to make up for the revenue loss from the exceptions granted in the code has driven up marginal tax rates and made the supply side of the economy even more tax-driven and less driven by underlying economics.

Of course, the more complex the code and the steeper the rate differentials, the greater the perception of unfairness. In 2012 America saw Warren Buffett, one of the country's richest men, complain that his average tax rate was lower than his secretary's. This sparked the widespread perception that the rich weren't paying enough, even though Buffett's situation was fairly unusual and he himself had arranged his affairs in a way to create his low tax position. It turns out that raising the statutory rate would have done little to raise Buffett's taxes. Moreover, the media coverage focused on Buffett's personal tax situation and ignored the really big tax dodge Buffett enjoyed: his firm, Berkshire Hathaway, was a conglomerate masquerading as an insurance company in a way that allowed him to take advantage of the special tax treatment of insurers known as reserve accounting. Again, the solution was not to fix that underlying problem but to raise rates still more on those whose income was not so sheltered.

The KISS System of Taxation

After three decades of watching all of this transpire, and America dig itself ever deeper into the morass, I have concluded that we need to go back to basics, in what I call the KISS system: Keep It Simple, Stupid! There are three basic rules to the KISS system. First, all money in the tax base should be treated the same. Second, there should be one and only one tax on the tax base. Third, ideally there should be one and only one rate at which the tax base should be taxed. If that is impossible (and given distributional concerns it probably is), there should be as few rates as possible and "gaming" the rates should be made difficult by keeping the rate structure simple. One tax base, one tax system, and as close to one rate as we can get. That is simple.

One single tax base. National income accounting has a concept known as national income. It is the value of all of the economic activity generated by all of the households and firms in the country. In it are wages, salaries, and other types of employee compensation, such as fringe benefits, that are used to compensate labor for the job workers perform. It also includes interest and dividends, and retained corporate profits. What all of these different types of compensation of labor and capital happen to be called should be immaterial, really. One can always hire clever lawyers, accountants, and lobbyists to have the tax code redefine what most people would think of as interest into a dividend or to turn wage income into a fringe benefit. And some forms of income do not fit neatly into any box. Are the products of human capital, such as ideas, concepts, and their legal manifestation in the form of patents, labor compensation or capital? If labor income and capital income are treated differently—and they are in the current code—then someone will be hired to make sure that the income is put into whatever box is most tax efficient.

So rather than think of income and how one defines it, the single concept in national income on which all GDP accounting is based is known as value added. The value added by a firm is simply the difference between what it sells its products for and what it pays other firms for products used in the production process. Consider the very first company I ever owned—a hot dog stand selling hot dogs and soda. The value added by the hot dog stand was its sales minus what it paid to other companies—the Schonland's Corporation for its hot dogs; the supermarket for its buns, ketchup, relish, mustard, and ingredients for sauerkraut and chili; the Coca-Cola company for the cans of soda; the local 7-Eleven where I bought the ice to keep the soda and the other ingredients cold; and the company where I bought the propane to run the hot dog steamer. Finally, there was the cost of the hot dog stand itself, which my partner and I had made by a local sheet metal shop.

That was it. The difference between what we collected from our customers and what we paid out to those other companies was our value added. It didn't matter whether we called the difference wages or dividends, it all came from the same place, and how we divided it up was arbitrary. If the tax code gave us a chance to call some of it by one name rather than another and that type of income was tax favored, we would choose the tax-favored label because it didn't matter to us what we called it.

Note also that all of the money we paid out that was subtracted from the money that came in was paid to other companies. Our expense was their revenue. That revenue went into their value-added calculation. So Schonland's Hot Dogs subtracted the cost of the meat and other ingredients that it bought from other companies to compute its value added. And the company that sold them the meat did the same. So all of the money that we subtracted to get our value added was value added to some other company. So all of the final sales that were made are taxed once and only once in this process—the taxes are paid by that particular company in the production chain that happened to add the value. And the way to determine which company added the value is quite simple: It's arithmetic, the difference between what comes in the door from customers and what goes out to other firms. Simple.

What about governments? They are really companies too, but the money that comes in doesn't come in voluntarily from other customers. It comes in because the tax man collects it. And it is far from certain that all the money that comes in is value added. Some is. Consider national defense, for example. Uncle Sam buys a plane from Boeing. Boeing added value and that value will be taxed to Boeing, and to its suppliers, the same way the stand's hot dogs were taxed. On the other hand, the money the government sends a Social Security recipient isn't value added. The government simply moved money from one place to another. Now the recipient will buy goods and services from other companies and those companies will pay value-added tax, but the Social Security check itself is not added value. The same is true for Medicare and Medicaid payments to hospitals and doctors. Those medical service providers are adding the value, which will be taxed to them. Paying a Medicare claim is therefore not value added.

The value added by government is really the cost of processing all of this. It is the salaries paid to the government workers who sign and monitor the defense contracts, the airmen who fly the planes, and the workers at the local Social Security offices who process all of the claims. Government's compensation of its employees is really its value added, much like the value added by the hot dog stand was paid to its employees. And if those employees were not adding value in the government, they would probably be adding value at some other employer who would be paying value-added tax. Again, it is conceptually quite simple.

There is one other important issue with regard to defining this tax base, and it involves goods and services produced overseas but sold in America, or goods and services produced in America and sold overseas. Consider the first case, known as imports. If I buy a car from Toyota of America, that company may have gotten the car from its Japanese parent. But that parent doesn't pay value-added tax. So Toyota of America should not get a subtraction for that cost. Subtractions for the cost of inputs used to obtain value added are done only when the company the input is purchased from puts its sale into its value-added base.

On the other hand, consider a company such as Caterpillar, which sells one of its tractors overseas. It cannot collect value-added tax from its overseas customer. So, that good should not be taxed to Caterpillar. This is known as border adjustability. It is a standard concept in international tax law. When a good enters a country, it is subject to that country's value-added tax. When it leaves a country, it is not subject to the exporting country's value-added tax, but is taxed by the importing country.

This is a very important point in international competitiveness and it is one that America and its current antiquated tax system neglects. Most countries in the world have value-added taxes. For example, the standard rate in Germany is 19 percent. So when a Mercedes leaves the port in Hamburg to be shipped to America, Daimler (the maker of Mercedes) gets a 19 percent rebate from the government on the good it ships. When it hits American shores the car is barely taxed at all. Its maker paid no income taxes or employment taxes to the US government on its production. Daimler therefore enjoys a huge competitive advantage over, say, Cadillac. On the other hand, when Cadillac ships a car to Germany, current tax law gives it no tax break, and that car is hit with a 19 percent tax as soon as it is off-loaded at the port in Hamburg. Shifting from an income-based tax system to one based on value added will end this discriminatory treatment.

One Single Tax on That Base

The big advantage of having a single tax base is that you can apply a single tax to the base. Many in Washington think of a value-added tax base as an addition to the current income taxes we have. That would be, quite frankly, a crazy idea. Already taxpayers, particularly companies, have to keep a variety of books. One is to keep the Securities and Exchange Commission happy about what a company reports to its shareholders. Call that the GAAP accounts, for generally accepted accounting principles. Then there is the corporation income tax accounting. This involves an entirely separate set of calculations, particularly with respect to how one treats capital investments, such as plant and equipment. But it also involves separate treatment of employee benefit programs ranging from stock options to pensions to health insurance. After that is an entirely separate set of accounts for employment taxes, such as Social Security and Medicare. These are applied only to labor income, at least if you are a Schedule C corporation, but not if you are a Schedule S. Benefit programs are generally excluded from the tax base, but not always. Adding yet another set of books to comply with yet another tax is exactly the wrong direction to go.

The KISS tax will lead to the abolition of the personal income tax, the corporate income tax, and the Social Security tax, commonly known as FICA. It will also end the newly imposed "Obamacare" tax, which began in 2013. That new tax, no surprise, involves yet another separate calculation to determine the tax base on which it is imposed. There will be one tax, and one tax only on income and production. The KISS tax does not necessarily end "user fee" taxes, such as the gas tax that pays for road building, and airline ticket taxes to pay for airport construction. It also does not end the inheritance tax, which is imposed for entirely separate reasons, though it could.

In 2011 the three taxes that a KISS tax would replace collected just under $2.1 trillion in revenue, about 90 percent of the total revenue collected by the federal government. As defined here, the tax base would have been about $12.5 trillion that year. So, a 17 percent tax on the base would have collected the same amount of revenue as was collected under the taxes that the KISS tax would have replaced. This gets to the heart of the question about what tax rate would be appropriate.

Let's stipulate in advance that this is too low a tax rate for a variety of reasons. Among them is that the current tax system does not collect enough revenue to avoid our headlong march into the morass. But there are other issues involved as well. For example, some of the tax base will escape the tax man's collection net, a figure we will assume to be 10 percent, although the broad net of the KISS tax makes it much harder to avoid or evade than the current tax system. But even if it is the case, a 20 percent tax rate on the same tax base would produce $135 billion more in revenue than was actually collected by the three taxes it is designed to replace. The actual tax rate depends on what one considers fair and on what one considers to be the appropriate revenue needs of the government.

A single (sort of) tax rate. The "right" tax rate also depends very much on what the American people will, over the long run, think is a fair tax rate. If Americans come to think a rate is too high or too low, the question of fairness will lead to attempts to change the underlying tax structure in ways that will undo all of the advantages of Keeping It Simple, Stupid. The good news is that what the American public thinks is fair is very much in line with the kind of tax rate that supports the revenue constraint described above. Typically the rate given to pollsters is 20 percent. I have asked that question to many audiences, but I ask it slightly differently: "How many days out of a five-day week should someone work for the government to pay their taxes before they start keeping what they make?" The answer invariably comes back that it is fine to work one day for the government and that is it.

Then I ask the question in a way that makes clear that I am not talking about the people in the audience but about some hypothetical rich person. "How many days is it fair to ask someone who makes lots of money, who is rich, to work to pay taxes to the government instead of working to support himself or herself and their family?" I typically start with Friday, meaning that someone should work all five days of the work week for the government, with nothing left over, and no one thinks that is fair. No one thinks Thursday is fair. No one thinks that working all day Wednesday for the government is fair either. A very few hands go up when I split the work week in half, and suggest Wednesday lunch. But that group typically composes less than 10 percent of the audience. A few more hands go up for the close of business on Tuesday, implying a 40 percent tax rate. Almost half the people think that Tuesday lunch is fair. In short, most Americans think that a tax rate of between 20 and 30 percent is the maximum *fair* rate of tax even for rich people.

This experience, and similar polling data, has caused me to create what I call the Monday Rule and the Tuesday Rule. Ordinary Americans should go home at the end of Monday knowing that they have paid all of their taxes. And even rich Americans should be able to go home Tuesday knowing that they have paid their taxes. Those are the maximum possible *fair* rates of tax.

As a practical matter, these basic rules also allow for a KISS tax rate system that produces more than enough revenue for the federal government. If one takes the base of the tax system as described above and applies a 20 percent rate to the whole base, it produces about $2.5 trillion in revenue. If we take away the 10 percent "slippage," the figure might be closer to $2.25 trillion. Then, to get to the "rich" and make the system more progressive, imagine a monthly income cutoff of $10,000 per month. After paying that basic 20 percent tax on the entire value added, a firm would be allowed to deduct the first $10,000 per month in earnings it paid to any individual worker. So, a worker making $5,000 per month would have his or her entire earnings deducted, and a worker making $20,000 a month would have only half of his or her earnings deducted. All earnings above that amount, plus any value added not paid to workers in earnings, would be put into a separate pot and subjected to a second 20 percent tax.

There is about $5 trillion in value added above the $10,000 per month threshold, or $4.5 trillion if we reduce the figure by 10 percent for avoidance. This figure would be reduced by value-added tax already paid, so the company would not have to pay tax on tax, leaving $2.25 trillion. The net tax collected at this second stage would be $450 billion. Of this, some should be rebated at the low end. One could, for example, maintain the existing Earned Income Tax Credit and give a $100 credit to every worker in America and still be left with roughly $2.5 trillion in KISS taxes, $400 billion more than was actually collected by the three taxes it was designed to replace. This amounts to almost a 20 percent tax increase. It is more than five times the revenue collected by raising the top two rates of the income tax at the start of 2013.

Comparison to Current Law

Whenever tax reform is considered, the big question for every special-interest group and every voter is: How will this affect me? That is why tax reform is so difficult to achieve. Groups whose taxes go up tend to fight it. One political problem with the KISS tax set at these levels is that *total* taxes go up by about $400 billion, based on 2011 economic data. But this is probably essential to escape the morass in which we find ourselves.

So, a comparison by most taxpayers of current law and the KISS tax would make the change look unfavorable on a like-for-like basis. But this neglects the fact that taxes are going to go up by roughly this amount at some point. Government cannot sustain itself unless they do. Moreover, spending needs to be cut from current levels and entitlements need to be reformed in a way to make them sustainable. But higher tax collections—enough to increase tax revenue by about 20 percent—will be a necessary piece of the solution. All in all, the tax increase under the KISS system is designed to keep the distribution of taxes roughly unchanged. A $400 billion tax increase is the equivalent of

$1,300 for every person in the country, or alternatively, an increase of about 3 percent in national income. So, a reasonable distribution test is how the KISS tax increase compares to either of these metrics.

In considering individual situations it is worth bearing in mind that none of these people would have to fill out a tax form. April 15 would become just another day on the calendar. All taxes would be paid at the company level based on the total value added of the firm. The computations below simply extrapolate that firm-paid value added to the employees of the firm to provide a basis for comparison.

Jessica is a single mother supporting her child on $10 per hour, or $20,000 per year. At present, she and her employer each pay 7.65 percent of this in FICA taxes, or a combined $3,060. She pays no federal income taxes and receives an Earned Income Tax Credit (EITC) of $2,561. Under this proposal, that EITC payment would be maintained. Her value added is represented by her $20,000 in pay plus the $1,530 in employer-paid payroll taxes and would be subject to a 20 percent tax, worth $4,306. This would be offset by a $1,000 per worker credit, meaning that her net taxes would be $3,306, $246 more than the $3,060 currently paid in payroll taxes. Note that on net her taxes would still be virtually zero since she would still receive an EITC payment. But the total change in her taxes would be about 1 percent of income, much less than average.

Bob and Joan would be considered a "traditional" middle-income family with two children. Dad works full-time and makes $60,000, and receives an additional $10,000 in untaxed fringe benefits. Under current law their income taxes amount to $2,500, low in large part because they own their own home and have a mortgage interest deduction and property tax deduction. In addition, the current tax law gives them a $1,000 credit for each of their two children. The payroll taxes on Dad's earnings amount to $9,180. Under this proposal, Bob's real value added is $70,000 and would be taxed at 20 percent, yielding $14,000. This is offset, as Dad would get a $1,000 credit. This family's taxes would go up by $1,320, or about 2 percent of their income.

Alice is a mid-level executive in a large firm getting $250,000 in taxable compensation and $25,000 in fringe benefits. She and her employer pay $25,000 in payroll taxes, of which the employer-paid half represents value added. Her income taxes are $60,000. Under this plan, her total value added is $287,500. The first $120,000 would be taxed to the firm at 20 percent, the rest at 40 percent, for a total value-added tax of $91,000, which would be reduced by a $1,000 credit. Her taxes would therefore rise by $5,000, or about 2 percent of her income.

While these tax changes are comparatively minor, some very-high-income taxpayers would see a substantial increase in their taxes. For example, Warren Buffett publicly stated that his taxes were only about 15 percent of his income. During the 2012 election it was reported that Mitt Romney's tax share was about the same. Under the KISS tax their effective tax rate would be roughly 40 percent. Of course the tax would be paid by the companies they own, control, or have investments in. But the ability of individuals to escape taxation is virtually eliminated. First, individuals do not control their own tax arrangements. Taxation is done at the company level. Second, because the KISS tax is based on a very straightforward invoicing system—the difference between what comes in the door and what goes out to other taxed entities—it is very difficult to manipulate.

Pro-Growth Aspects of the KISS Tax

Many economists harbor an illusion that growth is about more spending. That is why they are urging ever bigger deficits and more money creation at the moment. But in fact, growth is caused by something much different—it involves using the resources at one's disposal more wisely. A society can have the same amount of workers and the same industrial structure, but if those resources can be used more efficiently, more can be produced from the same amount of input. American living standards have not risen due to more inputs. We actually each work fewer hours than we did a half century ago, and many fewer hours than at the beginning of the twentieth century. Taxation affects growth because it distorts, and sometimes even camouflages, the most efficient way to do things. An efficient tax system, and most important, a simple tax system like the KISS tax structure, makes the efficient way of doing things more obvious.

Compliance costs. The most obvious example of this is the simple cost of complying with the tax code. The Tax Foundation, a nonpartisan nonprofit think tank in Washington, estimated that in 2011 the cost of complying with federal income taxation was $392 billion.[1] That is roughly 21 cents for every dollar of tax collected. Now in the naive view of growth, spending more on lawyers and accountants contributes to GDP. Of course it does in the narrow sense of the word. But those lawyers and accountants are dead wood. The money paid to them to pull the records together to pay taxes really doesn't make society better off. Growth is enhanced if those resources were deployed elsewhere.

The $392 billion figure is significant. For example, in 2011 we spent $337 billion on all the new homes built in America. We spent $328 billion on new cars and replacement parts for the existing ones. We spent $375 billion on new computers, peripherals, and software. Which do you think contributed more to living standards, or more to American economic growth, the money we spent on housing, or the money we spent on cars, or the money we spent on computers and software, or the money we spent on lawyers and accountants to comply with our tax system? Looked at another way, the total real growth in the US economy in 2011 was $225 billion. Stated differently, the cost of complying with the US income tax system was the equivalent of roughly two years of economic growth.

The KISS tax will not eliminate compliance costs, but it will substantially reduce them. First, households will be out of the tax compliance business completely. They will not file any returns, get information returns from businesses, or keep records on what they give money to in order to determine whether it is taxable. Second, firms who will actually write the checks to cover the taxes will see their compliance costs go down sharply since the data they will provide the government will be data they will be collecting anyway in the ordinary course of business. How much were our sales? How much did we pay each of our suppliers? The need to keep separate sets of books to run your business and pay your taxes will be eliminated.

Leveling the playing field between foreign and domestic production. This problem was discussed above. At present, goods and services produced abroad and exported to America receive very favorable tax treatment. The goods we export to other countries are not. The costs of producing in America are augmented by the high payroll and income taxes we pay, both at the personal level and at the corporate level. Then those goods are subjected to foreign value-added taxes when they hit their shores. Under the KISS system there will be no domestic income or payroll taxes, and the value-added tax collected on the production of the goods will be returned to the taxpayer in the form of a rebate upon export.

The numbers are significant. In 2011 we exported about $2.1 trillion of merchandise and imported about $2.7 trillion. If we take the typical European value-added tax rate of 19 percent as indicative, our exports faced about a $400 billion competitive disadvantage and our imports received $520 billion in export subsidies. That $900 billion difference is a measure of the competitive disadvantage under which our works and the businesses that employ them operate.

This is important for economic growth for two reasons. The first is what we might think of as "catch-up" growth. A leveling of the playing field between domestic and foreign companies will inevitably lead to a surge in US exports and gains for American companies that compete with subsidized foreign imports. The benefits of that are real, but they are temporary. The second gain to growth is long term. In an efficient world, taxes should not determine whether goods are produced in America or overseas, the underlying costs of production should. By eliminating the tax advantages to producing abroad and making the production decision based on economic fundamentals, Americans will focus on producing things where we have the greatest advantage. And basing decision-making on the underlying fundamentals allows us to get the most productivity out of our existing resources.

Debt versus equity. The choice of how a company finances itself is not generally thought of as a central focus of productivity and growth, but the past two decades have taught us that it really is. Our current tax system is strongly biased toward debt finance. Interest payments to service debt are tax deductible to the payer and taxable to the recipient. That means that the net flow of interest payments is a wash as far as taxes are concerned: One side gets a deduction, the other pays the taxes. Of course this can be exploited. Tax-favored or tax-exempt institutions, such as pension funds, naturally benefit from these types of investments since the return is based on the assumption that it is fully taxable and therefore being tax exempt is of maximum advantage. On the other hand, the returns to equity are taxed twice. Corporate profits are taxed at the company level, then when the profits are distributed to shareholders in the form of either dividends or capital gains, they are taxed again. In fact, back in the 1970s the public finance literature was full of papers saying that American companies did not borrow enough. They should increase their debt relative to their equity to take advantage of the relatively favorable tax treatment.

What we learned during the 1990s and the first decade of the twenty-first century was that debt may make sense for an individual company, but it can be catastrophic when it is carried to excess at the economy-wide level. Overleveraged firms and households were forced to either default on their loans or reschedule them, leading to a series of financial crises. Growth built on tax-subsidized leverage and excessive debt is not free. It actually involves a very high cost to society in the long run in terms of financial crises and the recessions that follow them.

The KISS system is indifferent to how firms finance themselves. The value added that produces the funds used to either pay interest or to pay dividends or to retain earnings and thus build capital gains for shareholders are all taxed exactly the same way. That means that decisions about debt and equity should be based on economic fundamentals and the risk profile of the firm, not on tax considerations. That will lead to a more economically efficient form of finance and a more productive allocation of society's resources.

In sum, the KISS system of taxation is probably the next Growth Experiment in taxation that is most likely to lead to productive gains and success. It will not be politically easy. But no successful experiment in tax design ever was. What works most in its favor is that eventually the American people will tire of the no-growth, dead-end morass into which current policies are leading us. As Winston Churchill said, "Americans always end up doing the right thing, after they have tried everything else first."

Notes

Introduction

1. George W. Bush, *Decision Points* (New York: Crown Books, 2010), 441–442.

Chapter 1

1. The consumer price index is compiled by the Bureau of Labor Statistics, US Department of Labor. Although there is some question about the precision of the index, it is easily the most commonly used measure of inflation and is used for adjusting Social Security payments, income tax brackets, and numerous labor contracts for inflation.

2. This figure is calculated by including the compounding of inflation for twelve months. Mathematically it is equal to $(1.014)^{12} - 1$. Multiplying 1.4 by 12 will understate the annual inflation resulting from 1.4 percent monthly increases.

3. *Economic Report of the President, 1981* (Washington, D.C.: Government Printing Office, 1981), 32.

4. This means that prices in December 1980 were 12.5 percent higher than they were in December 1979. On average in all of 1980, prices were 13.5 percent higher than they averaged in 1979.

5. Fortunately, this decline lasted only one quarter. During the Great Depression, the economy shrank 30 percent over four years, or at an 8.4 percent average annual rate.

6. After declining in the first few months of 1980, the M1 money supply expanded at a 16 percent annual rate between May and October.

7. Unemployment data is collected by the Bureau of Labor Statistics, US Department of Labor.

8. The Misery Index is now tracked for a number of countries by the *Economist* magazine.

9. The prime interest rate is set by the credit market. It is a base rate charged by banks to business customers. The quote of the rate is usually based on the prime charged by large New York banks. It rose to 21.5 percent in January 1981.

10. The average weekly earnings in private nonagricultural industry is the index used. It is compiled by the Bureau of Labor Statistics, US Department of Labor. It represents before-tax earnings adjusted for inflation of production on nonsupervisory workers.

11. Measured by employees on nonagricultural payrolls. These data are collected from establishments by the Bureau of Labor Statistics. It differs from the usual unemployment measure that surveys households.

12. To understand this reasoning, the reader should refer to any major introductory economics text. Texts such as Stanley Fischer, Rudiger Dornbusch, and Richard Schmalensee, *Economics*, 2d Edition (New York: McGraw-Hill, 1988) and R. Lipsey, P. Steiner, and D. Purvis, *Economics*, 8th Edition (New York: Harper & Row, 1987) are quite good.

13. Success and failure are always in the eye of the beholder. This author is struck by those commentators who talk about the "failed" policies of the 1980s, a decade that seems remarkably successful. As supporting evidence note that the unemployment rate rose from 5.9 percent in 1971 to 7.1 percent in 1980 while the inflation rate rose from 3.3 percent to 12.5 percent over the same period. By contrast, unemployment fell from 7.6 in 1981 to 5.3 percent as of this writing, while inflation fell from 8.9 percent in 1981 to under 5 percent.

14. The creator of the term is unknown, though it is obviously a combination of stagnation and inflation.

15. Keynes's quip was given in *A Tract on Monetary Reform* (London: MacMillan, 1923), 80.

16. *US News & World Report*, 4 August 1980, 40.

17. Walter Heller, "The Kemp-Roth-Laffer Free Lunch," *Wall Street Journal*, 12 July 1978, 20.

18. Some may say I'm being too easy a grader—on both schools. Here, I'm grading based on results, not on comparison to what the various schools promised. Some polemicists who called themselves supply-siders clearly oversold their goods. But their Keynesian critics should remember that they too oversold their product. Keynesian "fine-tuning" promised to repeal the business cycle, according to many in the 1960s, and usher in continued low unemployment and low inflation.

19. Paraphrased from *Keynes' General Theory of Employment and Money* (New York: Harcourt, Brace, and World, 1935), preface.

20. See a discussion of this in the 1981 *Economic Report of the President*, 57–68.

21. The period is 1982 to 1986. As later discussion will show, the first real reduction in taxes didn't occur until July 1982. Nineteen eighty-six was the last year in which ERTA, the 1981 tax bill, was in effect.

22. The impatient reader might skip forward to chapter 8. Or he might choose to read Martin Feldstein and Douglas Elmendorf, "Budget Deficits, Tax Incentives, and Inflation: A Surprising Lesson from the 1983–84 Recovery" in *Tax Policy and the Economy*, vol. 3, ed. Lawrence H. Summers (Cambridge: MIT Press, 1988).

23. The author gratefully acknowledges the help provided by the National Bureau of Economic Research TAXSIM model. A detailed description of this model and some of the author's contributions to the methodological study of the effect of taxes can be found in Lindsey, *Simulating the Effect of Tax Changes on Taxpayer Behavior*, unpublished doctoral dissertation at Harvard University, 1985. That dissertation won the Outstanding Doctoral Dissertation award from the National Tax Association. The thesis is obtainable from University Microfilm, Ann Arbor, Michigan, (313) 761–4700. Theses are available in hardcover, softcover, microfiche, or microfilm.

Chapter 2

1. This observation was first clearly demonstrated in Martin Feldstein and Charles Clotfelter, "Tax Incentives for Charitable Contributions in the United States," *Journal of Public Economics* 5 (1976): 1–26.

2. For a survey by the Gallup organization, see *The Independent Sector, Giving and Volunteering in the United States: Findings from a National Survey* (Washington, D.C.: Independent sector, 1988).

3. *McCulloch v. Maryland*, 17 US (4 Wheat.) 316, 4 L.Ed. 579 (1819). The actual tax varied with the size of the banknote, but averaged about 2 percent.

4. The concept of excess burden, also known as deadweight loss, is a very important one in microeconomic analysis. The reader interested in more detail with some background in economics might choose a good public finance text, such as Harvey Rosen, *Public Finance*, Chapter 12.

A more detailed description of the problems in measuring excess burden appears in Alan Auerbach and Harvey Rosen, "Will the Real Excess Burden Stand Up?" (National Bureau of Economic Research Working Paper No. 495, 1980). Readers not interested in technical details should think of excess burden as economic costs in excess of the tax revenue collected.

5. Richard Musgrave and Peggy Musgrave, *Public Finance in Theory and Practice* (New York: McGraw-Hill, 1973), 457–458.

6. For a sophisticated model of the sensitivity of the tax base, see Don Fullerton, "On the Possibility of an Inverse Relationship Between Tax Rates and Government Revenues," *Journal of Public Economics* 19 (October 1982): 3–22. Fullerton does not, however, incorporate into his model all the factors that affect the income tax base.

7. According to data compiled by the US Chamber of Commerce Research Center, the fringe share of compensation has risen continuously, along with marginal tax rates, over most of the past thirty years. Their study, *Employee Benefits*, is available from the Economic Policy Division, US Chamber of Commerce, 1615 H St. NW, Washington, D.C., 20067. The National Income and Products Accounts mirror this, indicating a sharp rise in non-wage labor compensation.

8. For historical data on the income tax, see *Historical Statistics of the United States, Colonial Times to 1970*, US Department of Commerce, Bureau of the Census, 1975. The *Statistics of Income* (Washington, D.C.: US Gov-

ernment Printing Office) series by the Internal Revenue Service is excellent and provides detailed breakdowns of income and taxes paid by income class. The 1943 *Statistics of Income* provides detailed data for the early income tax.

9. To preserve a family's relative position in the income distribution, its income must rise in real terms as well as with inflation. Real family incomes have roughly tripled since 1913 on top of the tenfold rise in prices.

10. Most taxpayers earning over $100,000 saw their rates rise from 7 or 8 percent to 64 or 68 percent. The very top rate rose fivefold from 15 percent to 77 percent.

11. Calvin Coolidge, State of the Union, 3 December 1924.

12. The personal exemption for both married couples and single individuals dropped by roughly one-third while personal income dropped 30 percent between 1931 and 1933. Thus, the decline in the exemption maintained the relative position of the threshold at which taxpayers owed tax.

13. The tax collected from taxpayers earning more than $100,000 dropped from $239 million in 1930 to $137 million in 1933, in spite of the 150 percent rise in tax rates.

Chapter 3

1. The difficulties turned out to be more apparent than real. While periodicals such as *Business Week* and *Time* mentioned slowdowns, the economy actually did quite nicely. Still, the stock market was scared. It plunged 27 percent during the first half of 1962.

2. *Business Week*, 9 February 1963, 120.

3. Data reported in the *Historical Tables of the Budget of the United States Government* (Washington, D.C.: US Government Printing Office, 1989).

4. Kennedy proposed a $13.5 billion tax rate reduction in his state of the union address, *Newsweek*, 21 January 1963. GNP that year was $606 billion.

5. *Business Week*, 2 February 1963, 25.

6. *Business Week*, 9 February 1963, 25.

7. Wilbur Mills, Democratic Chairman of Ways and Means, said, "The function of taxation is to raise revenue—I do not go along with economists who think of taxation primarily as an instrument for manipulating the economy," *Newsweek*, 14 January 1963, 15. Democratic Senator Harry Byrd, Chairman of the Senate Finance Committee, denounced Kennedy as "the

first President to deliberately ask for a tax reduction that would add to the deficit" (*Newsweek*, 24 December 1962).

8. *Newsweek*, 2 March 1964, 61.

9. Walter Heller, "The Kemp-Roth-Laffer Free Lunch," *Wall Street Journal*, 12 July 1978, 20.

10. These figures are all expressed in 1965 dollars. Real GNP in 1963 was 633.1. So, normal growth accounted for $44 billion of the $72 billion increase, or 61 percent was due to normal growth. We will attribute the residual to the tax cuts.

11. Budget outlays fell from $102.8 billion in FY64 to $101.7 billion in FY65. Spending growth averaged 6 percent between FY60 and FY64. Had the trend continued, spending would have been $109 billion, or $7.3 billion more than what Congress actually spent.

12. Donald W. Kiefer, "An Economic Analysis of the Kemp-Roth Tax Cut Bill, H.R. 8333: A Description and Examination of Its Rationale and Estimates of Its Economic Effects," *Congressional Record* (2 August 1978): H7777–H7778; also in *The Economics of the Tax Revolt: A Reader*, ed. Arthur Laffer and Jan P. Seymour (New York: Harcourt Brace Jovanovich, 1979), 13–27. Kiefer, who is an excellent analyst, would probably consider himself more of a Keynesian than a supply-sider. But, like most modern economists, he has a philosophy that combines aspects of both schools of thought.

13. See the *Statistics of Income* series compiled by the IRS, which provides detailed tables of the composition of income in these years by income bracket and type of income. The data used here are from the 1963, 1964, and 1965 *Statistics of Income* tabulated by the Internal Revenue Service (Washington, D.C.: US Government Printing Office).

14. These assumptions stack the analysis against the supply-side claim since they presume that the entire rise in income was due to demand-side effects.

15. There was a brief pause in 1966 that some considered a recession. However, data revisions have removed this slowdown from the list of recessions. In any event, the 1966 slowdown was due to a sharp upward spike in interest rates deliberately caused by the Federal Reserve in order to slow down a booming economy.

16. This was nonpartisan. Richard Nixon followed this course of policy with a vengeance. More than any president in memory, he perfected Keynesian fine-tuning to produce a glowing economic situation for the 1972 elec-

tions. The looming inflation was temporarily held in check by wage and price controls. When lifted, a rapid inflation followed by a deep recession quickly ensued.

17. *Economic Report of the President 1980* (Washington, D.C.: US Government Printing Office, 1980), 68.

18. *General Explanation of the Economic Recovery Tax Act of 1981* (Washington, D.C.: US Government Printing Office), 382–401.

19. Strictly speaking, the marriage penalty overtaxed the earnings of the lower-earning spouse, regardless of sex, in a two-earner family, but only a minority of American wives earn more than their husbands.

20. *General Explanation of the Economic Recovery Tax Act of 1981* (Washington, D.C.: US Government Printing Office), 38.

21. Between 1977 and 1981 personal tax receipts rose 76 percent while personal income grew just 57 percent. Furthermore, as note 17 indicated, it was the intention of the Carter administration to continue to use bracket creep to balance the budget.

22. As early as April 1981, Democrats had signed on to a cut in the top rate to 50 percent, *Business Week*, 13 April 1981, 135.

Chapter 4

1. This analysis was first presented in Lawrence Lindsey, "Simulating the Response of Taxpayers to Changes in Tax Rates" (Ph.D. diss., Harvard University, 1985), which won the Outstanding Doctoral Dissertation award from the National Tax Association. It is available through the University of Michigan but, like most doctoral dissertations, should be resorted to only by the inordinately dedicated. For a more readable though still technical analysis, see Lawrence Lindsey, "Estimating the Behavioral Responses of Taxpayers to Changes in Tax Rates: 1982–1984 with Implications for the Revenue-Maximizing Tax Rate," *Journal of Public Economics* (July 1987): 173–206. For those interested in a complete account of the analysis as applied in this chapter, using the numbers that were current when this chapter was written, see Manhattan Institute Associates, *Decomposing the Revenue Effects of a Tax Cut* (New York: Manhattan Institute, 1989). It is available from the Manhattan Institute, 42 E. 71st St., New York, NY 10021.

2. Both the Treasury Department and the Joint Committee on Taxation usually incorporate demand-side effects in their revenue estimates, but the

process is constrained by official forecasts. Technically all treasury estimates assume both that the administration's economic forecast is accurate and that the president's program will be adopted. The committee relies on an alternative forecast, usually that of the Congressional Budget Office. Neither agency explicitly separates demand-side effects from its overall revenue estimates.

3. Economists hedge this answer: Someone who gets a raise may choose to work less, as he is now richer he'll need to work fewer hours to enjoy the same level of consumption. Most evidence suggests, however, that over the range under discussion most people would work more.

4. There might be some additional labor supply, because workers might feel they were better off overall under the new deal. But that would be a supply-side response and any additional revenue that resulted would properly be part of a supply-side effect.

5. See Lawrence Lindsey, "Estimating the Behavioral Responses of Taxpayers to Changes in Tax Rates: 1982–1984 with Implications for the Revenue-Maximizing Tax Rate," *Journal of Public Economics* (July 1987): 173–206. A brief summary is in order here: Each income item in each of the 34,000 tax returns is increased by the growth in that item, per tax return, in the overall economy. For example, if the per-return level of wages rose 20 percent, then the reported wages on each return are increased 20 percent. The same procedure is repeated for wages, interest, dividends, capital gains, business income, farm income, unemployment compensation, and partnership income. A similar procedure is performed for itemized deductions in order to sort out changes in the income distribution caused by a rise in interest rates or unemployment, as distinct from tax-induced changes in taxpayer behavior. Each tax return is given a "sample weight" reflecting how many of the roughly 95 million total returns it represents. These sample weights are adjusted to reflect changes in the number of returns filed. Similar sample weight adjustments are made to returns receiving unemployment compensation in order to reflect changes in the unemployment rate. The extrapolation thus resembles as closely as possible the changes in macroeconomic conditions between the year of the sample (1979) and the years simulated (1981–85).

6. Otto Eckstein, *The DRI Model of the US Economy* (New York: McGraw-Hill, 1983), xx, 37.

7. See Gary Burtlass and Jerry Hausman, "The Effect of Taxation on Labor Supply: Evaluating the Gary Negative Income Tax Experiment," *Journal*

of Political Economy 6 (December 1986): 1103–30; Michael Boskin, "The Economics of Labor Supply," and Robert Hall, "Wages, Income, and Hours of the US Labor Force," in *Income Maintenance and Labor Supply*, ed. G. Cain and H. Watts (Chicago: Markham, 1973), 101–62; M. Kosters, "Effects of an Income Tax on Labor Supply," in *The Taxation of Income From Capital*, ed. Arnold Harberger and Michael Bailey (Washington, D.C.: Brookings Institution, 1967), 301–24; Harvey Rosen, "Taxes in a Labor Supply Model with Joint Wages-Hours Determination," *Econometric* 44, no. 3 (May 1976): 485ff.; Jerry Hausman, "Stochastic Problems in the Simulation of Labor Supply," in *Behavioral Simulation Methods in Tax Policy Analysis*, ed. Martin Feldstein (Chicago: University of Chicago Press, 1983), 47–82.

8. For a complete description of this test of the behavioral responses, see Lawrence Lindsey, "Did ERTA Raise the Share of Taxes Paid by Upper-Income Taxpayers? Will TRA86 Be a Repeat?" in *Tax Policy and the Economy*, ed. Lawrence H. Summers (Cambridge: MIT Press, 1988), 131–160.

9. Robert W. Turner, *The Effect of Taxes on Fringe Share of Compensation*, Colgate University Department of Economics Discussion Paper 88–05. Turner also wrote "Are Taxes Responsible for the Growth of Fringe Benefits?" *National Tax Journal* 40 (June 1987): 205–220.

10. The pecuniary effect has been the focus of some research. Lindsey's *Journal of Public Economics* article, as well as a series of pieces in *Tax Notes* (17 March 1986; 13 October 1986; and 4 May 1987) all focus on the pecuniary effect: "Estimating the Behavioral Response of Taxpayers to Changes in Tax Rates: 1982–84 with Implications for the Revenue Maximizing Rate," *Journal of Public Economics*, (July 1987): 173–206; "Criticizing the CBO Analysis of ERTA's Effect on the Distribution of Income and Taxes," *Tax Notes* (4 May 1987): 491–96; "Revenue Response to the 1982 Personal Tax Cuts—A Reply," *Tax Notes* (13 October 1986): 197–200; "Revenue Response to the 1982 Tax Cuts," *Tax Notes* (17 March 1986): 1157–1161.

11. This number may seem high as a figure for real returns but is consistent with current estimates; return on business investment by definition must be somewhat higher than the real rate on corporate bonds.

Chapter 5

1. The definition of "rich," like so much else, is in the eye of the beholder. According to income tax data, in 1981 the top 1 percent made $85,000 or

more. The top 10 percent made $38,000 or more. While "rich" on a relative basis, much of this latter group probably considered itself decidedly middle class. Since the entire rich-and-poor argument is a matter of appearances rather than fact, this discussion shall leave the definition of "rich" to the reader unless an explicit fact is being stated.

2. The poverty rate is the percent of the population living in families earning less than the poverty level. It is an admittedly imperfect measure. It is based on an index established by a federal interagency committee and is updated annually based on the consumer price index. Details can be found in the Commerce Department's Current Population Reports, series P-60, no. 160 (Washington, D.C.: US Government Printing Office). Since the poverty rate is the statistic most often used by Reagan critics, it is examined in further detail here.

3. Congressional Budget Office, "CBO Replies to Lindsey," *Tax Notes* (May 1987): 501. The CBO analysis focused only on the pecuniary effect and ignored the demand-side and supply-side effects discussed here.

4. The tax rate increase from 28 percent to 33 percent lowers the after-tax share received by taxpayers from 72 cents to 67 cents for each dollar earned. Lindsey, *Journal of Public Economics*, July 1987, found that a 7 percent cut in after-tax shares could easily cause a 10 percent shrinkage of the base.

Chapter 6

1. *Newsweek*, 2 March 1981, 24.

2. *Newsweek*, 2 March 1981, 34.

3. These data are for calendar years as compiled by the Bureau of Economic Analysis, US Department of Commerce. They reflect National Income and Product Account accounting, not budgetary accounting, though these differences are relatively minor.

4. Here, unlike the previous chapters, there is no "counterfactual" to worry about. We are looking at what actually occurred and comparing those events with history. Shares of GNP are used to make the historical comparisons meaningful. Not only does this avoid the problem that all numbers tend to go up over time, but percent of GNP is the standard measure of the amount of fiscal stimulus that a tax cut or spending increase involves.

5. In 1944, at the height of World War II, federal taxes still took only 19.4 percent of GNP. The only higher year was 1969, when federal receipts took 20.7 percent of GNP.

6. The Vietnam War had contributed only modestly to this figure; in the Kennedy years prior to Vietnam, defense spending already averaged 8.9 percent of GNP.

7. The author does not claim expertise in judging the efficacy of such expenditures. However, recent events around the world suggest that the money invested in defense has paid big dividends in advancing the cause of liberty.

8. These figures were calculated by taking the change in the deficit caused by these factors in each year and paying interest on them at the six-month T-bill rate.

9. *America's New Beginning: A Program for Economic Recovery* (Washington, D.C.: US Government Printing Office, 18 February 1981) includes a presidential address to the Congress and a detailed set of budget proposals.

10. *1983 Budget of the United States* (Washington, D.C.: US Government Printing Office, 1983), 3–6.

11. Reagan had called for total non-defense spending of 14.3 percent of GNP and 6.1 percent for defense. In fact, defense ended at 6.3 percent and non-defense at 18.2 percent. A small part of the reason for the higher shares of GNP was the recession of 1982, which produced a lower GNP in FY83.

Chapter 7

1. Both World War II and Korea involved single years of double-digit consumer price inflation, measured either year over year or December to December. The 1974 inflation similarly was in double digits for only a single year. The Carter inflation was in double digits for two years on a December-to-December basis and three years on a year-over-year basis.

2. *US News & World Report*, 4 August 1980, 40.

3. Walter Heller, "The Kemp-Roth-Laffer Free Lunch," *Wall Street Journal*, 12 July 1978, 20.

4. *US News & World Report*, 7 July 1980, 23.

5. We select this period as it represents the years that ERTA was in effect.

6. This equation is also expressed as MV = PT where T represents transactions.

7. The very astute reader might note that many checking accounts—called NOW accounts—do pay interest. There is some indication that the advent of NOW accounts changed the relationship between money and

interest. In fact, the definition of M1 was changed to reflect this. That is one of the reasons we use M2 in this exposition.

8. For example, between the end of 1982 and the end of 1986, the ratio of cash and checking account balances to money market fund balances rose from 1.67 to 1.91. The same period was one of sharply falling interest rates.

9. Over the same period, 1982–86, nonfinancial corporate businesses doubled their cash and checking deposits while the money market balances remained unchanged.

10. Federal Reserve Board, *Balance Sheets of the US Economy*. It is summarized in the *Economic Report of the President 1989*, table B.29.

11. See also Mankiw-Summers, "Money Demand and the Effects of Fiscal Policy," *Journal of Money Credit and Banking* (November 1986): 415–429.

12. This fact is certainly contrary to the conventional wisdom that the Reagan recovery was financed by massive consumer borrowing. The net borrowing by individuals in 1983, the first year of the recovery, was only 10.5 percent of personal income. In 1979 it was 13.6 percent of personal income. The "red ink" hypothesis will be discussed more in chapter 8.

13. The price of imports actually fell 8 percent between 1981 and 1986. The reason that the price didn't fall 64 percent was that foreign inflation pushed up production costs. The fact is the dollar's rise exceeded this foreign inflation, thereby causing a reduction in the dollar cost of imports.

14. The figure is obtained by multiplying the 11 percent share of imports by the 64 percent appreciation of the dollar. This is of course an oversimplification. Had the dollar not risen, both our GNP and our level of imports would have been different. However, it is unclear which direction the oversimplification biases the result. The import share in 1980, with a lower dollar, was actually higher than in 1985.

15. This is the proper period to analyze: 1973 and 1981 were both business cycle peaks. It is too early to tell whether 1989 was also a business cycle peak.

Chapter 8

1. Martin Feldstein and Douglas Elmendorf, "Budget Deficits, Tax Incentive, and Inflation: A Surprising Lesson from the 1983–84 Recovery," in *Tax Policy and the Economy*, vol. 3, ed. Lawrence H. Summers (Cambridge: MIT Press, 1988). This careful comparative study is the source of many of the facts presented here.

2. The economic literature on this problem is quite extensive. Particular academic attention was paid to this issue during the late 1970s and early 1980s when inflation was so high. Alan Auerbach and Dale Jorgenson wrote a very interesting and quite readable article, "Inflation-Proof Depreciation of Assets," *Harvard Business Review* 58 (1980): 113–18. The early analysis of this issue is provided by Robert Hall and Dale Jorgenson in "Tax Policy and Investment Behavior," *American Economic Review*, 57 (June 1967): 391–414.

3. For some critical detail on this issue some good sources are Jane Gravelle's "Effects of the 1981 Depreciation Revisions on the Taxation of Income from Business Capital," *National Tax Journal* 35 (March 1982): 1–20; Don Fullerton and Yolanda Henderson's "Investment Effects of Taxes on Income from Capital: Alternative Policies in the 1980s" in *The Legacy of Reagonomics: Prospects for Long-Term Growth*, ed. Charles Hulten and Thomas Sawhill (Washington, D.C.: Urban Institute Press, 1984).

The best summary volume is Mervyn King and Don Fullerton, eds., *The Taxation of Income from Capital* (Chicago: University of Chicago Press, 1984).

4. These data come from the 1982 *Economic Report of the President*, pp. 122–125. Table 5.3 provides the real after-tax return needed to make a 4 percent real hurdle. The hurdle rate presented here is obtained by adding the inflation rate to this real hurdle rate.

5. Feldstein and Elmendorf, "Budget Deficits," 12.

6. Some economists overlook this because they use figures that are not adjusted for inflation. For a wide variety of reasons the price of investment goods actually declined in the early 1980s while the price of most other goods continued to rise.

7. Steven F. Venti and David A. Wise, "The Determinants of IRA Contributions and the Effects of Limit Changes," in *Pensions and the US Economy*, ed. Zvi Bodie, John Shoven, and David Wise (Chicago: University of Chicago Press, 1988).

8. Popular belief is that the effect was horrible, so it isn't too hard for the facts to indicate a better result. Our purpose here is not to argue that Americans should save more. Rather, it is to point out that the doomsayers are quite wide off the mark.

9. Much of the gain in the value of the house is due to inflation. The individual is not richer to the extent of the inflation. What we do here is to take the inflationary gains into account by reducing the value of the house, and

other assets, by the rise in the consumer price index. This captures the real increase in the individual's wealth without counting the inflation.

10. *Balance Sheets for the US Economy* are obtainable from the Board of Governors of the Federal Reserve System, Washington, D.C. 20551.

11. These data were computed by taking the nominal net worth of households at the end of each year as calculated by the Fed and dividing by the consumer price index to get real net worth. Changes in real net worth represent the real saving of the household sector. This divided by real personal income provides the saving rate.

12. Internally generated funds as calculated by the Federal Reserve.

Chapter 9

1. *Wall Street Journal*, 17 March 1988.

2. Data compiled by the British Treasury is available from the Adam Smith Institute, 23 Great Smith St., London SW1P 3BL.

3. *The Economist*, 18 March 1989, 14.

4. Much of this discussion appeared in an article by your author in "Socialism and the Supply Side in Sweden," *Wall Street Journal*, 6 June 1988, European edition.

5. The expert on this subject is Alan Reynolds of Polyconomics, Morristown, New Jersey, who has written numerous articles on this subject.

6. "US Tax Cuts Go Global," *Fortune*, 29 November 1986, 131.

Chapter 10

1. *US News and World Report*, 3 March 1986, 50.

2. See Martin Feldstein, ed., *The Effects of Taxation on Capital Accumulation* (Chicago: University of Chicago Press, 1989); one of the best compendiums of serious research in this area, it is a compilation of papers given at a conference sponsored by the National Bureau of Economic Research in the midst of the debate over tax reform, February 1986.

3. *The Tax Reform Act of 1986* P.L. 99–514, 22 Oct. 1986, 2687.

4. Ibid., 2687.

5. The 33 percent bracket was created to raise the average tax rate on the rich to the level of the top marginal rate of 28 percent. To do this, zero-rated and low-rated income had to be taxed at higher rates. To do this, the "tax savings" from having part of one's income in the 15 percent bracket and the per-

sonal exemptions that taxpayers get for themselves and their children were eliminated. Taxpayers lost these features at a 5 percent rate, thus adding 5 points on top of the existing 28 percent rate, making it 33 percent. After the tax tables have taken away everything taxed at low rates, the regular 28 percent rate again applies. Amazingly, some congressmen have proposed eliminating the perceived unfairness of this 5 percent phase-out by raising the top rate to 33 percent directly.

6. Congressional Budget Office, *How Capital Gains Rates Affect Revenue: The Historical Evidence* (Washington, D.C.: US Congressional Budget Office, March 1988).

7. Roger H. Gordon, James R. Hines, and Lawrence H. Summers, "Notes on the Tax Treatment of Structures," in *The Effects of Taxation on Capital Accumulation*, ed. Martin Feldstein (Chicago: University of Chicago Press, 1989).

Chapter 11

1. This explanation of excess burden is intentionally simplified to provide the non-economist a flavor of what is involved. Those wishing a more detailed explanation might select a good public finance textbook, such as Harvey Rosen's *Public Finance* (Homewood, Illinois: Irwin, 1985), 275–99. A classic work on excess burden and income taxation is provided by Michael Boskin, "The Efficiency Aspects of the Differential Tax Treatment of Market and Household Economic Activities," *Journal of Public Economics* 4 (1975): 1–25.

2. Jude Wanniski, "Tax Revenues and the Laffer Curve," *The Public Interest* (Winter 1978): 4–5.

3. An exception might be a case in which the government wanted a certain tax base to shrink. Thus concern about cancer might justify a severe tax on cigarette sales, as an attempt to make that particular tax base shrink. But the tax would raise less revenue than the present lower rate. The government would still have to make the implicit decision that the loss in revenue was "worth it" to reduce shrinking.

4. A more technical explanation of taxpayer behavior is given by the Theory of Demand. The demand curve provides the number of units people will buy at a given price. When a tax is imposed, the price rises and individuals choose to buy fewer goods. The excess burden provides the value, to the consumer, in excess of price paid, absent the tax, of the goods not purchased. Note in figures 11.1 and 11.2, taxpayers would have been willing to pay *some*

tax on the goods not purchased. The tax that they would have been willing to pay had the rate been lower is a measure of how much excess burden (or forgone value) the higher rate imposes.

5. See Anthony Atkinson, *The Economics of Inequality* (Oxford: Oxford University Press, 1975), for a thorough explanation of the competing theories.

6. A classic work by John Stuart Mill is *Principles of Political Economy*, ed. W. J. Ashley (London: Langmans, 1921).

7. Though this prescription may sound statist, Mill was very much an individualist. His fundamental concept was that total social welfare was the sum of the welfare enjoyed by each individual in society. Utilitarianism, Mill's underlying philosophy, is an important underpinning of free market thinking.

8. James McCullough, cited in Dan T. Smith, *Federal Tax Reform* (New York: McGraw-Hill, 1961), 16.

Chapter 12

1. *The New Republic*, 17 October 1983, 4.

2. The estimate for FY89 as this book was going to press in 1989 was $161 billion.

3. See, for example, Richard and Peggy Musgrave's *Public Finance in Theory and Practice* (New York: McGraw-Hill, 1973), 551.

4. Consider, for example, the period 1965 to 1969, which saw a constant set of corporate tax rules (although a rate surcharge was imposed). While the economy grew 36.7 percent, corporate tax receipts, adjusted downward for the surcharge, grew 64.3 percent on an NIPA basis. That would imply an elasticity of roughly 1.6, not 1.4. In the 1982–85 expansion (where the law was constant) corporate taxes grew 55.7 percent while the economy grew 26.8 percent, implying an elasticity of almost 1.9. The 1.4 elasticity shown here is an extrapolation for a longer run expansion.

5. This was the average rate of interest paid on outstanding publicly held debt during 1989 according to the 1990 federal budget.

Chapter 13

1. Congressional Budget Office, "The Distribution of Household Income and Federal Taxes, 2008 and 2009," www.cbo.gov/publication/43373.

2. Congressional Budget Office, "The 2012 Long-Term Budget Outlook," Alternative Fiscal Scenario, www.cbo.gov/publication/43288.

3. Committee for Responsible Federal Budget, "Federal Deficit Reduction Plan Comparison Tool," http://crfb.org/compare.

4. Census Bureau, "Table H-2. Share of Aggregate Income Received by Each Fifth and Top 5 Percent of Households, All Races: 1967 to 2011," www .census.gov/hhes/www/income/data/historical/household/2011/H02AR _2011.xls.

5. Joint Committee on Taxation, "March 20, 2012 Memorandum," http://online.wsj.com/public/resources/documents/buffettrule20120321 .pdf.

6. Thomas Hungerford, "An Analysis of the 'Buffett Rule,'" Congressional Research Service, www.fas.org/sgp/crs/misc/R42043.pdf.

7. Census Bureau, "Table H-1. Income Limits for Each Fifth and Top 5 Percent of All Households: 1967 to 2011," www.census.gov/hhes/www/income /data/historical/household/2011/H01AR_2011.xls.

8. Census Bureau, "Historical Income Tables: Households." www.census .gov/hhes/www/income/data/historical/household/

Chapter 14

1. Lawrence Lindsey, *The Growth Experiment: How the New Tax Policy Is Transforming the US Economy* (New York: Basic Books, 1990).

2. Joint Committee on Taxation, "Estimated Budget Effects of the Revenue Provisions of H.R. 2264."

3. Office of Management and Budget, "Table 1.1—Summary of Receipts, Outlays, and Surpluses or Deficits (–): 1789–2017," www.whitehouse.gov /sites/default/files/omb/budget/fy2013/assets/hist01z1.xls.

4. Peter Young and M. Saltiel, "The Revenue and Growth Effects of Britain's High Personal Taxes" (London: Adam Smith Institute: March 2011).

5. The $250,000 threshold for the top bracket in 1994 is $390,000 in 2012 dollars.

6. Census Bureau, "Table H-2. Share of Aggregate Income Received by Each Fifth and Top 5 Percent of Households, All Races: 1967 to 2011," www .census.gov/hhes/www/income/data/historical/household/2011/H02AR _2011.xls.

7. Lawrence Lindsey with P. Bolster and A. Mitrusi, "Tax Induced Trading: The Effect of the 1986 Tax Reform Act on Stock Market Activity," *Journal of Finance* (June 1989): 327–344.

8. The $250,000 threshold for the top bracket in 1994 is $390,000 in 2012 dollars.

9. Lindsey, *The Growth Experiment*.

10. IRS Statistics of Income, "Table 1c.—Individual Income Tax, All Returns: Sources of Income, Adjustments, and Tax Items, in Constant 1990 Dollars, by Size of Real Adjusted Gross Income, Tax Year 1992."

11. Joint Committee on Taxation, "Estimated Budget Effects of the Revenue Provisions of H.R. 2264."

Chapter 15

1. Dave Gilson and C. Perot, "It's the Inequality, Stupid," www.motherjones .com/politics/2011/02/income-inequality-in-america-chart-graph.

2. Frederick Allen, "How Income Inequality Is Damaging the US," www.forbes.com/sites/frederickallen/2012/10/02/how-income-inequality-is-damaging-the-u-s.

3. Peter Lindert and J. Williamson, "American Incomes Before and After the Revolution," www.nber.org/papers/w17211.

4. "The Forbes 400: The Richest People in America," www.forbes.com /forbes-400.

Chapter 16

1. Federal Reserve, "Meeting of the Federal Open Market Committee September 24, 1996," 24–35, www.federalreserve.gov/monetarypolicy/files /FOMC19960924meeting.pdf.

2. Ibid., 30.

3. Federal Reserve, "Meeting of the Federal Open Market Committee December 17, 1996," 28–30, www.federalreserve.gov/monetarypolicy/files /FOMC19961217meeting.pdf.

4. Lawrence Lindsey, *Economic Puppetmasters: Lessons from the Halls of Power* (Washington, D.C.: AEI Press, 1998).

5. IRS Statistics of Income, "Table 1. All Returns: Sources of Income, Adjustments, Deductions and Exemptions, by Size of Adjusted Gross Income, Tax Year 2009."

6. IRS Statistics of Income, "All Returns: Selected Income and Tax Items," 2000–2002.

7. Ibid.

8. IRS Statistics of Income, "All Returns: Sources of Income, Adjustments, and Tax Items" for 2000–2002.

9. Ibid.

10. Allen Sinai., "Capital Gains Taxes and the Economy," http://accf.org /news/publication/capital-gains-taxes-and-the-economy.

11. Office of Management and Budget, "Table 1.1—Summary of Receipts, Outlays, and Surpluses or Deficits (–): 1789–2017," www .whitehouse.gov/sites/default/files/omb/budget/fy2013/assets/hist01z1.xl s, and "Table 1.2—Summary of Receipts, Outlays, and Surpluses or Deficits (–) as Percentages of GDP: 1930–2017," www.whitehouse.gov/sites/default /files/omb/budget/fy2013/assets/hist01z2.xls.

12. L. Lindsey, *Economic Puppetmasters: Lessons from the Halls of Power* (Washington, D.C.: AEI Press, 1998).

13. Ibid.

14. Data from Federal Reserve Flow of Fund Statistics, www.federal reserve.gov/releases/z1/Current/z1.pdf table B.100 line 48.

Chapter 17

1. Sir Mervyn King, "Monetary Policy Developments,'" www.bis.org /review/r121025a.pdf.

2. National Bureau of Economic Research, "US Business Cycle Expansions and Contractions," www.nber.org/cycles/cyclesmain.html.

3. Estimates developed from CBO's August 2012 report "An Update to the Economic and Budget Outlook: Fiscal Years 2012 to 2022," www.cbo.gov /publication/43539, and Office of Management and Budget's "Table 3.1— Outlays By Superfunction and Function: 1940–2017," www.whitehouse .gov/sites/default/files/omb/budget/fy2013/assets/hist03z1.xls.

4. Peter Wallsten, L. Montgomery, and S. Wilson, "Obama's Evolution: Behind the Failed 'Grand Bargain' on the Debt," *Washington Post*, March 15, 2012, www.washingtonpost.com/politics/obamas-evolution-behind-the -failed-grand-bargain-on-the-debt/2012/03/15/gIQAHyyfJS_story.html.

Chapter 18

1. The Tax Foundation, "Total Federal Income Tax Compliance Costs, 1990–2015," http://taxfoundation.org/article/total-federal-income-tax -compliance-costs-1990–2015.

Index